Shell Programming in Unix, Linux and OS X

Fourth Edition

Developer's Library

ESSENTIAL REFERENCES FOR PROGRAMMING PROFESSIONALS

Developer's Library books are designed to provide practicing programmers with unique, high-quality references and tutorials on the programming languages and technologies they use in their daily work.

All books in the *Developer's Library* are written by expert technology practitioners who are especially skilled at organizing and presenting information in a way that's useful for other programmers.

Key titles include some of the best, most widely acclaimed books within their topic areas:

PHP & MySQL Web Development
Luke Welling & Laura Thomson
ISBN-13: 978-0-321-83389-1

Python Essential Reference
David Beazley
ISBN-13: 978-0-672-32862-6

MySQL
Paul DuBois
ISBN-13: 978-0-672-32938-8

Programming in Objective-C
Stephen G. Kochan
ISBN-13: 978-0-321-56615-7

Linux Kernel Development
Robert Love
ISBN-13: 978-0-672-32946-3

Programming in C
Stephen G. Kochan
ISBN-13: 978-0-321-77641-9

Developer's Library books are available at most retail and online bookstores, as well as by subscription from Safari Books Online at **safari.informit.com**

**Developer's
Library**
informit.com/devlibrary

Shell Programming in Unix, Linux and OS X

Fourth Edition

Stephen G. Kochan
Patrick Wood

✦✦Addison-Wesley

800 East 96th Street, Indianapolis, Indiana 46240

Shell Programming in Unix, Linux and OS X, Fourth Edition

ISBN-13: 978-0-13-449600-9

ISBN-10: 0-13-449600-0

Printed in the United States of America

1   16

The Library of Congress Control Number is on file.

Trademarks

All terms mentioned in this book that are known to be trademarks or service marks have been appropriately capitalized. The publisher cannot attest to the accuracy of this information. Use of a term in this book should not be regarded as affecting the validity of any trademark or service mark.

Warning and Disclaimer

Every effort has been made to make this book as complete and as accurate as possible, but no warranty or fitness is implied. The information provided is on an "as is" basis. The author and the publisher shall have neither liability nor responsibility to any person or entity with respect to any loss or damages arising from the information contained in this book.

Special Sales

For information about buying this title in bulk quantities, or for special sales opportunities (which may include electronic versions; custom cover designs; and content particular to your business, training goals, marketing focus, or branding interests), please contact our corporate sales department at corpsales@pearsoned.com or (800) 382-3419.

For government sales inquiries, please contact

governmentsales@pearsoned.com

For questions about sales outside the U.S., please contact

international@pearsoned.com

Editor
Mark Taber

Copy Editor
Larry Sulky

Technical Editor
Brian Tiemann

Designer
Chuti Prasertsith

Page Layout
codeMantra

Contents at a Glance

Table of Contents

About the Authors

Stephen Kochan is the author or co-author of several best-selling titles on Unix and the C language, including *Programming in C*, *Programming in Objective-C*, *Topics in C Programming*, and *Exploring the Unix System*. He is a former software consultant for AT&T Bell Laboratories, where he developed and taught classes on Unix and C programming.

Patrick Wood is the CTO of the New Jersey location of Electronics for Imaging. He was a member of the technical staff at Bell Laboratories when he met Mr. Kochan in 1985. Together they founded Pipeline Associates, Inc., a Unix consulting firm, where he was vice president. They co-authored *Exploring the Unix System*, *Unix System Security*, *Topics in C Programming*, and *Unix Shell Programming*.

We Want to Hear from You!

As the reader of this book, *you* are our most important critic and commentator. We value your opinion and want to know what we're doing right, what we could do better, what areas you'd like to see us publish in, and any other words of wisdom you're willing to pass our way.

We welcome your comments. You can email or write directly to let us know what you did or didn't like about this book—as well as what we can do to make our books better.

Please note that we cannot help you with technical problems related to the topic of this book, and that due to the high volume of mail we receive, we might not be able to reply to every message.

When you write, please be sure to include this book's title and author, as well as your name and phone or email address.

Email: feedback@developers-library.info

Mail: Reader Feedback
           Addison-Wesley Developer's Library
           800 East 96th Street
           Indianapolis, IN 46240 USA

Reader Services

Visit our website and register this book at **www.informit.com/register** for convenient access to any updates, downloads, or errata that might be available for this book.

Introduction

It's no secret that the family of Unix and Unix-like operating systems has emerged over the last few decades as the most pervasive, most widely used group of operating systems in computing today. For programmers who have been using Unix for many years, this came as no surprise: The Unix system provides an elegant and efficient environment for program development. That's exactly what Dennis Ritchie and Ken Thompson sought to create when they developed Unix at Bell Laboratories way back in the late 1960s.

> **Note**
>
> Throughout this book we'll use the term Unix to refer generically to the broad family of Unix-based operating systems, including true Unix operating systems such as Solaris as well as Unix-like operating systems such as Linux and Mac OS X.

One of the strongest features of the Unix system is its wide collection of programs. More than 200 basic commands are distributed with the standard operating system and Linux adds to it, often shipping with 700–1000 standard commands! These commands (also known as *tools*) do everything from counting the number of lines in a file, to sending electronic mail, to displaying a calendar for any desired year.

But the real strength of the Unix system comes not from its large collection of commands but from the elegance and ease with which these commands can be combined to perform far more sophisticated tasks.

The standard user interface to Unix is the command line, which actually turns out to be a *shell*, a program that acts as a buffer between the user and the lowest levels of the system itself (the *kernel*). The shell is simply a program that reads in the commands you type and converts them into a form more readily understood by the system. It also includes core programming constructs that let you make decisions, loop, and store values in variables.

The standard shell distributed with Unix systems derives from AT&T's distribution, which evolved from a version originally written by Stephen Bourne at Bell Labs. Since then, the IEEE has created standards based on the Bourne shell and the other more recent shells. The current version of this standard, as of this writing, is the Shell and Utilities volume of IEEE Std 1003.1-2001, also known as the POSIX standard. This shell is what we use as the basis for the rest of this book.

The examples in this book were tested on a Mac running Mac OS X 10.11, Ubuntu Linux 14.0, and an old version of SunOS 5.7 running on a Sparcstation Ultra-30. All examples, with the exception of some Bash examples in Chapter 14, were run using the Korn shell, although all of them also work fine with Bash.

Because the shell offers an interpreted programming language, programs can be written, modified, and debugged quickly and easily. We turn to the shell as our first choice of programming language and after you become adept at shell programming, you will too.

How This Book Is Organized

This book assumes that you are familiar with the fundamentals of the system and command line; that is, that you know how to log in; how to create files, edit them, and remove them; and how to work with directories. In case you haven't used the Linux or Unix system for a while, we'll examine the basics in Chapter 1, "A Quick Review of the Basics." In addition, filename substitution, I/O redirection, and pipes are also reviewed in the first chapter.

Chapter 2, "What Is the Shell?," reveals what the shell really is, how it works, and how it ends up being your primary method of interacting with the operating system itself. You'll learn about what happens every time you log in to the system, how the shell program gets started, how it parses the command line, and how it executes other programs for you. A key point made in Chapter 2 is that the shell is just another program; nothing more, nothing less.

Chapter 3, "Tools of the Trade," provides tutorials on tools useful in writing shell programs. Covered in this chapter are cut, paste, sed, grep, sort, tr, and uniq. Admittedly, the selection is subjective, but it does set the stage for programs that we'll develop throughout the remainder of the book. Also in Chapter 3 is a detailed discussion of regular expressions, which are used by many Unix commands, such as sed, grep, and ed.

Chapters 4 through 9 teach you how to put the shell to work for writing programs. You'll learn how to write your own commands; use variables; write programs that accept arguments; make decisions; use the shell's for, while, and until looping commands; and use the read command to read data from the terminal or from a file. Chapter 5, "Can I Quote you on That?", is devoted entirely to a discussion of one of the most intriguing (and often confusing) aspects of the shell: the way it interprets quotes.

By that point in the book, all the basic programming constructs in the shell will have been covered, and you will be able to write shell programs to solve your particular problems.

Chapter 10, "Your Environment," covers a topic of great importance for a real understanding of the way the shell operates: the *environment*. You'll learn about local and exported variables; subshells; special shell variables, such as HOME, PATH, and CDPATH; and how to set up your .profile file.

Chapter 11, "More on Parameters," and Chapter 12, "Loose Ends," tie up some loose ends, and Chapter 13, "Rolo Revisited," presents a final version of a phone directory program called rolo that is developed throughout the book.

A Quick Review
of the Basics

This chapter provides a review of the Unix system, including the file system, basic commands, filename substitution, I/O redirection, and pipes.

Some Basic Commands

Displaying the Date and Time: The `date` Command

The `date` command tells the system to print the date and time:

```
$ date
Thu Dec  3 11:04:09 MST 2015
$
```

`date` prints the day of the week, month, day, time (24-hour clock, the system's time zone), and year. Throughout the code examples in this book, whenever we use **boldface type like this**, it's to indicate what you, the user, type in. Normal face type like this is used to indicate what the Unix system prints. *Italic type* is used for comments in interactive sequences.

Every Unix command is submitted to the system with the pressing of the `Enter` key. `Enter` says that you are finished typing things in and are ready for the Unix system to do its thing.

Finding Out Who's Logged In: The `who` Command

The `who` command can be used to get information about all users currently logged in to the system:

```
$ who
pat       tty29    Jul 19 14:40
ruth      tty37    Jul 19 10:54
steve     tty25    Jul 19 15:52
$
```

Here, three users are logged in: pat, ruth, and steve. Along with each user ID is listed the *tty* number of that user and the day and time that user logged in. The tty number is a unique identification number the Unix system gives to each terminal or network device that a user is on when they log into the system.

The who command also can be used to get information about yourself:

```
$ who am i
pat        tty29   Jul 19 14:40
$
```

who and who am i are actually the same command: who. In the latter case, the am and i are *arguments* to the who command. (This isn't a good example of how command arguments work; it's just a curiosity of the who command.)

Echoing Characters: The echo Command

The echo command prints (or *echoes*) at the terminal whatever else you happen to type on the line (there are some exceptions to this that you'll learn about later):

```
$ echo this is a test
this is a test
$ echo why not print out a longer line with echo?
why not print out a longer line with echo?
$ echo
                                    A blank line is displayed
$ echo one         two    three         four   five
one two three four five
$
```

You will notice from the preceding example that echo squeezes out extra blanks between words. That's because on a Unix system, the words are important while the blanks are only there to separate the words. Generally, the Unix system ignores extra blanks (you'll learn more about this in the next chapter).

Working with Files

The Unix system recognizes only three basic types of files: *ordinary* files, *directory* files, and *special* files. An ordinary file is just that: any file on the system that contains data, text, program instructions, or just about anything else. Directories, or folders, are described later in this chapter. Finally, as its name implies, a special file has a special meaning to the Unix system and is typically associated with some form of I/O.

A filename can be composed of just about any character directly available from the keyboard (and even some that aren't) provided that the total number of characters contained in the name is not greater than 255. If more than 255 characters are specified, the Unix system simply ignores the extra characters.

The Unix system provides many tools that make working with files easy. Here we'll review some of the basic file manipulation commands.

Listing Files: The `ls` Command

To see what files you have stored in your directory, you can type the `ls` command:

```
$ ls
READ_ME
names
tmp
$
```

This output indicates that three files called READ_ME, names, and tmp are contained in the current directory. (Note that the output of ls may vary from system to system. For example, on many Unix systems ls produces multicolumn output when sending its output to a terminal; on others, different colors may be used for different types of files. You can always force single-column output with the -1 option—that's the number one.)

Displaying the Contents of a File: The `cat` Command

You can examine the *contents* of a file by using the cat command. (That's short for "concatenate," if you're thinking feline thoughts.) The argument to cat is the name of the file whose contents you want to examine.

```
$ cat names
Susan
Jeff
Henry
Allan
Ken
$
```

Counting the Number of Words in a File: The `wc` Command

With the wc command, you can get a count of the total number of lines, words, and characters contained in a file. Once again, the name of the file is expected to be specified as the argument to this command:

```
$ wc names
        5        7       27 names
$
```

The wc command lists three numbers followed by the filename. The first number represents the number of lines in the file (5), the second the number of words (7), and the third the number of characters (27).

Command Options

Most Unix commands allow the specification of *options* at the time a command is executed. These options generally follow the same format:

```
-letter
```

That is, a command option is a minus sign followed immediately by a single letter. For example, to count just the number of lines contained in a file, the option -l (that's the letter l) is given to the wc command:

```
$ wc -l names
        5 names
$
```

To count just the number of characters in a file, the -c option is specified:

```
$ wc -c names
       27 names
$
```

Finally, the -w option can be used to count the number of words contained in the file:

```
$ wc -w names
        7 names
$
```

Some commands require that the options be listed before the filename arguments. For example, sort names -r is acceptable, whereas wc names -l is not. Still, the former is unusual and most Unix commands are designed for you to specify command options first, as exemplified by wc -l names.

Making a Copy of a File: The cp Command

To make a copy of a file, use the cp command. The first argument to the command is the name of the file to be copied (known as the *source file*), and the second argument is the name of the file to place the copy into (known as the *destination file*). You can make a copy of the file names and call it saved_names as follows:

```
$ cp names saved_names
$
```

Execution of this command causes the contents of the file names to be copied into a new file named saved_names. As with many Unix commands, the fact that no output other than a command prompt was displayed after the cp command was typed indicates that the command executed successfully.

Renaming a File: The mv Command

A file can be renamed with the mv ("move") command. The arguments to the mv command follow the same format as the cp command. The first argument is the name of the file to be renamed, and the second argument is the new name. So, to change the name of the file saved_names to hold_it, for example, the following command would do the trick:

```
$ mv saved_names hold_it
$
```

Be careful! When executing an mv or cp command, the Unix system does not care whether the file specified as the second argument already exists. If it does, the contents of the file will be lost. For example, if a file called old_names exists, executing the command

```
cp names old_names
```

would copy the filenames to old_names, destroying the previous contents of old_names in the process. Similarly, the command

```
mv names old_names
```

would rename names to old_names, even if the file old_names existed prior to execution of the command.

Removing a File: The rm Command

Use the rm command to remove a file from the system. The argument to rm is simply the name of the file to be removed:

```
$ rm hold_it
$
```

You can remove more than one file at a time with the rm command by simply specifying all such files on the command line. For example, the following would remove the three files wb, collect, and mon:

```
$ rm wb collect mon
$
```

Working with Directories

Suppose that you had a set of files consisting of various memos, proposals, and letters. Further suppose that you had another set of files that were computer programs. It would seem logical to group this first set into a directory called documents and the latter into a directory called programs. Figure 1.1 illustrates such a directory organization.

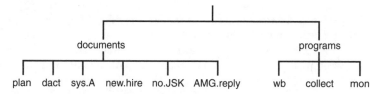

Figure 1.1   Example directory structure

The file directory `documents` *contains* the files `plan`, `dact`, `sys.A`, `new.hire`, `no.JSK`, and `AMG.reply`. The directory `programs` contains the files `wb`, `collect`, and `mon`. At some point, you may decide to further categorize the files in a directory. This can be done by creating subdirectories and then placing each file into the appropriate subdirectory. For example, you might want to create subdirectories called `memos`, `proposals`, and `letters` inside your `documents` directory, as shown in Figure 1.2.

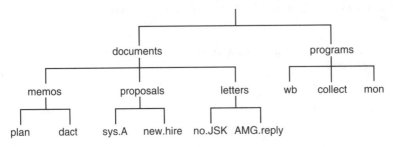

Figure 1.2   Directories containing subdirectories

`documents` contains the subdirectories `memos`, `proposals`, and `letters`. Each of these subdirectories in turn contains two files: `memos` contains `plan` and `dact`; `proposals` contains `sys.A` and `new.hire`; and `letters` contains `no.JSK` and `AMG.reply`.

Although each file in a given directory must have a unique name, files contained in different directories do not. So you could have a file in your `programs` directory called `dact`, even though a file by that name also exists in the `memos` subdirectory.

The Home Directory and Pathnames

The Unix system always associates each user of the system with a particular directory. When you log in to the system, you are placed automatically into your own directory (called your *home* directory).

Although the location of users' home directories can vary from one system to the next, let's assume that your home directory is called `steve` and that this directory is actually a subdirectory of a directory called `users`. Therefore, if you had the directories `documents` and `programs`, the overall directory structure would actually look something like Figure 1.3. A special directory named / (pronounced "slash") is shown at the top of the directory tree. This directory is known as the *root.*

Whenever you are "inside" a particular directory (called your *current working directory*), the files contained within that directory are immediately accessible, without specifying any path information. If you want to access a file from another directory, you can either first issue a command to "change" to the appropriate directory and then access the particular file, or you can specify the particular file by its *pathname.*

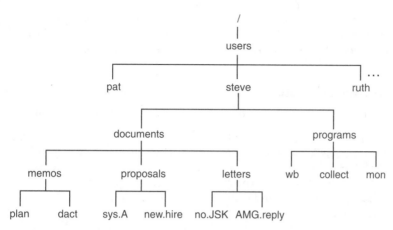

Figure 1.3   Hierarchical directory structure

A pathname enables you to uniquely identify a particular file to the Unix system. In the specification of a pathname, successive directories along the path are separated by the slash character /. A pathname that *begins* with a slash character is known as a *full* or *absolute* pathname because it specifies a complete path from the root. For example, the pathname /users/steve identifies the directory steve contained within the directory users. Similarly, the pathname /users/steve/documents references the directory documents as contained in the directory steve within users. As a final example, the pathname /users/steve/documents/letters/AMG.reply identifies the file AMG.reply contained along the appropriate directory path.

To help reduce the typing that would otherwise be required, Unix provides certain notational conveniences. A pathname that does not begin with a slash is known as a *relative* pathname: the path is relative to your current working directory. For example, if you just logged in to the system and were placed into your home directory /users/steve, you could directly reference the directory documents simply by typing documents. Similarly, the relative pathname programs/mon could be typed to access the file mon contained inside your programs directory.

By convention, .. always references the directory that is one level higher than the current directory, known as the parent directory. For example, if you were in your home directory /users/steve, the pathname .. would reference the directory users. If you had issued the appropriate command to change your working directory to documents/letters, the pathname .. would reference the documents directory, ../.. would reference the directory steve, and ../proposals/new.hire would reference the file new.hire contained in the proposals directory. There is usually more than one way to specify a path to a particular file, a very Unix-y characteristic.

Another notational convention is the single period ., which always refers to the current directory. That'll become more important later in the book when you want to specify a shell script in the current directory, not one in the PATH. We'll explain this in more detail soon.

Displaying Your Working Directory: The pwd Command

The pwd command is used to help you "get your bearings" by telling you the name of your current working directory.

Recall the directory structure from Figure 1.3. The directory that you are placed in after you log in to the system is called your home directory. You can assume from Figure 1.3 that the home directory for the user steve is /users/steve. Therefore, whenever steve logs in to the system, he will automatically be placed inside this directory. To verify that this is the case, the pwd (print working directory) command can be issued:

```
$ pwd
/users/steve
$
```

The output from the command verifies that steve's current working directory is /users/ steve.

Changing Directories: The cd Command

You can change your current working directory by using the cd command. This command takes as its argument the name of the target or destination directory.

Let's assume that you just logged in to the system and were placed in your home directory, /users/steve. This is depicted by the arrow in Figure 1.4.

You know that two directories are directly "below" steve's home directory: documents and programs. This can be easily verified at the terminal by issuing the ls command:

```
$ ls
documents
programs
$
```

The ls command lists the two directories documents and programs the same way it listed other ordinary files in previous examples.

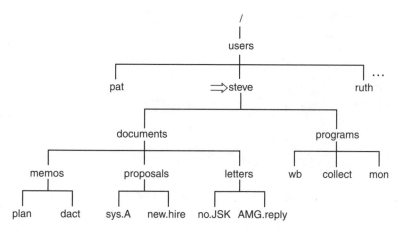

Figure 1.4   Current working directory is `steve`

To change your current working directory, issue the `cd` command, followed by the name of the new directory:

```
$ cd documents
$
```

After executing this command, you will be placed inside the `documents` directory, as depicted in Figure 1.5.

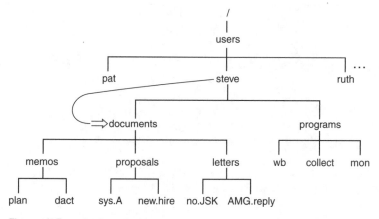

Figure 1.5   `cd documents`

You can verify at the terminal that the working directory has been changed by using the pwd command:

```
$ pwd
/users/steve/documents
$
```

The easiest way to move up one level in a directory is to reference the . . shortcut with the command

```
cd ..
```

because by convention . . always refers to the directory one level up (see Figure 1.6).

```
$ cd ..
$ pwd
/users/steve
$
```

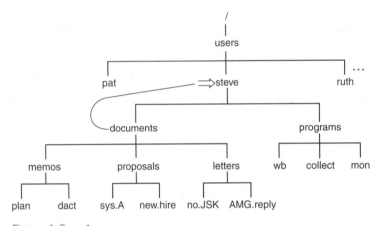

Figure 1.6 cd ..

If you wanted to change to the letters directory, you could get there with a single cd command by specifying the relative path documents/letters (see Figure 1.7):

```
$ cd documents/letters
$ pwd
/users/steve/documents/letters
$
```

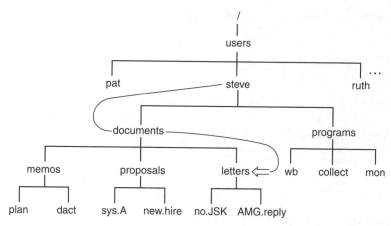

Figure 1.7 `cd documents/letters`

You can get back up to your home directory by using a single `cd` command to go up two directories as shown:

```
$ cd ../..
$ pwd
/users/steve
$
```

Or you can get back to the home directory using a full pathname rather than a relative one:

```
$ cd /users/steve
$ pwd
/users/steve
$
```

Finally, there is a third way to get back to the home directory that is also the easiest. Typing the command `cd` *without* an argument *always* moves you back to your home directory, no matter where you are in the file system:

```
$ cd
$ pwd
/users/steve
$
```

More on the `ls` Command

When you type the `ls` command, the files contained in the current working directory are listed. But you can also use `ls` to obtain a list of files in other directories by supplying an argument to the command. First let's get back to your home directory:

```
$ cd
$ pwd
/users/steve
$
```

Now let's take a look at the files in the current working directory:

```
$ ls
documents
programs
$
```

If you supply the name of one of these directories to the ls command, you can get a list of the contents of that directory. So you can find out what's contained in the documents directory by typing the command **ls documents**:

```
$ ls documents
letters
memos
proposals
$
```

To take a look at the subdirectory memos, you can follow a similar procedure:

```
$ ls documents/memos
dact
plan
$
```

If you specify a nondirectory file argument to the ls command, you simply get that filename echoed back at the terminal:

```
$ ls documents/memos/plan
documents/memos/plan
$
```

Confused? There's an option to the ls command that lets you determine whether a particular file is a directory, among other things. The -1 option (the letter l) provides a more detailed description of the files in a directory. If you were currently in steve's home directory, here's what the -1 option to the ls command produces:

```
$ ls -l
total 2
drwxr-xr-x    5 steve    DP3725      80 Jun 25 13:27 documents
drwxr-xr-x    2 steve    DP3725      96 Jun 25 13:31 programs
$
```

The first line of the display is a count of the total number of *blocks* (1,024 bytes) of storage that the listed files use. Each successive line displayed by the ls -1 command contains detailed information about a file in the directory. The first character on each line indicates what type of file it is: d for a directory, - for a file, b, c, l, or p for a special file.

The next nine characters on the line define the access permissions of that particular file or directory. These *access modes* apply to the file's owner (the first three characters), other users in the same *group* as the file's owner (the next three characters), and finally all other users on the system (the last three characters). Generally, they indicate whether the specified class of user can read the file, write to the file, or execute the contents of the file (in the case of a program or shell script).

The `ls -l` command then shows the *link* count (see "Linking Files: The `ln` Command," later in this chapter), the owner of the file, the group owner of the file, how large the file is (that is, how many characters are contained in it), and when the file was last modified. The information displayed last on the line is the filename itself.

> **Note**
>
> Many modern Unix systems have gone away from using groups, so while those permissions are still shown, the group owner for a specific file or directory is often omitted in the output of the ls command.

You should now be able to glean a lot of information from the `ls -l` output for a directory full of files:

```
$ ls -l programs
total 4
-rwxr-xr-x    1 steve     DP3725      358 Jun 25 13:31 collect
-rwxr-xr-x    1 steve     DP3725     1219 Jun 25 13:31 mon
-rwxr-xr-x    1 steve     DP3725       89 Jun 25 13:30 wb
$
```

The dash in the first column of each line indicates that the three files `collect`, `mon`, and `wb` are ordinary files and not directories. Now, can you figure out how big are they?

Creating a Directory: The `mkdir` Command

Use `mkdir` to create directories. The argument to this command is simply the name of the directory you want to create. For example, assume that you are still working with the directory structure depicted in Figure 1.7 and that you want to create a new directory called `misc` *at the same level* as the directories `documents` and `programs`. If you were currently in your home directory, typing the command **mkdir misc** would achieve the desired effect:

```
$ mkdir misc
$
```

Now if you run **ls**, you will have the new directory listed:

```
$ ls
documents
misc
programs
$
```

The directory structure now appears as shown in Figure 1.8.

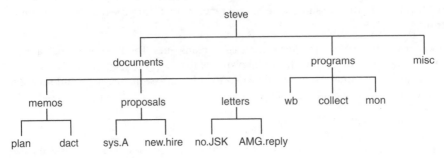

Figure 1.8   Directory structure with newly created `misc` directory

Copying a File from One Directory to Another

The `cp` command can be used to copy a file from one directory into another. For example, you can copy the file `wb` from the `programs` directory into a file called `wbx` in the `misc` directory as follows:

```
$ cp programs/wb misc/wbx
$
```

Because the two files are in different directories, they can safely have the exact same name:

```
$ cp programs/wb misc/wb
$
```

When the destination file is going to have the same name as the source file (in a different directory, of course), it is necessary to specify only the destination directory as the second argument:

```
$ cp programs/wb misc
$
```

When this command gets executed, the Unix system recognizes that the second argument is a directory and copies the source file into that directory. The new file is given the same name as the source file.

You can copy more than one file into a directory by listing the files to be copied prior to the name of the destination directory. If you were currently in the `programs` directory, the command

```
$ cp wb collect mon ../misc
$
```

would copy the three files `wb`, `collect`, and `mon` into the `misc` directory, with the same filenames.

To copy a file from another directory into your current location in the file system and give the file the same name, use the handy "." shortcut for the current directory:

```
$ pwd
/users/steve/misc
$ cp ../programs/collect .
$
```

The preceding command copies the file collect from the directory ../programs into the current directory (/users/steve/misc).

Moving Files Between Directories

You recall that the mv command can be used to rename a file. Indeed, there is no "rename" command in Unix. However, when the two arguments reference different directories, the file is actually moved from the first directory into the second.

To demonstrate, go from the home directory to the documents directory:

```
$ cd documents
$
```

Suppose that now you decide that the file plan contained in the memos directory is really a proposal so you want to move it from the memos directory into the proposals directory. The following would do the trick:

```
$ mv memos/plan proposals/plan
$
```

As with the cp command, if the source file and destination file have the same name, only the name of the destination directory need be supplied, so there's an easier way to move this file:

```
$ mv memos/plan proposals
$
```

Also like the cp command, a group of files can be simultaneously moved into a directory by simply listing all files to be moved before the name of the destination directory:

```
$ pwd
/users/steve/programs
$ mv wb collect mon ../misc
$
```

This would move the three files wb, collect, and mon into the directory misc.

You can also use the mv command to change the name of a directory, as it happens. For example, the following renames the programs directory to bin.

```
$ mv programs bin
$
```

Linking Files: The `ln` Command

So far everything we've talked about with file management has assumed that a given collection of data has one and only one filename, wherever it may be located in the file system. It turns out that Unix is more sophisticated than that and can assign multiple filenames to the same collection of data.

The main command for creating these duplicate names for a given file is the `ln` command.

The general form of the command is

```
ln from to
```

This links the file *from* to the file *to*.

Recall the structure of `steve`'s `programs` directory from Figure 1.8. In that directory, he has stored a program called `wb`. Suppose that he decides that he'd also like to call the program `writeback`. The most obvious thing to do would be to simply create a copy of `wb` called `writeback`:

```
$ cp wb writeback
$
```

The drawback with this approach is that now twice as much disk space is being consumed by the program. Furthermore, if `steve` ever changes `wb`, he may forget to duplicate the change in `writeback`, resulting in two different, out of sync copies of what he thinks is the same program. Not so good, Steve!

By linking the file `wb` to the new name, these problems are avoided:

```
$ ln wb writeback
$
```

Now instead of two copies of the file existing, only one exists with two different names: `wb` and `writeback`. The two files have been logically linked by the Unix system.

As far as you're concerned, it appears as though you have two *different* files. Executing an `ls` command shows the two files separately:

```
$ ls
collect
mon
wb
writeback
$
```

Where it gets interesting is when you use `ls -l`:

```
$ ls -l
total 5
-rwxr-xr-x   1 steve    DP3725     358 Jun 25 13:31 collect
-rwxr-xr-x   1 steve    DP3725    1219 Jun 25 13:31 mon
-rwxr-xr-x   2 steve    DP3725      89 Jun 25 13:30 wb
-rwxr-xr-x   2 steve    DP3725      89 Jun 25 13:30 writeback
$
```

Look closely at the second column of the output: The number shown is 1 for collect and mon and 2 for wb and writeback. This is the number of links to a file, normally 1 for nonlinked, nondirectory files. Because wb and writeback are linked, however, this number is 2 for these files (or, more correctly, this file with two names).

You can remove either of the two linked files at any time, and the other will not be removed:

```
$ rm writeback
$ ls -l
total 4
-rwxr-xr-x   1 steve     DP3725      358 Jun 25 13:31 collect
-rwxr-xr-x   1 steve     DP3725     1219 Jun 25 13:31 mon
-rwxr-xr-x   1 steve     DP3725       89 Jun 25 13:30 wb
$
```

Note that the number of links on wb went from 2 to 1 because one of its links was removed.

Most often, ln is used to allow a file to appear in more than one directory simultaneously. For example, suppose that pat wanted to have access to steve's wb program. Instead of making a copy for himself (subject to the same data sync problems described previously) or including steve's programs directory in his PATH (which has security risks as described in Chapter 10, "Your Environment"), he can simply link to the file from his own program directory:

```
$ pwd
/users/pat/bin                    pat's program directory
$ ls -l
total 4
-rwxr-xr-x   1 pat       DP3822     1358 Jan 15 11:01 lcat
-rwxr-xr-x   1 pat       DP3822      504 Apr 21 18:30 xtr
$ ln /users/steve/wb .            link wb to pat's bin
$ ls -l
total 5
-rwxr-xr-x   1 pat       DP3822     1358 Jan 15 11:01 lcat
-rwxr-xr-x   2 steve     DP3725       89 Jun 25 13:30 wb
-rwxr-xr-x   1 pat       DP3822      504 Apr 21 18:30 xtr
$
```

Note that steve is still listed as the owner of wb, even when viewing the contents of pat's directory. This makes sense, because there's really only one copy of the file and it's owned by steve.

The only stipulation on linking files is that for ordinary links the files to be linked together must reside on the same *file system*. If they don't, you'll get an error from ln when you try to link them. (To determine the different file systems on your system, execute the df command. The first field on each line of output is the name of a file system.)

To create links to files on different file systems (or on different networked systems), you can use the -s option to the ln command. This creates a *symbolic* link. Symbolic links behave a lot like regular links, except that the symbolic link points to the original file; if the original file is removed, the symbolic link no longer works.

Let's see how symbolic links work with the previous example:

```
$ rm wb
$ ls -l
total 4
-rwxr-xr-x   1 pat      DP3822     1358 Jan 15 11:01 lcat
-rwxr-xr-x   1 pat      DP3822      504 Apr 21 18:30 xtr
$ ln -s /users/steve/wb ./symwb               Symbolic link to wb
$ ls -l
total 5
-rwxr-xr-x   1 pat      DP3822     1358 Jan 15 11:01 lcat
lrwxr-xr-x   1 pat      DP3822       15 Jul 20 15:22 symwb -> /users/steve/wb
-rwxr-xr-x   1 pat      DP3822      504 Apr 21 18:30 xtr
$
```

Note that pat is listed as the owner of symwb, and the file type shown as the very first character in the ls output is l, which indicates a symbolic link. The size of the symbolic link is 15 (the file actually contains the string /users/steve/wb), but if we attempt to access the contents of the file, we are presented with the contents of the file it's linked to, /users/steve/wb:

```
$ wc symwb
        5        9       89 symwb
$
```

The -L option to the ls command can be used with the -l option to get a detailed list of information on the file the symbolic link points to:

```
$ ls -Ll
total 5
-rwxr-xr-x   1 pat      DP3822     1358 Jan 15 11:01 lcat
-rwxr-xr-x   2 steve    DP3725       89 Jun 25 13:30 wb
-rwxr-xr-x   1 pat      DP3822      504 Apr 21 18:30 xtr
$
```

Removing the file that a symbolic link points to invalidates the symbolic link (because symbolic links are maintained as filenames), but it doesn't remove it:

```
$ rm /users/steve/wb               Assume pat can remove this file
$ ls -l
total 5
-rwxr-xr-x   1 pat      DP3822     1358 Jan 15 11:01 lcat
lrwxr-xr-x   1 pat      DP3822       15 Jul 20 15:22 wb -> /users/steve/wb
-rwxr-xr-x   1 pat      DP3822      504 Apr 21 18:30 xtr
$ wc wb
Cannot open wb: No such file or directory
$
```

This type of file is called a *dangling symbolic link* and should be removed unless you have a specific reason to keep it around (for example, if you intend to replace the removed file).

One last note before leaving this discussion: The `ln` command follows the same general format as `cp` and `mv`, meaning that you can create links to a bunch of files within a specific target directory using the format

```
ln files directory
```

Removing a Directory: The `rmdir` Command

You can remove a directory with the `rmdir` command. Rather than let you accidentally remove dozens or hundreds of files, however, `rmdir` won't let you proceed unless the specified directory is completely empty of files and subdirectories.

To remove the directory `/users/pat`, we could use the following:

```
$ rmdir /users/pat
rmdir: pat: Directory not empty
$
```

Phew! That would have been a mistake! Instead, let's remove the `misc` directory that you created earlier:

```
$ rmdir /users/steve/misc
$
```

Once again, the preceding command works only if no files or directories are contained in the `misc` directory; otherwise, the following happens, as also shown earlier:

```
$ rmdir /users/steve/misc
rmdir: /users/steve/misc: Directory not empty
$
```

If you still want to remove the `misc` directory, you would first have to remove all the files contained in that directory before reissuing the `rmdir` command.

As an alternative method for removing a directory and its contents, you can use the `-r` option to the `rm` command. The format is simple:

```
rm -r dir
```

where `dir` is the name of the directory that you want to remove. `rm` removes the indicated directory and *all* files (including directories) in it, so be careful with this powerhouse command.

Want to go full turbo? Add the `-f` flag and it forces the action without prompting you on a command-by-command basis. It can completely trash your system if you're not careful, however, so many admins simply avoid `rm -rf` entirely!

Filename Substitution

The Asterisk

One powerful feature of the Unix system that is handled by the shell is *filename substitution*. Let's say that your current directory has these files in it:

```
$ ls
chapt1
chapt2
chapt3
chapt4
$
```

Suppose that you want to display their contents en masse. Easy: `cat` allows you to display the contents of as many files as you specify on the command line. Like this:

```
$ cat chapt1 chapt2 chapt3 chapt4
    . . .
$
```

But that's tedious. Instead, you can take advantage of filename substitution by simply typing:

```
$ cat *
    . . .
$
```

The shell automatically *substitutes* the names of all the files in the current directory that match the pattern `*`. The same substitution occurs if you use `*` with another command too, of course. How about `echo`?

```
$ echo *
chapt1 chapt2 chapt3 chapt4
$
```

Here the `*` is again replaced with the names of all the files contained in the current directory, and the `echo` command simply displays that list to you.

Any place that `*` appears on the command line, the shell performs its substitution:

```
$ echo * : *
chapt1 chapt2 chapt3 chapt4 : chapt1 chapt2 chapt3 chapt4
$
```

The `*` is part of a rich file substitution language, actually, and it can also be used in combination with other characters to limit which filenames are matched.

For example, let's say that in your current directory you have not only chapt1 through chapt4 but also files a, b, and c:

```
$ ls
a
b
```

```
c
chapt1
chapt2
chapt3
chapt4
$
```

To display the contents of just the files beginning with chap, you can type in

```
$ cat chap*
    .
    .
    .
$
```

The chap* matches any filename that *begins* with chap. All such filenames matched are substituted on the command line before the specified command is even invoked.

The * is not limited to the end of a filename; it can be used at the beginning or in the middle as well:

```
$ echo *t1
chapt1
$ echo *t*
chapt1 chapt2 chapt3 chapt4
$ echo *x
*x
$
```

In the first echo, the *t1 specifies all filenames that end in the characters t1. In the second echo, the first * matches everything up to a t and the second everything after; thus, all filenames containing a t are printed. Because there are no files ending with x, no substitution occurs in the last case. Therefore, the echo command simply displays *x.

Matching Single Characters

The asterisk (*) matches *zero* or more characters, meaning that x* matches the file x as well as x1, x2, xabc, and so on. The question mark (?) matches exactly one character. So cat ? will display all files that have filenames of exactly one character, just as cat x? prints all files with two-character names beginning with x. Here we see this behavior illustrated again with echo:

```
$ ls
a
aa
aax
alice
b
bb
c
cc
```

```
report1
report2
report3
$ echo ?
a b c
$ echo a?
aa
$ echo ??
aa bb cc
$ echo ??*
aa aax alice bb cc report1 report2 report3
$
```

In the preceding example, the ?? matches two characters, and the * matches zero or more characters up to the end. The net effect is to match all filenames of two or more characters.

Another way to match a single character is to give a list of characters to match within square brackets [ ]. For example, [abc] matches the letter a, b, or c. It's similar to the ?, but it allows you to choose which characters are valid matches.

You can also specify a logical range of characters with a dash, a huge convenience! For example, [0-9] matches the characters 0 *through* 9. The only restriction in specifying a *range* of characters is that the first character must be alphabetically less than the last character, so that [z-f] is not a valid range specification, while [f-z] is.

By mixing and matching ranges and characters in the list, you can perform complicated substitutions. For example, [a-np-z]* matches all files that start with the letters a through n *or* p through z (or more simply stated, any filename that doesn't start with the lowercase letter o).

If the first character following the [is a !, the sense of the match is inverted. That is, any character is matched *except* those enclosed in the brackets. So

[!a-z]

matches any character except a lowercase letter, and

*[!o]

matches any file that doesn't end with the lowercase letter o.

Table 1.1 gives a few more examples of filename substitution.

Table 1.1 **Filename Substitution Examples**

Command	Description
echo a*	Print the *names* of the files beginning with a
cat *.c	Print the contents of all files ending in .c
rm *.*	Remove all files containing a period
ls x*	List the names of all files beginning with x

`rm *`	Remove *all* files in the current directory (No??? Be careful when you use this.)
`echo a*b`	Print the names of all files beginning with `a` and ending with `b`
`cp ../programs/* .`	Copy all files from `../programs` into the current directory
`ls [a-z]*[!0-9]`	List files that begin with a lowercase letter and don't end with a digit

Filename Nuances

Spaces in Filenames

A discussion of command lines and filenames wouldn't be complete without talking about the bane of old-school Unix people and very much the day-to-day reality of Linux, Windows, and Mac users: spaces in filenames.

The problem arises from the fact that the shell uses spaces as delimiters between words. In other words the phrase `echo hi mom` is properly parsed as an invocation to the command `echo`, with two arguments `hi` and `mom`.

Now imagine you have a file called `my test document`. How do you reference it from the command line? How do you view it or display it using the `cat` command?

```
$ cat my test document
cat: my: No such file or directory
cat: test: No such file or directory
cat: document: No such file or directory
```

That definitely doesn't work. Why? Because `cat` wants a filename to be specified and instead of seeing one, it sees three: `my`, `test`, and `document`.

There are two standard solutions for this: Either escape every space by using a backslash, or wrap the entire filename in quotes so that the shell understands that it's a single word with spaces, rather than multiple words.

```
$ cat "my test document"
This is a test document and is full
of scintillating information to edify
and amaze.
$ cat my\ test\ document
This is a test document and is full
of scintillating information to edify
and amaze.
```

That solves the problem and is critical to know as you proceed with file systems that quite likely have lots of directories and files that contain spaces as part of their filenames.

Other Weird Characters

While the space might be the most difficult and annoying of special characters that can appear in filenames, occasionally you'll find others show up that can throw a proverbial monkey-wrench into your command line efforts.

For example, how would you deal with a filename that contains a question mark? In the next section, you'll learn that the character "?" has a specific meaning to the shell. Most modern shells are smart enough to sidestep the duplication of meaning, but, again, quoting the filename or using backslashes to denote that the special character is part of the filename is required:

```
$ ls -l who\ me\?
-rw-r--r--  1 taylor  staff  0 Dec  4 10:18 who me?
```

Where this really gets interesting is if you have a backslash or quote as part of the filename, something that can happen inadvertently, particularly for files created by graphically oriented programs on a Linux or Mac system. The trick? Use single quotes to escape a filename that includes a double quote, and vice versa. Like this:

```
$ ls -l "don't quote me" 'She said "yes"'
-rw-r--r--  1 taylor  staff  0 Dec  4 10:18 don't quote me
-rw-r--r--  1 taylor  staff  0 Dec  4 10:19 She said "yes"
```

This topic will come up again as we proceed, but now you know how to side-step problems with directories or files that contain spaces or other non-standard characters.

Standard Input/Output, and I/O Redirection

Standard Input and Standard Output

Most Unix system commands take input from your screen and send the resulting output back to your screen. In Unix nomenclature, the screen is generally called the *terminal*, a reference that harkens back to the earliest days of computing. Nowadays it's more likely to be a terminal *program* you're running within a graphical environment, whether it's a Linux window manager, a Windows computer, or a Mac system.

A command normally reads its input from *standard input*, which is your computer keyboard by default. It's a fancy way of clarifying that you "type in" your information. Similarly, a command normally writes its output to *standard output*, which is also your terminal or terminal app by default. This concept is depicted in Figure 1.9.

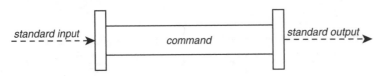

Figure 1.9 Typical Unix command

As an example, recall that executing the who command results in the display of all users that are currently logged-in. More formally, the who command writes a list of the logged-in users to standard output. This is depicted in Figure 1.10.

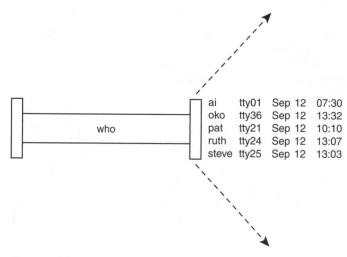

ai	tty01	Sep 12	07:30
oko	tty36	Sep 12	13:32
pat	tty21	Sep 12	10:10
ruth	tty24	Sep 12	13:07
steve	tty25	Sep 12	13:03

Figure 1.10 who command

It turns out that just about every single Unix command can take the output of a previous command or file as its input too, and can even send its output to another command or program. This concept is hugely important to understanding the power of the command line and why it's so helpful to know all of these commands even when a graphical interface might be also available for your use.

Before we get there, however, consider this: if the sort command is invoked *without* a filename argument, the command takes its input from standard input. As with standard output, this is your terminal (or keyboard) by default.

When input is entered this way, an end-of-file sequence must be specified after the last line is typed, and, by Unix convention, that's *Ctrl+d*; that is, the sequence produced by simultaneously pressing the *Control* (or *Ctrl*, depending on your keyboard) key and the *d* key.

As an example, let's use the sort command to sort the following four names: Tony, Barbara, Harry, Dirk. Instead of first entering the names into a file, we'll enter them directly from the terminal:

```
$ sort
Tony
Barbara
Harry
Dirk
Ctrl+d
```

```
Barbara
Dirk
Harry
Tony
$
```

Because no filename was specified to the `sort` command, the input was taken from standard input, the terminal. After the fourth name was typed in, the *Ctrl* and *d* keys were pressed to signal the end of the data. At that point, the `sort` command sorted the four names and displayed the results on the standard output device, which is also the terminal. This is depicted in Figure 1.11.

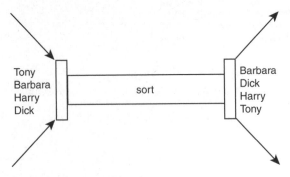

```
Tony
Barbara          sort          Barbara
Harry                          Dick
Dick                           Harry
                               Tony
```

Figure 1.11 `sort` command

The `wc` command is another example of a command that takes its input from standard input if no filename is specified on the command line. The following shows an example of this command used to count the number of lines of text entered from the terminal:

```
$ wc -l
This is text that
is typed on the
standard input device.
Ctrl+d
      3
$
```

Note that the `Ctrl+d` that is used to terminate the input is not counted as a separate line by the `wc` command because it's interpreted by the shell, not handed to the command. Furthermore, because the `-l` flag was specified to the `wc` command, only the count of the number of lines (3) is presented as the output of the command.

Output Redirection

The output from a command normally intended for standard output can be easily "diverted" to a file instead. This capability is known as *output redirection* and is also essential to understanding the power of Unix.

If the notation > `file` is appended to *any* command that normally writes its output to standard output, the output of that command will be written to the file `file` instead:

```
$ who > users
$
```

This command causes the who command to be executed and its output to be written into the file `users`. Notice that no output appears. This is because the output has been *redirected* from the default standard output device (the terminal) into the specified file. We can check this, of course:

```
$ cat users
oko    tty01   Sep 12 07:30
ai     tty15   Sep 12 13:32
ruth   tty21   Sep 12 10:10
pat    tty24   Sep 12 13:07
steve  tty25   Sep 12 13:03
$
```

If a command has its output redirected to a file and the file already contains some data, that data will be overwritten and lost.

```
$ echo line 1 > users
$ cat users
line 1
$
```

But now consider this example, remembering that users already contains the output of the earlier who command:

```
$ echo line 2 >> users
$ cat users
line 1
line 2
$
```

If you're paying close attention you'll notice that this echo command uses a different type of output redirection, indicated by the characters >>. This character pair causes the standard output from the command to be *appended* to the contents of the specified file. The previous contents are not lost; the new output simply gets added to the end.

By using the redirection append characters >>, you can use cat to append the contents of one file onto the end of another:

```
$ cat file1
This is in file1.
$ cat file2
This is in file2.
$ cat file1 >> file2          Append file1 to file2
$ cat file2
This is in file2.
This is in file1.
$
```

Recall that specifying more than one filename to `cat` results in the display of the first file followed immediately by the second file, and so on. This means there's a second way to accomplish the same result:

```
$ cat file1
This is in file1.
$ cat file2
This is in file2.
$ cat file1 file2
This is in file1.
This is in file2.
$ cat file1 file2 > file3          Redirect it instead
$ cat file3
This is in file1.
This is in file2.
$
```

In fact, that's where the `cat` command gets its name: When used with more than one file, its effect is to *concatenate* the files together.

Input Redirection

Just as the output of a command can be redirected to a file, so can the input of a command be redirected *from* a file. And as the greater-than character > is used for output redirection, the less-than character < is used to redirect the input of a command. Of course, only commands that normally take their input from standard input can have their input redirected from a file in this manner.

To redirect input, type the < character followed by the name of the file that the input is to be read from. To count the number of lines in the file `users`, for example, you already know that you can execute the command `wc -l users`:

```
$ wc -l users
      2 users
$
```

It turns out that you can also count the number of lines in the file by redirecting standard input for the `wc` command:

```
$ wc -l < users
      2
$
```

Note that there is a difference in the output produced by the two forms of the `wc` command. In the first case, the name of the file `users` is listed with the line count; in the second case, it is not.

This points out a subtle distinction between the execution of the two commands. In the first case, `wc` knows that it is reading its input from the file `users`. In the second case, it only sees the raw data which is being fed to it via standard input. The shell redirects the input so that it comes from the file `users` and not the terminal (more about this in the next chapter). As far as `wc` is concerned, it doesn't know whether its input is coming from the terminal or from a file, so it can't report the filename!

Pipes

As you will recall, the file `users` that was created previously contains a list of all the users currently logged in to the system. Because you know that there will be one line in the file for each user logged in to the system, you can easily determine the *number* of login sessions by counting the number of lines in the `users` file:

```
$ who > users
$ wc -l < users
      5
$
```

This output indicates that currently five users are logged in or that there are five login sessions, the difference being that users, particularly administrators, often log in more than once. Now you have a command sequence you can use whenever you want to know how many users are logged in.

Another approach to determine the number of logged-in users bypasses the intermediate file. As referenced earlier, Unix lets you "connect" two commands together. This connection is known as a *pipe*, and it enables you to take the output from one command and feed it directly into the input of another. A pipe is denoted by the character |, which is placed between the two commands. To create a pipe between the `who` and `wc -l` commands, you type `who | wc -l`:

```
$ who | wc -l
     5
$
```

The pipe that is created between these two commands is depicted in Figure 1.12.

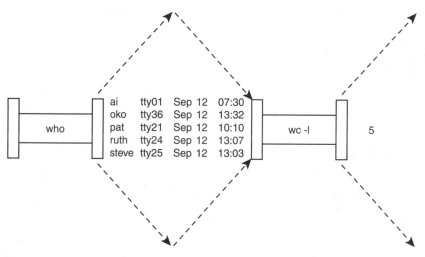

Figure 1.12   Pipeline process: `who  |  wc  -l`

When a pipe is established between two commands, the standard output from the first command is connected directly to the standard input of the second command. You know that the who command writes its list of logged-in users to standard output. Furthermore, you know that if no filename argument is specified to the wc command, it takes its input from standard input. Therefore, the list of logged-in users that is output from the who command automatically becomes the input to the wc command. Note that you never see the output of the who command at the terminal because it is piped directly into the wc command. This is depicted in Figure 1.13.

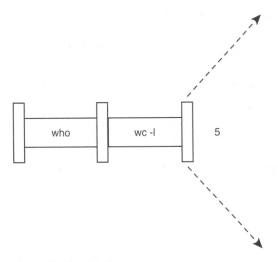

Figure 1.13   Pipeline process

A pipe can be made between *any* two programs, provided that the first program writes its output to standard output, and the second program reads its input from standard input.

As another example, suppose you wanted to count the number of files contained in your directory. Knowledge of the fact that the ls command displays one line of output per file enables you to use the same type of approach as before:

```
$ ls | wc -l
    10
$
```

The output indicates that the current directory contains 10 files.

It is also possible to create a more complicated *pipeline* that consists of more than two programs, with the output of one program feeding into the input of the next. As you become a more sophisticated command line user, you'll find many situations where pipelines can be tremendously powerful.

Filters

The term *filter* is often used in Unix terminology to refer to any program that can take input from standard input, perform some operation on that input, and write the results to standard output. More succinctly, a filter is any program that can be used to modify the output of other programs in a pipeline. So in the pipeline in the previous example, wc is considered a filter. ls is not because it does not read its input from standard input. As other examples, cat and sort are filters, whereas who, date, cd, pwd, echo, rm, mv, and cp are not.

Standard Error

In addition to standard input and standard output, there is a third virtual device known as *standard error*. This is where most Unix commands write their error messages. And as with the other two "standard" places, standard error is associated with your terminal or terminal app by default. In most cases, you never know the difference between standard output and standard error:

```
$ ls n*                          List all files beginning with n
n* not found
$
```

Here the "not found" message is actually being written to standard error by the ls command. You can verify that this message is not being written to standard output by redirecting the ls command's output:

```
$ ls n* > foo
n* not found
$
```

As you can see, the message is still printed out at the terminal and was not added to the file foo, even though you redirected standard output.

The preceding example shows the raison d'être for standard error: so that error messages will still get displayed at the terminal even if standard output is redirected to a file or piped to another command.

You can also redirect standard error to a file (for instance, if you're logging a program's potential errors during long-term operation) by using the slightly more complex notation

```
command 2> file
```

Note that *no space is permitted* between the 2 and the >. Any error messages normally intended for standard error will be diverted into the specified *file*, similar to the way standard output gets redirected.

```
$ ls n* 2> errors
$ cat errors
n* not found
$
```

More on Commands

Typing More Than One Command on a Line

You can type more than one command on a line provided that you separate them with a semicolon. For example, you can find out the current time and your current working directory by typing in the `date` and `pwd` commands on the same line:

```
$ date; pwd
Sat Jul 20 14:43:25 EDT 2002
/users/pat/bin
$
```

You can string out as many commands as you want on the line, as long as each command is delimited by a semicolon.

Sending a Command to the Background

Normally, you type in a command and then wait for the results of the command to be displayed at the terminal. For all the examples you have seen thus far, this waiting time is typically short—a fraction of a second.

Sometimes, however, you may have to run commands that require a few minutes or longer to complete. In those cases, you'll have to wait for the command to finish executing before you can proceed further, *unless you execute the command in the background.*

It turns out that while your Unix or Linux system seems like it's focused completely on what you're doing, all systems are actually multitasking, running multiple commands simultaneously at any given time. If you're on an Ubuntu system, for example, it might have the window manager, a clock, a status monitor and your terminal window all running simultaneously. You too can run multiple commands simultaneously from the command line. That's the idea of putting a command "into background," letting you work on other tasks while it completes.

The notational convention for pushing a command or command sequence into background is to append the ampersand character &. This means that the command will no longer tie up your terminal, and you can then proceed with other work. The standard *output* from the command will still be directed to your terminal, though in most cases the standard *input* will be dissociated from your terminal. If the command does try to read from standard input, it will stop and wait for you to bring it to the foreground (we'll discuss this in more detail in Chapter 14, "Interactive and Nonstandard Shell Features").

Here's an example:

```
$ sort bigdata > out &      Send the sort to the background
[1] 1258                     Process id
$ date                      Your terminal is immediately available to do other work
Sat Jul 20 14:45:09 EDT 2002
$
```

When a command is sent to the background, the Unix system automatically displays two numbers. The first is called the command's *job number* and the second the *process ID*, or *PID*. In the preceding example, 1 is the job number and 1258 the process ID. The job number is used as a shortcut for referring to a specific background job by some shell commands. (You'll learn more about this in Chapter 14.) The process ID uniquely identifies the command that you sent to the background and can be used to obtain status information about the command. This is done with the processor status—ps—command.

The `ps` Command

The `ps` command gives you information about the processes running on the system. Without any options, it prints the status of just your processes. If you type in `ps` at your terminal, you'll get a few lines back describing the processes you have running:

```
$ ps
   PID TTY          TIME CMD
 13463 pts/16   00:00:09 bash
 19880 pts/16   00:00:00 ps
$
```

The `ps` command (typically; your system might vary) prints out four columns of information: `PID`, the process ID; `TTY`, the terminal number that the process was run from; `TIME`, the amount of computer time in minutes and seconds that process has used; and `CMD`, the name of the process. (The `bash` process in the preceding example is the shell that was started when we logged in, and it's used 9 seconds of computer time.) Until the command is finished, it shows up in the output of the `ps` command as a running process, so process 19880 in the preceding example is the `ps` command itself.

When used with the `-f` option, `ps` prints out more information about your processes, including the *parent* process ID (`PPID`), the time the process started (`STIME`), and the command arguments:

```
$ ps -f
UID        PID   PPID  C STIME TTY          TIME CMD
steve    13463  13355  0 12:12 pts/16   00:00:09 bash
steve    19884  13463  0 13:39 pts/16   00:00:00 ps -f
$
```

Command Summary

Table 1.2 summarizes the commands reviewed in this chapter. In this table, *file* refers to a file, *file(s)* to one or more files, *dir* to a directory, and *dir(s)* to one or more directories.

Table 1.2   **Command Summary**

Command	Description
cat *file(s)*	Display contents of *file(s)* or standard input if not supplied
cd *dir*	Change working directory to *dir*
cp *file$_1$ file$_2$*	Copy *file$_1$* to *file$_2$*
cp *file(s) dir*	Copy *file(s)* into *dir*
date	Display the date and time
echo *args*	Display *args*
ln *file$_1$ file$_2$*	Link *file$_1$* to *file$_2$*
ln *file(s) dir*	Link *file(s)* into *dir*
ls *file(s)*	List *file(s)*
ls *dir(s)*	List files in *dir(s)* or in current directory if *dir(s)* is not specified
mkdir *dir(s)*	Create directory *dir(s)*
mv *file$_1$ file$_2$*	Move *file$_1$* to *file$_2$* (simply rename it if both reference the same directory)
mv *file(s) dir*	Move *file(s)* into directory *dir*
ps	List information about active processes
pwd	Display current working directory path
rm *file(s)*	Remove *files(s)*
rmdir *dir(s)*	Remove empty directory *dir(s)*
sort *file(s)*	Sort lines of *file(s)* or standard input if *file(s)* not supplied
wc *file(s)*	Count the number of lines, words, and characters in *file(s)* or standard input if *file(s)* not supplied
who	Display who's logged in

2

What Is the Shell?

In this chapter you'll learn what the Unix command shell is, what it does and why it's a vital part of every power user's toolbox.

The Kernel and the Utilities

The Unix system is logically divided into two different areas: the *kernel* and the *utilities* (see Figure 2.1). Or, if you prefer, the kernel and everything else, generally all accessed through the shell.

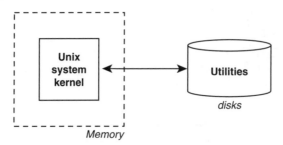

Figure 2.1   The Unix system

The kernel is the heart of the Unix system and resides in the computer's memory from the time the computer is turned on and *booted* until the time it is shut down.

The various tools and utilities that make up the full Unix system experience reside on the computer's disk and are only brought into memory and executed as requested. Virtually every Unix command you know is a utility; therefore, the program resides on the disk and is only brought into memory at your request. So, for example, when you execute the `date` command, the Unix system loads the program called `date` from the computer's disk into memory and begins reading its code to take the specified action or actions.

The shell is also a utility program and is loaded into memory for execution as part of your login sequence. In fact, it's worth learning the precise sequence of events that occurs when the first shell on a terminal or window starts up.

The Login Shell

In the old days, terminals were physical devices that were connected to the Unix hardware through a direct wire. Nowadays, however, terminal programs let you stay within your Linux, Mac or Windows environment and interact with the system over the network in a managed window. Generally you launch a program such as Terminal or xterm, then connect to remote systems as needed using programs such as ssh, telnet, or rlogin.

For each physical terminal on a system, a program called getty will be active. This is depicted in Figure 2.2.

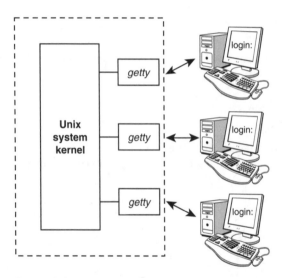

Figure 2.2 The getty process

The Unix system—more precisely a program called init—automatically starts up a getty program on each terminal port whenever the system is allowing users to log in. getty is essentially a device driver, letting the login program display the message login: at its assigned terminal and wait for someone to type in something.

If you connect via a program like ssh, you'll be assigned a pseudo-terminal or pseudo-tty, in Unix parlance. That's why when you typed in who you saw entries like ptty3 or pty1.

In both instances, there is the program that reads your account and password information, and the program that validates it and invokes whatever login programs are needed for you to "log in" if everything checks out and is correct.

As soon as someone types in some characters followed by the Enter key, the login program finishes the process of logging in (see Figure 2.3).

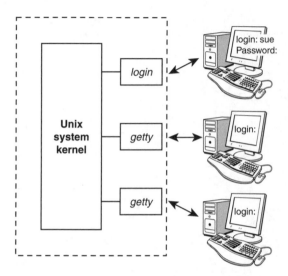

Figure 2.3   `login` started on `sue`'s terminal

When `login` begins execution, it displays the string `Password:` at the terminal and then waits for you to type your password. After you have typed it and pressed `Enter` (you won't see any output as you type, for security reasons), `login` then proceeds to verify your login name and password against the corresponding entry in the file `/etc/passwd`. This file contains an entry for each user account that specifies, among other things, the login name, home directory, and program to start up when that user logs in. The last bit of information (the login shell) is stored after the *last* colon of each line. If nothing follows the last colon, the *standard* shell `/bin/sh` is assumed by default.

If you log in through a terminal program, the data handshake might involve a program like `ssh` on your system and `sshd` on the server, and if you're opening up a window on your Unix computer, it will likely just instantly log you in without you having to again type in your password. Handy!

But back to the password file. The following three lines show typical lines from `/etc/passwd` for three users of the system: `sue`, `pat`, and `bob`:

```
sue:*:15:47::/users/sue:
pat:*:99:7::/users/pat:/bin/ksh
bob:*:13:100::/users/data:/users/data/bin/data_entry
```

After `login` validates an encrypted version of the password you typed in against the encrypted password for the specified account as stored in `/etc/shadow`, it then checks for the name of the login program to execute. In most cases, this will be `/bin/sh`, `/bin/ksh`, or `/bin/bash`. In other cases, it may be a special custom-designed program or `/bin/nologin` for accounts that don't include interactive access (common for file ownership management). The idea underlying them all is that you can set up a login account to automatically run any program whatsoever whenever someone logs in to the system. The shell is the program most often selected because of its general utility, but it's not the only game in town.

Back to Sue. Once she's validated, login essentially kills itself, handing off control of Sue's terminal connection to the standard shell and then vanishing from memory (see Figure 2.4).

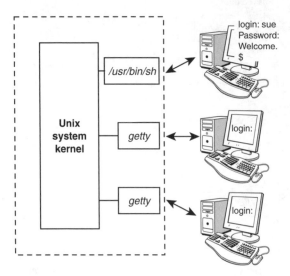

Figure 2.4   login executes /usr/bin/sh

According to the other entries from /etc/passwd shown previously, pat gets the program ksh stored in /bin (this is the Korn shell), and bob gets the specialized program data_entry (see Figure 2.5).

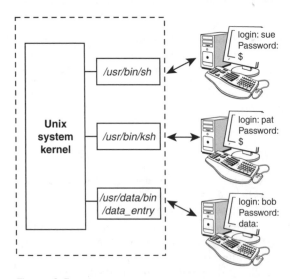

Figure 2.5   Three users logged in

As mentioned earlier, the `init` program runs programs similar to `getty` for networked connections. For example, `sshd`, `telnetd`, and `rlogind` answer connection requests via `ssh`, `telnet`, and `rlogin`, respectively. Instead of being tied directly to a specific, physical terminal or modem line, these programs connect users' shells to *pseudo-ttys*. You can see this whether you're logged in to your system over a network, on an X Windows screen, or through a networked terminal connection program with the `who` command:

```
$ who
phw      pts/0    Jul 20 17:37         Logged in with rlogin
$
```

Typing Commands to the Shell

When the shell starts up, it displays a command prompt—typically a dollar sign $—at your terminal and then waits for you to type in a command (Figure 2.6, Steps 1 and 2). Each time you type in a command and press the `Enter` key (Step 3), the shell analyzes what you typed and proceeds to carry out your request (Step 4).

If you ask the shell to invoke a particular program, it searches the disk, stepping through all the directories you've specified in your PATH until it finds the named program. When the program is found, the shell creates a clone of itself (known as a *subshell*) and asks the kernel to replace the subshell with the specified program; then the login shell "goes to sleep" until the program has finished (Step 5). The kernel copies the specified program into memory and begins its execution. This copied program is called a *process*; in this way, the distinction is made between a program that is kept in a file on the disk and a process that is in memory and being executed, line by line.

If the program writes output to standard output, that output will appear at your terminal unless redirected or piped into another command. Similarly, if the program reads input from standard input, it will wait for you to type in that input unless redirected from a file or piped from another command (Step 6).

When the command finishes execution, it vanishes and control once again returns to the login shell, which prompts for your next command (Steps 7 and 8).

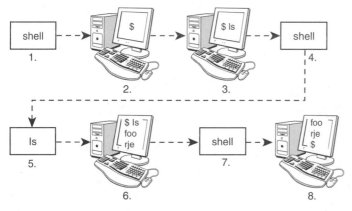

Figure 2.6   Command cycle

Note that this cycle continues as long as you're logged in. When you log off the system, execution of the shell then terminates and the system starts up a new getty (or rlogind, and so on) and waits for someone else to log in. This cycle is illustrated in Figure 2.7.

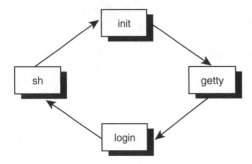

Figure 2.7   Login cycle

It's important to recognize that the shell is just a program. It has no special privileges on the system, meaning that anyone with sufficient expertise and enthusiasm can create their own shell. That's why so many different variations or "flavors" of the shell exist today, including the older Bourne shell, developed by Stephen Bourne; the Korn shell, developed by David Korn; the "Bourne again shell," mainly used on Linux systems; and the C shell, developed by Bill Joy. They were all designed to serve specific purposes and have their own unique capabilities and personalities.

The Shell's Responsibilities

Now you know that the shell analyzes (to use proper computer parlance, it *parses*) each line you type in and initiates execution of the selected program. It's during the parsing phase that filename expansion special characters like * are expanded, as discussed in the previous chapter.

The shell also has other responsibilities, as outlined in Figure 2.8.

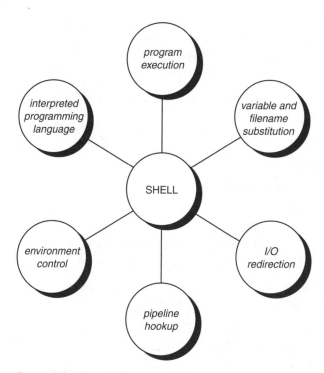

Figure 2.8   The shell's responsibilities

Program Execution

The shell is responsible for the execution of all programs that you request from your terminal.

Each time you type in a line to the shell, the shell analyzes the line and then determines what to do. As far as the shell is concerned, each line follows the same basic format:

```
program-name arguments
```

The line that is typed to the shell is known more formally as the *command line*. The shell scans this command line and determines the name of the program to be executed and what arguments to pass to the program.

The shell uses special characters to determine where the program name starts and ends, and where each argument starts and ends. These characters are collectively called *whitespace characters*, and are the space character, the horizontal tab character, and the end-of-line character, known more formally as the *newline character*. Multiple occurrences of whitespace characters are ignored by the shell. When you type the command

```
mv     tmp/mazewars games
```

the shell scans the command line and takes everything from the start of the line to the first whitespace character as the name of the program to execute: mv. Subsequent whitespace (the extra spaces) are ignored and the set of characters up to the next whitespace character is the first argument to mv: tmp/mazewars. The characters up to the next whitespace character—in this case, the newline character—is the second argument to mv: games. After parsing the command line, the shell then proceeds to execute the mv command, giving it the two specified arguments tmp/mazewars and games (see Figure 2.9).

Figure 2.9   Execution of mv with two arguments

As mentioned, multiple occurrences of whitespace characters are ignored by the shell. This means that when the shell processes this command line:

```
echo            when    do          we      eat?
```

it passes four arguments to the echo program: when, do, we, and eat? (see Figure 2.10).

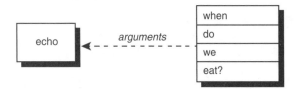

Figure 2.10   Execution of echo with four arguments

Because echo takes its arguments and simply displays them at the terminal, adding an individual space between each argument, the output from the following becomes a lot more legible:

```
$ echo          when    do          we      eat?
when do we eat?
$
```

It turns out the echo command never sees those blank spaces; they have been "gobbled up" by the shell. When we discuss quotes in Chapter 5, you'll see how you can include blank spaces in arguments to programs, but usually having extras vanish is exactly the behavior you want.

We mentioned earlier that the shell searches the disk until it finds the program you want to execute and then asks the Unix kernel to initiate its execution. This is true most of the time. However, there are some commands that are actually built into the shell itself. These built-in commands include cd, pwd, and echo. Before the shell searches the disk for a command, it first determines whether it's a built-in command, and if so executes the command directly.

But there's a bit more the shell does before individual programs are invoked, so let's talk about those for just a moment too.

Variable and Filename Substitution

Like a more formal programming language, the shell lets you assign values to variables. Whenever you specify one of these variables on the command line preceded by a dollar sign, the shell substitutes the value assigned to the variable. This topic is covered in much more detail in Chapter 4.

The shell also performs filename substitution on the command line. In fact, the shell scans the command line looking for filename substitution characters *, ?, or [...] before determining the name of the program to execute and its arguments.

Suppose that your current directory contains these files:

```
$ ls
mrs.todd
prog1
shortcut
sweeney
$
```

Now let's use filename substitution (*) for the echo command:

```
$ echo *            List all files
mrs.todd prog1 shortcut sweeney
$
```

How many arguments were passed to the echo program, one or four? Because the shell performs the filename substitution, the answer is four. When the shell analyzes the line

```
echo *
```

it recognizes the special character * and substitutes the names of all files in the current directory (it even alphabetizes them for you):

```
echo mrs.todd prog1 shortcut sweeney
```

Then the shell determines what arguments to pass to the actual command. So echo never sees the asterisk and as far as it's concerned, four arguments were typed on the command line (see Figure 2.11).

Figure 2.11   Execution of echo

I/O Redirection

It is also the shell's responsibility to take care of input and output redirection. It scans each entered command line for occurrences of the special redirection characters <, >, or >> (in case you're curious, there is a << redirection sequence, as you'll learn in Chapter 12).

When you type the command

```
echo Remember to record The Walking Dead > reminder
```

the shell recognizes the special output redirection character > and takes the next word on the command line as the name of the file to which the output should be redirected. In this case, the file is called `reminder`. If `reminder` already exists and you have write access, the previous contents are overwritten. If you don't have write access to the file or its directory, the shell will produce an error message.

Before the shell starts execution of the desired program, it redirects the standard output of the program to the indicated file. In almost every case, the program never knows that its output is being redirected. It just goes on its merry way writing to standard output (which is normally your terminal, you'll recall), unaware that the shell has redirected that information to a file.

Let's take another look at two nearly identical commands:

```
$ wc -l users
      5 users
$ wc -l < users
      5
$
```

In the first case, the shell parses the command line and determines that the name of the program to execute is wc and passes it two arguments: -l and users (see Figure 2.12).

Figure 2.12 Execution of wc -l users

When wc begins execution, it sees that it was passed the two arguments. The first, -l, tells it to count the number of lines. The second argument specifies the name of the file whose lines are to be counted. So wc opens the file users, counts its lines, and then prints the resultant count along with the filename.

Operation of wc in the second case is slightly different. The shell spots the input redirection character < when it scans the command line. The word that follows on the command line is therefore interpreted as the name of the file from which input is to be redirected. Having "gobbled up" the < users from the command line, the shell then starts execution of the wc program, redirecting its standard input from the file users and passing it only the single argument -l (see Figure 2.13).

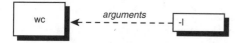

Figure 2.13   Execution of wc -l < users

When wc begins execution this time, it sees that it was passed the single argument -l. Because no filename was specified, wc decides that the number of lines coming in from standard input should be counted instead. So wc -l counts the number of lines, unaware that it's actually counting the number of lines in the file users. The final tally is displayed as usual, but without the name of a file because wc wasn't given one.

The difference in execution of the two commands is important for you to understand. If you're still unclear on this point, review the preceding section one more time before proceeding.

Hooking up a Pipeline

Just as the shell scans the command line looking for redirection characters, it also looks for the pipe character |. For each match, it connects the standard output from the preceding command to the standard input of the subsequent one, then initiates execution of both programs.

So when you type

who | wc -l

the shell finds the pipe symbol separating the commands who and wc. It connects the standard output of the former command to the standard input of the latter, then initiates execution of both. When the who command executes, it produces a list of who's logged in and writes the results to standard output, unaware that this is not going to the terminal but to another command instead.

When the wc command executes, it recognizes that no filename was specified and counts the lines on standard input, unaware that standard input is not coming from the terminal but from the output of the who command.

As we proceed, you'll see that not only can you have two-command pipelines; you can string together three, four, five, or more commands in really complicated pipelines too. It's a bit tricky to figure out, but that's really where some of the greatest power of the Unix system hides.

Environment Control

The shell provides certain commands that let you customize your environment. Your environment includes your home directory, the characters that the shell displays to prompt you to type in a command, and a list of the directories to be searched whenever you request that a program be executed. You'll learn more about this in Chapter 10.

Interpreted Programming Language

The shell has its own built-in programming language. This language is *interpreted*, meaning that the shell analyzes each statement as encountered, then executes any valid commands found. This differs from programming languages like C++ and Swift, in which the programming statements are typically compiled into a machine-executable form before they are executed.

Programs developed in interpreted programming languages are typically easier to debug and modify than compiled ones. However, they can take longer to execute than their compiled equivalents.

The shell programming language provides features you'd find in most other programming languages. It has looping constructs, decision-making statements, variables, and functions, and is procedure-oriented. Modern shells based on the IEEE POSIX standard have many other features including arrays, data typing, and built-in arithmetic operations.

Tools of the Trade

This chapter provides detailed descriptions of some commonly used shell programming tools. Covered are cut, paste, sed, tr, grep, uniq, and sort. The more proficient you become at using these tools, the easier it will be to write efficient shell scripts.

Regular Expressions

Before getting into the tools, you need to learn about *regular expressions*. Regular expressions are used by many different Unix commands, including ed, sed, awk, grep, and, to a more limited extent, the vi editor. They provide a convenient and consistent way of specifying *patterns* to be matched.

Where this gets confusing is that the shell recognizes a limited form of regular expressions with filename substitution. Recall that the asterisk (*) specifies zero or more characters to match, the question mark (?) specifies any single character, and the construct [...] specifies any character enclosed between the brackets. But that's not the same thing as the more formal regular expressions we'll explore. For example, the shell sees ? as a match for any single character, while a regular expression—commonly abbreviated regex—uses a period (.) for the same purpose.

True regular expressions are far more sophisticated than those recognized by the shell and there are entire books written about how to assemble really complex regex statements. Don't worry, though, you won't need to become an expert to find great value in regular expressions!

Throughout this section, we assume familiarity with a line-based editor such as ex or ed. See Appendix B for more information on these editors if you're not familiar with them, or check the appropriate man page.

Matching Any Character: The Period (.)

A period in a regular expression matches any single character, no matter what it is. So the regular expression

r.

matches an r followed by any single character.

The regular expression

`.x.`

matches an x that is surrounded by any two characters, not necessarily the same.

We can demonstrate a lot of regular expressions by using the simple ed editor, an old-school line-oriented editor that has been around as long as Linux have been around.

For example, the ed command

`/ ... /`

searches forward in the file you are editing for the first line that contains any three characters surrounded by blanks. But before we demonstrate that, notice in the very beginning of this example that ed shows the number of characters in the file (248) and that commands like print (p) can be prefixed with a range specifier, with the most basic being 1,$, which is the first through last line of the file:

```
$ ed intro
248
1,$p                            Print all the lines
The Unix operating system was pioneered by Ken
Thompson and Dennis Ritchie at Bell Laboratories
in the late 1960s.  One of the primary goals in
the design of the Unix system was to create an
environment that promoted efficient program
development.
```

That's our working file. Now let's try some regular expressions:

```
/ ... /                         Look for three chars surrounded by blanks
The Unix operating system was pioneered by Ken
/                               Repeat last search
Thompson and Dennis Ritchie at Bell Laboratories
1,$s/p.o/XXX/g                  Change all p.os to XXX
1,$p                            Let's see what happened
The Unix operating system was XXXneered by Ken
ThomXXXn and Dennis Ritchie at Bell Laboratories
in the late 1960s.  One of the primary goals in
the design of the Unix system was to create an
environment that XXXmoted efficient XXXgram
development.
```

In the first search, ed started searching from the beginning of the file and found that the sequence "was" in the first line matched the indicated pattern and printed it.

Repeating the search (the ed command /) resulted in the display of the second line of the file because "and" matched the pattern. The substitute command s that followed specified that all occurrences of the character p, followed by any single character, followed by the character o were to be replaced by the characters XXX. The prefix 1,$ indicates that it should be applied to all lines in the file, and the substitution is specified with the structure s/*old*/*new*/g, where s indicates it's a substitution, the slashes delimit the old and new values, and `g` indicates it should be applied as many times as needed for each line, not just once per line.

Matching the Beginning of the Line: The Caret (^)

When the caret character `^` is used as the first character in a regular expression, it matches the beginning of the line. So the regular expression

`^George`

matches the characters `George` *only if they occur at the beginning of the line*. This is actually known as "left-rooting" in the regex world, for obvious reasons.

Let's have a look:

```
$ ed intro
248
/the/
>>in the late 1960s.  One of the primary goals in
>>the design of the Unix system was to create an
/^the/                          Find the line that starts with the
the design of the Unix system was to create an
1,$s/^/>>/                      Insert >> at the beginning of each line
1,$p
>>The Unix operating system was pioneered by Ken
>>Thompson and Dennis Ritchie at Bell Laboratories
>>in the late 1960s.  One of the primary goals in
>>the design of the Unix system was to create an
>>environment that promoted efficient program
>>development.
```

The preceding example also shows how the regular expression `^` can be used to match the beginning of the line. Here it is used to insert the characters `>>` at the start of each line. A command like

`1,$s/^/    /`

is also commonly used to insert spaces at the start of each line (in this case four spaces would be inserted).

Matching the End of the Line: The Dollar Sign $

Just as the `^` is used to match the beginning of the line, so the dollar sign `$` is used to match the end of the line. So the regular expression

`contents$`

matches the characters `contents` *only if they are the last characters on the line*. What do you think would be matched by the regular expression

`.$`

Would this match a period character that ends a line? No. Recall that the period matches any character, so this would match any single character at the end of the line (including a period).

So how do you match a period? In general, if you want to match any of the characters that have a special meaning in regular expressions, precede the character by a backslash (\) to override its special meaning. For example, the regular expression

`\.$`

matches any line that ends in a period, and the regular expression

`^\.`

matches any line that starts with a period.

Want to specify a backslash as an actual character? Use two backslashes in a row: \\.

```
$ ed intro
248
/\.$/                      Search for a line that ends with a period
development.
1,$s/$/>>/                 Add >> to the end of each line
1,$p
The Unix operating system was pioneered by Ken>>
Thompson and Dennis Ritchie at Bell Laboratories>>
in the late 1960s.  One of the primary goals in>>
the design of the Unix system was to create an>>
environment that promoted efficient program>>
development.>>
1,$s/..$//                 Delete the last two characters from each line
1,$p
The Unix operating system was pioneered by Ken
Thompson and Dennis Ritchie at Bell Laboratories
in the late 1960s.  One of the primary goals in
the design of the Unix system was to create an
environment that promoted efficient program
development.
```

A common use of ^ and $ is the regular expression

`^$`

which matches any line that contains *no* characters at all. Note that this regular expression is different from

`^ $`

which matches any line that consists of a single space character.

Matching a Character Set: The [. . .] Construct

Suppose that you are editing a file and want to search for the first occurrence of the characters the. In ed, this is easy: You simply type the command

`/the/`

This causes ed to search forward in its buffer until it finds a line containing the indicated sequence. The first line that matches will be displayed by ed:

```
$ ed intro
248
/the/                                   Find line containing the
in the late 1960s.  One of the primary goals in
```

Notice that the first line of the file also contains the word the, except it begins with a capital T. A regular expression that searches for either the *or* The can be built using a character set: the characters [and] can be used to specify that one of the enclosed character set is to be matched. The regular expression

`[tT]he`

would match a lower- or uppercase t followed immediately by the characters he:

```
$ ed intro
248
/[tT]he/                     Look for the or The
The Unix operating system was pioneered by Ken
/                            Continue the search
in the late 1960s.  One of the primary goals in
/                            Once again
the design of the Unix system was to create an
1,$s/[aeiouAEIOU]//g         Delete all vowels
1,$p
Th nx prtng systm ws pnrd by Kn
Thmpsn nd Dnns Rtch t Bll Lbrtrs
n th lt 1960s. n f th prmry gls n
th dsgn f th nx systm ws t crt n
nvrnmnt tht prmtd ffcnt prgrm
dvlpmnt.
```

Notice the example in the above of [aeiouAEIOU] which will match a single vowel, either uppercase or lowercase. That notation can get rather clunky, however, so a range of characters can be specified inside the brackets instead. This can be done by separating the starting and ending characters of the range by a dash (-). So, to match any digit character 0 through 9, you could use the regular expression

`[0123456789]`

or, more succinctly, you could write

`[0-9]`

To match an uppercase letter, use

```
[A-Z]
```

To match an upper- or lowercase letter, you write

```
[A-Za-z]
```

Here are some examples with ed:

```
$ ed intro
248
/[0-9]/                         Find a line containing a digit
in the late 1960s. One of the primary goals in
/^[A-Z]/                        Find a line that starts with an uppercase letter
The Unix operating system was pioneered by Ken
/                               Again
Thompson and Dennis Ritchie at Bell Laboratories
1,$s/[A-Z]/*/g                  Change all uppercase letters to *s
1,$p
*he *nix operating system was pioneered by *en
*hompson and *ennis *itchie at *ell *aboratories
in the late 1960s. *ne of the primary goals in
the design of the *nix system was to create an
environment that promoted efficient program
development.
```

As you'll learn below, the asterisk is a special character in regular expressions. However, you don't need to put a backslash before it in the replacement string of the substitute command because the substitution's replacement string has a different expression language (we did mention that this can be a bit tricky at times, right?).

In the ed editor, regular expression sequences such as *, ., [...], $, and ^ are only meaningful in the search string and have no special meaning when they appear in the replacement string.

If a caret (^) appears as the first character after the left bracket, the sense of the match is *inverted*. (By comparison, the shell uses the ! for this purpose with character sets.) For example, the regular expression

```
[^A-Z]
```

matches any character *except* an uppercase letter. Similarly,

```
[^A-Za-z]
```

matches any non-alphabetic character. To demonstrate, let's remove all non-alphabetic characters from the lines in our test file:

```
$ ed intro
248
1,$s/[^a-zA-Z]//g               Delete all non-alphabetic characters
1,$p
TheUnixoperatingsystemwaspioneeredbyKen
ThompsonandDennisRitchieatBellLaboratories
```

```
InthelatesOneoftheprimarygoalsin
ThedesignoftheUnixsystemwastocreatean
Environmentthatpromotedefficientprogram
development
```

Matching Zero or More Characters: The Asterisk (*)

The asterisk is used by the shell in filename substitution to match zero or more characters. In forming regular expressions, the asterisk is used to match zero or more occurrences of the *preceding* element of the regular expression (which may itself be another regular expression).

So, for example, the regular expression

X*

matches zero, one, two, three, … capital X's while the expression

XX*

matches one or more capital X's, because the expression specifies a single X followed by zero or more X's. You can accomplish the same effect with a + instead: it matches *one or more* of the preceding expression, so XX* and X+ are identical in function.

A similar type of pattern is frequently used to match one or more blank spaces in a line:

```
$ ed lotsaspaces
85
1,$p
This        is    an example   of a
file    that  contains      a lot
of   blank spaces               Change multiple blanks to single blanks
1,$s/  */ /g
1,$p
This is an example of a
file that contains a lot
of blank spaces
```

The ed command

```
1,$s/  */ /g
```

told the program to substitute all occurrences of a space followed by zero or more spaces with a single space—in other words, to collapse all whitespace into single spaces. If it matches a single space, there's no change. But if it matches three spaces, say, they'll all be replaced by a single space.

The regular expression

```
.*
```

is often used to specify zero or more occurrences of *any* characters. Bear in mind that a regular expression matches the *longest* string of characters that match the pattern. Therefore, used by itself, this regular expression always matches the *entire* line of text.

As another example of the combination of . and *, the regular expression

e.*e

matches all the characters from the first e on a line to the last one.

Note that it doesn't necessarily match only lines that start and end with an e, however, because it's not left- or right-rooted (that is, it doesn't use ^ or $ in the pattern).

```
$ ed intro
248
1,$s/e.*e/+++/
1,$p
Th+++n
Thompson and D+++S
in th+++ primary goals in
th+++ an
+++nt program
d+++nt.
```

Here's an interesting regular expression. What do you think it matches?

[A-Za-z][A-Za-z]*

This matches any alphabetic character followed by zero or more alphabetic characters. This is pretty close to a regular expression that matches words and can be used as shown below to replace all words with the letter X while retaining all spaces and punctuation.

```
$ ed intro
248
1,$s/[A-Za-z][A-Za-z]*/X/g
1,$p
X X X X X X X
X X X X X X
X X X 1960X.  X X X X X
X X X X X X X X X
X X X X X
X.
```

The only thing it didn't match in this example was the numeric sequence 1960. You can change the regular expression to also consider a sequence of digits as a word too, of course:

```
$ ed intro
248
1,$s/[A-Za-z0-9][A-Za-z0-9]*/X/g
1,$p
X X X X X X X
X X X X X X
X X X.  X X X X X
X X X X X X X X X
X X X X X
X.
```

We could expand on this to consider hyphenated and contracted words (for example, *don't*), but we'll leave that as an exercise for you. As a point to note, if you want to match a dash character inside a bracketed choice of characters, you must put the dash immediately after the left bracket (but after the inversion character ^ if present) or immediately before the right bracket for it to be properly understood. That is, either of these expressions

```
[-0-9]
[0-9-]
```

matches a single dash or digit character.

In a similar fashion, if you want to match a right bracket character, it must appear after the opening left bracket (and after the ^ if present). So

```
[]a-z]
```

matches a right bracket or a lowercase letter.

Matching a Precise Number of Subpatterns: \{ . . . \}

In the preceding examples, you saw how to use the asterisk to specify that *one* or more occurrences of the preceding regular expression are to be matched. For instance, the regular expression

XX*

means match an x followed by zero or more subsequent occurrences of the letter x. Similarly,

XXX*

means match at least *two* consecutive x's.

Once you get to this point, however, it ends up rather clunky, so there is a more general way to specify a precise number of characters to be matched: by using the construct

\{*min,max*\}

where *min* specifies the minimum number of occurrences of the preceding regular expression to be matched, and *max* specifies the maximum. Notice that you need to *escape* the curly brackets by preceding each with a backslash.

The regular expression

X\{1,10\}

matches from one to 10 consecutive x's. Whenever there's a choice, the largest pattern is matched, so if the input text contains eight consecutive x's, that is how many will be matched by the preceding regular expression.

As another example, the regular expression

[A-Za-z]\{4,7\}

matches a sequence of alphabetic letters from four to seven characters long.

Let's try a substitution using this notation:

```
$ ed intro
248
1,$s/[A-Za-z]\{4,7\}/X/g
1,$p
The X Xng X was Xed by Ken
Xn and X X at X XX
in the X 1960s.  One of the X X in
the X of the X X was to X an
XX X Xd Xnt X
XX.
```

This invocation is a specific instance of a global search and replace in ed (and, therefore, also in vi): s/*old*/*new*/. In this case, we add a range of 1,$ beforehand and the g flag is appended to ensure that multiple substitutions will occur on each line, as appropriate.

A few special cases of this special construct are worth noting. If only one number is enclosed by braces, as in

`\{10\}`

that number specifies that the preceding regular expression must be matched *exactly* that many times. So

`[a-zA-Z]\{7\}`

matches exactly seven alphabetic characters; and

`.\{10\}`

matches exactly 10 characters no matter what they are:

```
$ ed intro
248
1,$s/^.\{10\}//            Delete the first 10 chars from each line
1,$p
perating system was pioneered by Ken
nd Dennis Ritchie at Bell Laboratories
e 1960s. One of the primary goals in
 of the Unix system was to create an
t that promoted efficient program
t.
1,$s/.\{5\}$//            Delete the last 5 chars from each line
1,$p
perating system was pioneered b
nd Dennis Ritchie at Bell Laborat
e 1960s. One of the primary goa
 of the Unix system was to crea
t that promoted efficient pr
t.
```

Note that the last line of the file didn't have five characters when the last substitute command was executed; therefore, the match failed on that line and thus was left alone because we specified that *exactly* five characters were to be deleted.

If a single number is enclosed in the braces, followed immediately by a comma, then at *least* that many occurrences of the previous regular expression must be matched, but no upper limit is set. So

+\{5,\}

matches at least five consecutive plus signs. If more than five occur sequentially in the input data, the largest number is matched.

```
$ ed intro
248
1,$s/[a-zA-Z]\{6,\}/X/g          Change words at least 6 letters long to X
1,$p
The Unix X X was X by Ken
X and X X at Bell X
in the late 1960s. One of the X goals in
the X of the Unix X was to X an
X that X X X
X.
```

Saving Matched Characters: \ (. . . \)

It is possible to reference the characters matched against a regular expression by enclosing those characters inside backslashed parentheses. These captured characters are stored in pre-defined variables in the regular expression parser called *registers*, which are numbered 1 through 9.

This gets a bit confusing, so take this section slowly!

As a first example, the regular expression

^\(.\)

matches the first character on the line, whatever it is, and stores it into register 1.

To retrieve the characters stored in a particular register, the construct \n is used, where n is a digit from 1 to 9. So the regular expression

^\(.\)\1

initially matches the first character on the line and stores it in register 1, then matches whatever is stored in register 1, as specified by the \1. The net effect of this regular expression is to match the first two characters on a line *if they are both the same character*. Tricky, eh?

The regular expression

^\(.\).*\1$

matches all lines in which the first character on the line (^.) is the same as the last character on the line (\1$). The .* matches all the characters in-between.

Let's break this one down. Remember ^ is the beginning of line and $ the end of line. The simplified pattern is then `..*` which is the first character of the line (the first `.`) followed by the `.*` for the rest of the line. Add the `\( \)` notation to push that first character into register 1 and `\1` to then reference the character, and it should make sense to you.

Successive occurrences of the `\(...\)` construct get assigned to successive registers. So when the following regular expression is used to match some text

`^\(...\)\(...\)`

the first three characters on the line will be stored into register 1, and the next three characters into register 2. If you appended `\2\1` to the pattern, you would match a 12-character string in which characters 1–3 matched characters 10–12, and in which characters 4–6 matched characters 7–9.

When using the substitute command in ed, a register can also be referenced as part of the replacement string, which is where this can be really powerful:

```
$ ed phonebook
114
1,$p
Alice Chebba     973-555-2015
Barbara Swingle  201-555-9257
Liz Stachiw      212-555-2298
Susan Goldberg   201-555-7776
Tony Iannino     973-555-1295
1,$s/\(.*\)     \(.*\)/\2 \1/          Switch the two fields
1,$p
973-555-2015 Alice Chebba
201-555-9257 Barbara Swingle
212-555-2298 Liz Stachiw
201-555-7776 Susan Goldberg
973-555-1295 Tony Iannino
```

The names and the phone numbers are separated from each other in the phonebook file by a single tab character. The regular expression

`\(.*\)     \(.*\)`

says to match all the characters up to the first tab (that's the character sequence `.*` between the `\(` and the `\)` and assign them to register 1, and to match all the characters that follow the tab character and assign them to register 2. The replacement string

`\2 \1`

specifies the contents of register 2, followed by a space, followed by the contents of register 1.

When ed applies the substitute command to the first line of the file:

```
Alice Chebba     973-555-2015
```

it matches everything up to the tab (`Alice Chebba`) and stores it into register 1, and everything after the tab (`973-555-2015`) and stores it into register 2. The tab itself is lost because it's not surrounded by parentheses in the regex. Then `ed` substitutes the characters that were matched (the entire line) with the contents of register 2 (`973-555-2015`), followed by a space, followed by the contents of register 1 (`Alice Chebba`):

```
973-555-2015 Alice Chebba
```

As you can see, regular expressions are powerful tools that enable you to match and manipulate complex patterns, albeit with a slight tendency to look like a cat ran over your keyboard at times!

Table 3.1 summarizes the special characters recognized in regular expressions to help you understand any you encounter and so you can build your own as needed.

Table 3.1   **Regular Expression Characters**

Notation	Meaning	Example	Matches
.	*Any* character	`a..`	a followed by any two characters
^	Beginning of line	`^wood`	wood only if it appears at the beginning of the line
$	End of line	`x$`	x only if it is the last character on the line
		`^INSERT$`	A line containing just the characters `INSERT`
		`^$`	A line that contains **no** characters

*	Zero or more occurrences of previous regular expression	`x*`
		`xx*`
		`.*`
		`w.*s`
			Zero or more consecutive x's
			One or more consecutive x's
			Zero or more characters w followed by zero or more characters followed by an s

+	One or more occurrences of previous regular expression	`x+`
		`xx+`
		`.+`
		`w.+s`
			One or more consecutive x's
			Two or more consecutive x's
			One or more characters w followed by one or more characters followed by an s

[*chars*]	Any character in *chars*	`[tT]`
		`[a-z]`
		`[a-zA-Z]`
			Lower- or uppercase t
			Lowercase letter Lower- or uppercase letter

[^*chars*]	Any character *not* in *chars*	`[^0-9]` `[^a-zA-Z]`	Any non-numeric character Any non-alphabetic character

(Continued)

Notation	Meaning	Example	Matches
\{min,max\}	At least min and at most max occurrences of previous regular expression	x\{1,5\} [0-9]\{3,9\} [0-9]\{3\} [0-9]\{3,\}	At least 1 and at most 5 x's Anywhere from 3 to 9 successive digits Exactly 3 digits At least 3 digits
\(...\)	Save characters matched between parentheses in next register (1-9)	^\(.\) ^\(.\)\1 ^\(.\)\(.\)	First character on the line; stores it in register 1 First and second characters on the line if they're the same First and second characters on the line; stores first character in register 1 and second character in register 2

cut

This section teaches you about a useful command known as cut. This command comes in handy when you need to extract (that is, "cut out") various fields of data from a data file or the output of a command. The general format of the cut command is

`cut -cchars file`

where *chars* specifies which characters (by position) you want to extract from each line of *file*. This can consist of a single number, as in -c5 to extract the fifth character from each line of input; a comma-separated list of numbers, as in -c1,13,50 to extract characters 1, 13, and 50; or a dash-separated range of numbers, as in -c20-50 to extract characters 20 through 50, inclusive. To extract characters to the end of the line, you can omit the second number of the range so

`cut -c5- data`

extracts characters 5 through the end of the line from each line of data and writes the results to standard output.

If *file* is not specified, cut reads its input from standard input, meaning that you can use cut as a filter in a pipeline.

Let's take another look at the output from the who command:

```
$ who
root     console Feb 24 08:54
steve    tty02   Feb 24 12:55
george   tty08   Feb 24 09:15
dawn     tty10   Feb 24 15:55
$
```

As shown, four people are logged in. Suppose that you just want to know the names of the logged-in users and don't care about what terminals they are on or when they logged in. You can use the cut command to cut out just the usernames from the who command's output:

```
$ who | cut -c1-8            Extract the first 8 characters
root
steve
george
dawn
$
```

The −c1-8 option to cut specifies that characters 1 through 8 are to be extracted from each line of input and written to standard output.

The following shows how you can tack a sort to the end of the preceding pipeline to get a sorted list of the logged-in users:

```
$ who | cut -c1-8 | sort
dawn
george
root
steve
$
```

Note, this is our first three-command pipe. Once you get the concept of output connected to subsequent input, pipes of three, four or more commands are logical and easy to assemble.

If you wanted to see which terminals were currently being used or which pseudo or virtual terminals were in use, you could cut out just the tty field from the who command output:

```
$ who | cut -c10-16
console
tty02
tty08
tty10
$
```

How did you know that who displays the terminal identification in character positions 10 through 16? Simple! You executed the who command at your terminal and *counted* out the appropriate character positions.

You can use cut to extract as many different characters from a line as you want. Here, cut is used to display just the username and login time of all logged-in users:

```
$ who | cut -c1-8,18-
root      Feb 24 08:54
steve     Feb 24 12:55
george    Feb 24 09:15
dawn      Feb 24 15:55
$
```

The option -c1-8,18- specifies "extract characters 1 through 8 (the username) and also characters 18 through the end of the line (the login time)."

The -d and -f Options

The cut command with its -c flag is useful when you need to extract data from a file or command, provided that file or command has a fixed format.

For example, you could use cut with the who command because you know that the usernames are always displayed in character positions 1–8, the terminal in 10–16, and the login time in 18–29. Unfortunately, not all your data will be so well organized!

For instance, take a look at the /etc/passwd file:

```
$ cat /etc/passwd
root:*:0:0:The Super User:/:/usr/bin/ksh
cron:*:1:1:Cron Daemon for periodic tasks:/:
bin:*:3:3:The owner of system files:/:
uucp:*:5:5::/usr/spool/uucp:/usr/lib/uucp/uucico
asg:*:6:6:The Owner of Assignable Devices:/:
steve:*.:203:100::/users/steve:/usr/bin/ksh
other:*:4:4:Needed by secure program:/:
$
```

/etc/passwd is the master file that contains the usernames of all users on your computer system. It also contains other information such as user ID, home directory, and the name of the program to start up when that particular user logs in.

Quite clearly, the data in this file does not line up anywhere near as neatly as the who's output does. Therefore extracting a list of all the users of your system from this file cannot be done using the -c option to cut.

Upon closer inspection of the file, however, it's clear that fields are separated by a colon character. Although each field may not be the same length from one line to the next, you can "count colons" to get the same field from each line.

The -d and -f options are used with cut when you have data that is delimited by a particular character, with -d specifying the field seperator delimiter and -f the field or fields you want extracted. The invocation of the cut command becomes

```
cut -ddchar -ffields file
```

where dchar is the character that delimits each field of the data, and fields specifies the fields to be extracted from file. Field numbers start at 1, and the same type of formats can be used to specify field numbers as was used to specify character positions before (for example, -f1,2,8, -f1-3, -f4-).

To extract the names of all users from /etc/passwd, you could type the following:

```
$ cut -d: -f1 /etc/passwd          Extract field 1
root
cron
bin
```

```
uucp
asg
steve
other
$
```

Given that the home directory of each user is in field 6, you can match up each user of the system with their home directory:

```
$ cut -d: -f1,6 /etc/passwd          Extract fields 1 and 6
root:/
cron:/
bin:/
uucp:/usr/spool/uucp
asg:/
steve:/users/steve
other:/
$
```

If the cut command is used to extract fields from a file and the -d option is not supplied, cut uses the tab character as the default field delimiter.

The following depicts a common pitfall when using the cut command. Suppose that you have a file called phonebook that has the following contents:

```
$ cat phonebook
Alice Chebba      973-555-2015
Barbara Swingle 201-555-9257
Jeff Goldberg     201-555-3378
Liz Stachiw       212-555-2298
Susan Goldberg  201-555-7776
Tony Iannino      973-555-1295
$
```

If you just want to get the names of the people in your phone book, your first impulse would be to use cut as shown:

```
$ cut -c1-15 phonebook
Alice Chebba    97
Barbara Swingle
Jeff Goldberg   2
Liz Stachiw     212
Susan Goldberg
Tony Iannino    97
$
```

Not quite what you want! This happened because the name is separated from the phone number by a tab character, not a set of spaces. As far as cut is concerned, tabs count as a single character when using the -c option. Therefore cut extracts the first 15 characters from each line, producing the results shown.

In a situation where the fields are separated by tabs, you should use the -f option to
cut instead:

```
$ cut -f1 phonebook
Alice Chebba
Barbara Swingle
Jeff Goldberg
Liz Stachiw
Susan Goldberg
Tony Iannino
$
```

Recall that you don't have to specify the delimiter character with the -d option because
cut defaults to a tab character delimiter.

How do you know in advance whether fields are delimited by blanks or tabs? One way to find
out is by trial and error, as shown previously. Another way is to type the command

```
sed -n l file
```

at your terminal. If a tab character separates the fields, \t will be displayed instead of the tab:

```
$ sed -n l phonebook
Alice Chebba\t973-555-2015
Barbara Swingle\t201-555-9257
Jeff Goldberg\t201-555-3378
Liz Stachiw\t212-555-2298
Susan Goldber\t201-555-7776
Tony Iannino\t973-555-1295
$
```

The output verifies that each name is separated from each phone number by a tab character.
The stream editor sed is covered in more detail a bit later in this chapter.

paste

The paste command is the inverse of cut: Instead of breaking lines apart, it puts them
together. The general format of the paste command is

```
paste files
```

where corresponding lines from each of the specified files are "pasted" or merged together
to form single lines that are then written to standard output. The dash character - can also be
used in the files sequence to specify that input is from standard input.

Suppose that you have a list of names in a file called names:

```
$ cat names
Tony
Emanuel
Lucy
```

```
Ralph
Fred
$
```

Suppose that you also have a second file called `numbers` that contains corresponding phone numbers for each name in `names`:

```
$ cat numbers
(307) 555-5356
(212) 555-3456
(212) 555-9959
(212) 555-7741
(212) 555-0040
$
```

You can use `paste` to print the names and numbers side-by-side as shown:

```
$ paste names numbers                    Paste them together
Tony    (307) 555-5356
Emanuel (212) 555-3456
Lucy    (212) 555-9959
Ralph   (212) 555-7741
Fred    (212) 555-0040
$
```

Each line from `names` is displayed with the corresponding line from `numbers`, separated by a tab.

The next example illustrates what happens when more than two files are specified:

```
$ cat addresses
55-23 Vine Street, Miami
39 University Place, New York
17 E. 25th Street, New York
38 Chauncey St., Bensonhurst
17 E. 25th Street, New York
$ paste names addresses numbers
Tony    55-23 Vine Street, Miami      (307) 555-5356
Emanuel 39 University Place, New York (212) 555-3456
Lucy    17 E. 25th Street, New York   (212) 555-9959
Ralph   38 Chauncey St., Bensonhurst  (212) 555-7741
Fred    17 E. 25th Street, New York   (212) 555-0040
$
```

The -d Option

If you don't want the output fields separated by tab characters, you can specify the -d option to specify the output delimiter:

-dchars

where *chars* is one or more characters that will be used to separate the lines pasted together. That is, the first character listed in *chars* will be used to separate lines from the first file that are pasted with lines from the second file; the second character listed in *chars* will be used to separate lines from the second file from lines from the third, and so on.

If there are more files than there are characters listed in *chars*, paste "wraps around" the list of characters and starts again at the beginning.

In the simplest form of the -d option, specifying just a single delimiter character causes that character to be used to separate *all* pasted fields:

```
$ paste -d'+' names addresses numbers
Tony+55-23 Vine Street, Miami+(307) 555-5356
Emanuel+39 University Place, New York+(212) 555-3456
Lucy+17 E. 25th Street, New York+(212) 555-9959
Ralph+38 Chauncey St., Bensonhurst+(212) 555-7741
Fred+17 E. 25th Street, New York+(212) 555-0040
```

Notice that it's always safest to enclose the delimiter characters in single quotes. The reason why will be explained shortly.

The -s Option

The -s option tells paste to paste together lines from the same file, not from alternate files. If just one file is specified, the effect is to merge all the lines from the file together, separated by tabs, or by the delimiter characters specified with the -d option.

```
$ paste -s names          Paste all lines from names
Tony    Emanuel Lucy    Ralph   Fred
$ ls | paste -d' ' -s -   Paste ls's output, use space as delimiter
addresses intro lotsaspaces names numbers phonebook
$
```

In the former example, the output from ls is piped to paste which merges the lines (-s option) from standard input (-), separating each field with a space (-d' ' option). You'll recall from Chapter 1 that the command

```
echo *
```

would have also listed all the files in the current directory, perhaps *slightly* less complicated than ls | paste.

sed

sed is a program used for editing data in a pipe or command sequence. It stands for *stream editor*. Unlike ed, sed cannot be used interactively, though its commands are similar. The general form of the sed command is

```
sed command file
```

where *command* is an ed-style command applied to *each* line of the specified `file`. If no file is specified, standard input is assumed.

As `sed` applies the indicated command or commands to each line of the input, it writes the results to standard output.

Let's have a look. First, the `intro` file again:

```
$ cat intro
The Unix operating system was pioneered by Ken
Thompson and Dennis Ritchie at Bell Laboratories
in the late 1960s. One of the primary goals in
the design of the Unix system was to create an
environment that promoted efficient program
development.
$
```

Suppose that you want to change all occurrences of "Unix" in the text to "UNIX." This can be easily done in `sed` as follows:

```
$ sed 's/Unix/UNIX/' intro        Substitute Unix with UNIX
The UNIX operating system was pioneered by Ken
Thompson and Dennis Ritchie at Bell Laboratories
in the late 1960s. One of the primary goals in
the design of the UNIX system was to create an
environment that promoted efficient program
development.
$
```

Get into the habit of enclosing your `sed` command in single quotes. Later, you'll know when the quotes are necessary and when it's better to use double quotes instead.

The `sed` command s/Unix/UNIX/ is applied to every line of `intro`. Whether or not the line is modified, it gets written to standard output. Since it's in the data stream also note that `sed` makes no changes to the original input file.

To make the changes permanent, you must redirect the output from `sed` into a temporary file and then replace the original file with the newly created one:

```
$ sed 's/Unix/UNIX/' intro > temp    Make the changes
$ mv temp intro                      And now make them permanent
$
```

Always make sure that the correct changes were made to the file before you overwrite the original; a `cat` of `temp` would have been smart before the `mv` command overwrote the original data file.

If your text included more than one occurrence of "Unix" on a line, the above `sed` would have changed just the first occurrence to "UNIX." By appending the *global* option g to the end of the substitute command s, you can ensure that multiple occurrences on a line will be changed.

In this case, the sed command would read

```
$ sed 's/Unix/UNIX/g' intro > temp
```

Now suppose that you wanted to extract just the usernames from the output of who. You already know how to do that with the cut command:

```
$ who | cut -c1-8
root
ruth
steve
pat
$
```

Alternatively, you can use sed to delete all the characters from the first space (which marks the end of the username) through the end of the line by using a regular expression:

```
$ who | sed 's/ .*$//'
root
ruth
steve
pat
$
```

The sed command substitutes a blank space followed by any characters up through the end of the line (.*$) with *nothing* (//); that is, it deletes the characters from the first blank to the end of the line for each input line.

The -n Option

By default, sed writes each line of input to standard output, whether or not it gets changed. Sometimes, however, you'll want to use sed just to extract specific lines from a file. That's what the -n flag is for: it tells sed that you don't want it to print any lines by default. Paired with that, use the p command to print whichever lines match your specified range or pattern. For example, to print just the first two lines from a file:

```
$ sed -n '1,2p' intro          Just print the first 2 lines
The UNIX operating system was pioneered by Ken
Thompson and Dennis Ritchie at Bell Laboratories
$
```

If, instead of line numbers, you precede the p command with a sequence of characters enclosed in slashes, sed prints just the lines from standard input that match that pattern. The following example shows how sed can be used to display just the lines that contain a particular string:

```
$ sed -n '/UNIX/p' intro       Just print lines containing UNIX
The UNIX operating system was pioneered by Ken
the design of the UNIX system was to create an
$
```

Deleting Lines

To delete lines of text, use the d command. By specifying a line number or range of numbers, you can delete specific lines from the input. In the following example, sed is used to delete the first two lines of text from intro:

```
$ sed '1,2d' intro          Delete lines 1 and 2
in the late 1960s. One of the primary goals in
the design of the UNIX system was to create an
environment that promoted efficient program
development.
$
```

Remembering that by default sed writes all lines of the input to standard output, the remaining lines in text—that is, lines 3 through the end—simply get written to standard output.

By preceding the d command with a pattern, you can used sed to delete all lines that contain that text. In the following example, sed is used to delete all lines of text containing the word UNIX:

```
$ sed '/UNIX/d' intro          Delete all lines containing UNIX
Thompson and Dennis Ritchie at Bell Laboratories
in the late 1960s. One of the primary goals in
environment that promoted efficient program
development.
$
```

The power and flexibility of sed goes far beyond what we've shown here. sed has facilities that enable you to loop, build text in a buffer, and combine many commands into a single editing script. Table 3.2 shows some more examples of sed commands.

Table 3.2   sed **Examples**

sed **Command**	**Description**
sed '5d'	Delete line 5
sed '/[Tt]est/d'	Delete all lines containing Test or test
sed -n '20,25p' text	Print only lines 20 through 25 from text
sed '1,10s/unix/UNIX/g' intro	Change unix to UNIX wherever it appears in the first 10 lines of intro
sed '/jan/s/-1/-5/'	Change the first -1 to -5 in all lines containing jan
sed 's/...//' data	Delete the first three characters from each line of data
sed 's/...$//' data	Delete the last 3 characters from each line of data
sed -n 'l' text	Print all lines from text, showing non-printing characters as \nn (where nn is the octal value of the character), and tab characters as \t

tr

The `tr` filter is used to translate characters from standard input. The general form of the command is

```
tr from-chars to-chars
```

where *from-chars* and *to-chars* are one or more characters or a set of characters. Any character in *from-chars* encountered on the input will be translated into the corresponding character in *to-chars*. The result of the translation is written to standard output.

In its simplest form, `tr` can be used to translate one character into another. Recall the file `intro` from earlier in this chapter:

```
$ cat intro
The UNIX operating system was pioneered by Ken
Thompson and Dennis Ritchie at Bell Laboratories
in the late 1960s. One of the primary goals in
the design of the UNIX system was to create an
environment that promoted efficient program
development.
$
```

The following shows how `tr` can be used to translate all letter e's to x's:

```
$ tr e x < intro
Thx UNIX opxrating systxm was pionxxrxd by Kxn
Thompson and Dxnnis Ritchix at Bxll Laboratorixs
in thx latx 1960s. Onx of thx primary goals in
thx dxsign of thx UNIX systxm was to crxatx an
xnvironmxnt that promotxd xfficixnt program
dxvxlopmxnt.
$
```

The input to `tr` must be redirected from the file `intro` because `tr` always expects its input to come from standard input. The results of the translation are written to standard output, leaving the original file untouched. Showing a more practical example, recall the pipeline that you used to extract the usernames and home directories of everyone on the system:

```
$ cut -d: -f1,6 /etc/passwd
root:/
cron:/
bin:/
uucp:/usr/spool/uucp
asg:/
steve:/users/steve
other:/
$
```

You can translate the colons into tab characters to produce a more readable output simply by tacking an appropriate `tr` command to the end of the pipeline:

```
$ cut -d: -f1,6 /etc/passwd | tr : '    '
root    /
cron    /
bin     /
uucp    /usr/spool/uucp
asg     /
steve   /users/steve
other   /
$
```

Enclosed between the single quotes is a tab character (even though you can't see it—just take our word for it). It must be enclosed in quotes to keep it from being parsed and discarded by the shell as extraneous whitespace.

Working with characters that aren't printable? The octal representation of a character can be given to `tr` in the format

nnn

where *nnn* is the octal value of the character. This isn't used too often, but can be handy to remember.

For example, the octal value of the tab character is 11, so another way to accomplish the colon-to-tab transformation is to use the `tr` command

```
tr : '\11'
```

Table 3.3 lists characters that you'll often want to specify in octal format.

Table 3.3   **Octal Values of Some ASCII Characters**

Character	Octal value
Bell	7
Backspace	10
Tab	11
Newline	12
Linefeed	12
Formfeed	14
Carriage Return	15
Escape	33

In the following example, `tr` takes the output from `date` and translates all spaces into newline characters. The net result is that each field of output appears on a different line:

```
$ date | tr ' ' '\12'          Translate spaces to newlines
Sun
```

```
Jul
28
19:13:46
EDT
2002
$
```

`tr` can also translate ranges of characters. For example, the following shows how to translate all lowercase letters in `intro` to their uppercase equivalents:

```
$ tr '[a-z]' '[A-Z]' < intro
THE UNIX OPERATING SYSTEM WAS PIONEERED BY KEN
THOMPSON AND DENNIS RITCHIE AT BELL LABORATORIES
IN THE LATE 1960S. ONE OF THE PRIMARY GOALS IN
THE DESIGN OF THE UNIX SYSTEM WAS TO CREATE AN
ENVIRONMENT THAT PROMOTED EFFICIENT PROGRAM
DEVELOPMENT.
$
```

The character ranges [a-z] and [A-Z] are enclosed in quotes to keep the shell from interpreting the pattern. Try the command without the quotes and you'll quickly see that the result isn't quite what you seek.

By reversing the two arguments to `tr`, you can use the command to translate all uppercase letters to lowercase:

```
$ tr '[A-Z]' '[a-z]' < intro
the unix operating system was pioneered by ken
thompson and dennis ritchie at bell laboratories
in the late 1960s. one of the primary goals in
the design of the unix system was to create an
environment that promoted efficient program
development.
$
```

For a more interesting example, try to guess what this `tr` invocation accomplishes:

```
tr '[a-zA-Z]' '[A-Za-z]'
```

Figured it out? This turns uppercase letters into lowercase, and lowercase letters into uppercase.

The -s Option

You can use the -s option to "squeeze" out multiple consecutive occurrences of characters in *to-chars*. In other words, if more than one consecutive occurrence of a character specified in *to-chars* occurs after the translation is made, the characters will be replaced by a single character.

For example, the following command translates all colons into tab characters, replacing multiple tabs with single tabs:

```
tr -s ':' '\11'
```

So one colon or several consecutive colons on the input will be replaced by a *single* tab character on the output.

Note that '\t' can work in many instances instead of '\11', so be sure to try that if you want things to be a bit more readable!

Suppose that you have a file called lotsaspaces that has contents as shown:

```
$ cat lotsaspaces
This        is    an example  of a
file   that contains        a   lot
of    blank spaces.
$
```

You can use tr to squeeze out the multiple spaces by using the -s option and by specifying a single space character as the first and second argument:

```
$ tr -s ' ' ' ' < lotsaspaces
This is an example of a
file that contains a lot
of blank spaces.
$
```

This tr command in effect says, "translate occurrences of space with another space, replacing multiple spaces in the output with a single space."

The −d Option

tr can also be used to delete individual characters from the input stream. The format of tr in this case is

```
tr -d from-chars
```

where any character listed in *from-chars* will be deleted from standard input. In the following example, tr is used to delete all spaces from the file intro:

```
$ tr -d ' ' < intro
TheUNIXoperatingSystemwaspioneeredbyKen
ThompsonandDennisRitchieatBellLaboratories
inthelate1960s.Oneoftheprimarygoalsin
thedesignoftheUNIXSystemwastocreatean
environmentthatpromotedefficientprogram
development.
$
```

You probably realize that you could have also used sed to achieve the same results:

```
$ sed 's/ //g' intro
TheUNIXoperatingsystemwaspioneeredbyKen
ThompsonandDennisRitchieatBellLaboratories
inthelate1960s.Oneoftheprimarygoalsin
thedesignoftheUNIXsystemwastocreatean
environmentthatpromotedefficientprogram
```

```
development.
$
```

This is not atypical for the Unix system; there's almost always more than one approach to solving a particular problem. In the case we just saw, either approach is satisfactory (that is, tr or sed), but tr is probably a better choice because it is a much smaller program and likely to execute faster.

Table 3.4 summarizes how to use tr for translating and deleting characters. Bear in mind that tr works only on *single* characters. So if you need to translate anything longer than a single character (say all occurrences of unix to UNIX), you have to use a different program, such as sed, instead.

Table 3.4   tr **Examples**

tr **Command**	Description
tr 'X' 'x'	Translate all capital X's to small x's.
tr '()' '{}'	Translate all open parentheses to open braces, all closed parentheses to closed braces
tr '[a-z]' '[A-Z]'	Translate all lowercase letters to uppercase
tr '[A-Z]' '[N-ZA-M]'	Translate uppercase letters A–M to N–Z, and N–Z to A–M, respectively
tr ' ' ' '	Translate all tabs (character in first pair of quotes) to spaces
tr -s ' ' ' '	Translate multiple spaces to single spaces
tr -d '\14'	Delete all formfeed (octal 14) characters
tr -d '[0-9]'	Delete all digits

grep

grep allows you to search one or more files for a pattern you specify. The general format of this command is

```
grep pattern files
```

Every line of each file that contains *pattern* is displayed at the terminal. If more than one file is specified to grep, each line is also preceded by the name of the file, thus enabling you to identify the particular file that the pattern was found in.

Let's say that you want to find every occurrence of the word shell in the file ed.cmd:

```
$ grep shell ed.cmd
files, and is independent of the shell.
to the shell, just type in a q.
$
```

This output indicates that two lines in the file ed.cmd contain the word shell.

If the pattern does not exist in the specified file(s), the grep command simply displays nothing:

```
$ grep cracker ed.cmd
$
```

You saw in the section on sed how you could print all lines containing the string UNIX from the file intro with the command

```
sed -n '/UNIX/p' intro
```

But you could also use the following grep command to achieve the same result:

```
grep UNIX intro
```

Recall the phonebook file from before:

```
$ cat phonebook
Alice Chebba     973-555-2015
Barbara Swingle  201-555-9257
Jeff Goldberg    201-555-3378
Liz Stachiw      212-555-2298
Susan Goldberg   201-555-7776
Tony Iannino     973-555-1295
$
```

When you need to look up a particular phone number, the grep command comes in handy:

```
$ grep Susan phonebook
Susan Goldberg   201-555-7776
$
```

The grep command is particularly useful when you have a lot of files and you want to find out which ones contain certain words or phrases. The following example shows how the grep command can be used to search for the word shell in *all* files in the current directory:

```
$ grep shell *
cmdfiles:shell that enables sophisticated
ed.cmd:files, and is independent of the shell.
ed.cmd:to the shell, just type in a q.
grep.cmd:occurrence of the word shell:
grep.cmd:$ grep shell *
grep.cmd:every use of the word shell.
$
```

As noted, when more than one file is specified to grep, each output line is preceded by the name of the file containing that line.

As with expressions for sed and patterns for tr, it's a good idea to enclose your grep pattern inside a pair of *single* quotes to "protect" it from the shell. Here's an example of what can happen if you don't: say you want to find all the lines containing asterisks inside the file stars; typing

```
grep * stars
```

doesn't work as you'd hope because the shell sees the asterisk and automatically substitutes the names of all the files in your current directory!

```
$ ls
circles
polka.dots
squares
stars
stripes
$ grep * stars
$
```

In this case, the shell took the asterisk and substituted the list of files in your current directory. Then it started execution of grep, which took the first argument (circles) and tried to find it in the files specified by the remaining arguments, as shown in Figure 3.1.

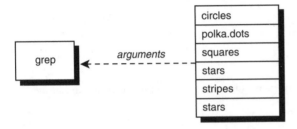

Figure 3.1 grep * stars

Enclosing the asterisk in quotes, however, blocks it from being parsed and interpreted by the shell:

```
$ grep '*' stars
The asterisk (*) is a special character that
**********
5 * 4 = 20
$
```

The quotes told the shell to leave the enclosed characters alone. It then started execution of grep, passing it the two arguments * (*without* the surrounding quotes; the shell removes them in the process) and stars (see Figure 3.2).

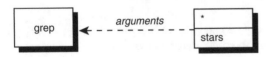

Figure 3.2 grep '*' stars

There are characters other than * that have a special meaning to the shell and must be quoted when used in a pattern. The whole topic of how quotes are handled by the shell is admittedly tricky; an entire chapter—Chapter 5—is devoted to it.

grep takes its input from standard input if no filename is specified. So you can use grep as part of a pipe to scan through the output of a command for lines that match a specific pattern. Suppose that you want to find out whether the user jim is logged in. You can use grep to search through who's output:

```
$ who | grep jim
jim        tty16          Feb 20 10:25
$
```

Note that by not specifying a file to search, grep automatically scans standard input. Naturally, if the user jim were not logged in, you would get a new command prompt without any preceding output:

```
$ who | grep jim
$
```

Regular Expressions and grep

Let's take another look at the intro file:

```
$ cat intro
The UNIX operating system was pioneered by Ken
Thompson and Dennis Ritchie at Bell Laboratories
in the late 1960s. One of the primary goals in
the design of the UNIX system was to create an
environment that promoted efficient program
development.
$
```

grep allows you to specify your pattern using regular expressions as in ed. Given this information, it means that you can specify the pattern

[tT]he

to have grep search for either a lower- or uppercase T followed by the characters he.

Here's how to use grep to list all the lines containing the characters the or The:

```
$ grep '[tT]he' intro
The UNIX operating system was pioneered by Ken
in the late 1960s.  One of the primary goals in
the design of the UNIX system was to create an
$
```

A smarter alternative might be to utilize the -i option to grep which makes patterns case insensitive. That is, the command

```
grep -i 'the' intro
```

tells grep to ignore the difference between upper and lowercase when matching the pattern against the lines in intro. Therefore, lines containing the or The will be printed, as will lines containing THE, THe, tHE, and so on.

Table 3.5 shows other types of regular expressions that you can specify to grep and the types of patterns they'll match.

Table 3.5 **Some** grep **Examples**

Command	Prints
grep '[A-Z]' list	Lines from list containing a capital letter
grep '[0-9]' data	Lines from data containing a digit
grep '[A-Z]...[0-9]' list	Lines from list containing five-character patterns that start with a capital letter and end with a digit
grep '\.pic$' filelist	Lines from filelist that end with .pic

The -v Option

Sometimes you're interested not in finding the lines that contain a specified pattern, but those that *don't*. That's what the -v option is for with grep: to *reverse* the logic of the matching task. In the next example, grep is used to find all the lines in intro that don't contain the pattern UNIX.

```
$ grep -v 'UNIX' intro              Print all lines that don't contain UNIX
Thompson and Dennis Ritchie at Bell Laboratories
in the late 19605.  One of the primary goals in
environment that promoted efficient program
development.
$
```

The -l Option

At times, you may not want to see the actual lines that match a pattern but just seek the names of the files that contain the pattern. For example, suppose that you have a set of C programs in your current directory (by convention, these filenames end with the filename suffix .c), and you want to know which use a variable called Move_history. Here's one way of finding the answer:

```
$ grep 'Move_history' *.c              Find Move_history in all C source files
exec.c:MOVE     Move_history[200] = {0};
exec.c:      cpymove(&Move_history[Number_half_moves -1],
exec.c: undo_move(&Move_history[Number_half_moves-1],;
exec.c: cpymove(&last_move,&Move_history[Number_half_moves-1]);
exec.c: convert_move(&Move_history[Number_half_moves-1]),
exec.c:      convert_move(&Move_history[i-1]),
```

```
exec.c: convert_move(&Move_history[Number_half_moves-1]),
makemove.c:IMPORT MOVE Move_history[];
makemove.c:      if ( Move_history[j].from != BOOK (i,j,from) OR
makemove.c:           Move_history[j] .to != BOOK (i,j,to) )
testch.c:GLOBAL MOVE Move_history[100] = {0};
testch.c:    Move_history[Number_half_moves-1].from = move.from;
testch.c:    Move_history[Number_half_moves-1].to = move.to;
$
```

Sifting through the preceding output, you discover that three files—exec.c, makemove.c, and testch.c—use the variable.

Add the -l option to grep and you instead get a list of files that contain the specified pattern, not the matching lines from the files:

```
$ grep -l 'Move_history' *.c          List the files that contain Move_history
exec.c
makemove.c
testch.c
$
```

Because grep conveniently lists the files one per line, you can pipe the output from grep -l into wc to count the *number* of *files* that contain a particular pattern:

```
$ grep -l 'Move_history' *.c | wc -l
     3
$
```

The preceding command shows that precisely three C program files reference the variable Move_history. Now, just to make sure you're paying attention, what are you counting if you use grep *without* the -l option and pipe the output to wc -l?

The -n Option

If the -n option is used with grep, each line from the file that matches the specified pattern is preceded by its corresponding line number. From previous examples, you saw that the file testch.c was one of the three files that referenced the variable Move_history; the following shows how you can pinpoint the precise lines in the file that reference the variable:

```
$ grep -n 'Move_history' testch.c          Precede matches with line numbers
13:GLOBAL MOVE Move_history[100] = {0};
197:    Move_history[Number_half_moves-1].from = move.from;
198:    Move_history[Number_half_moves-1].to = move.to;
$
```

As you can see, Move_history is used on lines 13, 197, and 198 in testch.c.

For Unix experts, grep is one of the most commonly used programs because of its flexibility and sophistication with pattern matching. It's one well worth studying.

sort

At its most basic, the `sort` command is really easy to understand: give it lines of input and it'll sort them alphabetically, with the result appearing as its output:

```
$ sort names
Charlie
Emanuel
Fred
Lucy
Ralph
Tony
Tony
$
```

By default, `sort` takes each line of the specified input file and sorts it into ascending order.

Special characters are sorted according to the internal encoding of the characters. For example, the space character is represented internally as the number 32, and the double quote as the number 34. This means that the former would be sorted before the latter. Particularly for other languages and locales the sorting order can vary, so although you are generally assured that `sort` will perform as expected on alphanumeric input, the ordering of foreign language characters, punctuation, and other special characters is not always what you might expect.

`sort` has many options that provide more flexibility in performing your sort. We'll just describe a few of the options here.

The -u Option

The -u option tells `sort` to eliminate duplicate lines from the output.

```
$ sort -u names
Charlie
Emanuel
Fred
Lucy
Ralph
Tony
$
```

Here you see that the duplicate line that contained `Tony` was eliminated from the output. A lot of old-school Unix people accomplish the same thing by using the separate program `uniq`, so if you read system shell scripts you'll often see sequences like `sort | uniq`. Those can be replaced with `sort -u`!

The -r Option

Use the -r option to *reverse* the order of the sort:

```
$ sort -r names          Reverse sort
Tony
Tony
Ralph
Lucy
Fred
Emanuel
Charlie
$
```

The -o Option

By default, sort writes the sorted data to standard output. To have it go into a file, you can use output redirection:

```
$ sort names > sorted_names
$
```

Alternatively, you can use the -o option to specify the output file. Simply list the name of the output file right after the -o:

```
$ sort names -o sorted_names
$
```

This sorts names and writes the results to sorted_names.

What's the value of the -o option? Frequently, you want to sort the lines in a file and have the sorted data replace the original. But typing

```
$ sort names > names
$
```

won't work—it ends up wiping out the names file! However, with the -o option, it is okay to specify the same name for the output file as the input file:

```
$ sort names -o names
$ cat names
Charlie
Emanuel
Fred
Lucy
Ralph
Tony
Tony
$
```

> **Tip**
>
> Be careful if your filter or process is going to replace your original input file and make sure that it's all working as you expect prior to having the data overwritten. Unix is good at a lot of things, but there's no *unremove* command to recover lost data or lost files.

The -n Option

Suppose that you have a file containing pairs of (*x*, *y*) data points as shown:

```
$ cat data
5       27
2       12
3       33
23      2
-5      11
15      6
14      -9
$
```

And suppose that you want to feed this data into a plotting program called plotdata, but that the program requires that the incoming data pairs be sorted in increasing value of *x* (the first value on each line).

The -n option to sort specifies that the first field on the line is to be considered a *number*, and the data is to be sorted arithmetically. Compare the output of sort used without the -n option and then with it:

```
$ sort data
-5      11
14      -9
15      6
2       12
23      2
3       33
5       27
$ sort -n data          Sort arithmetically
-5      11
2       12
3       33
5       27
14      -9
15      6
23      2
$
```

Skipping Fields

If you had to sort your data file by the y value—that is, the second number in each line—you could tell sort to start with the second field by using the option

-k2n

instead of -n. The -k2 says to skip the first field and start the sort analysis with the second field of each line. Similarly, -k5n would mean to start with the fifth field on each line and then sort the data numerically.

```
$ sort -k2n data          Start with the second field in the sort
14       -9
23       2
15       6
-5       11
2        12
5        27
3        33
$
```

Fields are delimited by space or tab characters by default. If a different delimiter is to be used, the -t option must be used.

The -t Option

As mentioned, if you skip over fields, sort assumes that the fields are delimited by space or tab characters. The -t option can indicate otherwise. In this case, the character that follows the -t is taken as the delimiter character.

Consider the sample password file again:

```
$ cat /etc/passwd
root:*:0:0:The super User:/:/usr/bin/ksh
steve:*:203:100::/users/steve:/usr/bin/ksh
bin:*:3:3:The owner of system files:/:
cron:*:1:1:Cron Daemon for periodic tasks:/:
george:*:75:75::/users/george:/usr/lib/rsh
pat:*:300:300::/users/pat:/usr/bin/ksh
uucp:nc823ciSiLiZM:5:5::/usr/spool/uucppublic:/usr/lib/uucp/uucico
asg:*:6:6:The Owner of Assignable Devices:/:
sysinfo:*:10:10:Access to System Information:/:/usr/bin/sh
mail:*:301:301::/usr/mail:
$
```

If you wanted to sort this file by username (the first field on each line), you could just issue the command

```
sort /etc/passwd
```

To sort the file instead by the third colon-delimited field (which contains what is known as your *user ID*), you would want an arithmetic sort, starting with the third field (-k3), and specifying the colon character as the field delimiter (-t:):

```
$ sort -k3n -t: /etc/passwd            Sort by user id
root:*:0:0:The Super User:/:/usr/bin/ksh
cron:*:1:1:Cron Daemon for periodic tasks:/:
bin:*:3:3:The owner of system files:/:
uucp:*:5:5::/usr/spool/uucppublic:/usr/lib/uucp/uucico
asg:*:6:6:The Owner of Assignable Devices:/:
sysinfo:*:10:10:Access to System Information:/:/usr/bin/sh
george:*:75:75::/users/george:/usr/lib/rsh
steve:*:203:100::/users/steve:/usr/bin/ksh
pat:*:300:300::/users/pat:/usr/bin/ksh
mail:*:301:301::/usr/mail: .
$
```

Here we've bolded the third field of each line so that you can easily verify that the file was sorted correctly by user *ID*.

Other Options

Other options to `sort` enable you to skip characters within a field, specify the field to *end* the sort on, merge sorted input files, and sort in "dictionary order" (only letters, numbers, and spaces are used for the comparison). For more details on these options, look under `sort` in your *Unix User's Manual*.

uniq

The `uniq` command is useful when you need to find or remove duplicate lines in a file. The basic format of the command is

```
uniq in_file out_file
```

In this format, `uniq` copies *in_file* to *out_file*, removing any duplicate lines in the process. `uniq`'s definition of duplicated lines is *consecutive lines that match exactly.*

If *out_file* is not specified, the results will be written to standard output. If *in_file* is also not specified, `uniq` acts as a filter and reads its input from standard input.

Here are some examples to see how `uniq` works. Suppose that you have a file called `names` with contents as shown:

```
$ cat names
Charlie
Tony
Emanuel
Lucy
```

```
Ralph
Fred
Tony
$
```

You can see that the name `Tony` appears twice in the file. You can use `uniq` to remove such duplicate entries:

```
$ uniq names              Print unique lines
Charlie
Tony
Emanuel
Lucy
Ralph
Fred
Tony
$
```

Oops! `Tony` still appears twice in the preceding output because the multiple occurrences are not *consecutive* in the file, and thus `uniq`'s definition of duplicate is not satisfied. To remedy this situation, `sort` is often used to get the duplicate lines adjacent to each other, as mentioned earlier in the chapter. The result of the sort is then run through `uniq`:

```
$ sort names | uniq
Charlie
Emanuel
Fred
Lucy
Ralph
Tony
$
```

The `sort` moves the two `Tony` lines together, and then `uniq` filters out the duplicate line (but recall that `sort` with the `-u` option performs precisely this function).

The -d Option

Frequently, you'll be interested in finding just the duplicate entries in a file. The `-d` option to `uniq` can be used for such purposes: It tells `uniq` to write *only* the duplicated lines to `out_file` (or standard output). Such lines are written just once, no matter how many consecutive occurrences there are.

```
$ sort names | uniq -d          List duplicate lines
Tony
$
```

As a more practical example, let's return to our `/etc/passwd` file. This file contains information about each user on the system. It's conceivable that over the course of adding and removing users from this file that perhaps the same username has been inadvertently entered more than once. You can easily find such duplicate entries by first sorting `/etc/passwd` and piping the results into `uniq -d` as done previously:

```
$ sort /etc/passwd | uniq -d          Find duplicate entries in /etc/passwd
$
```

There are no duplicate full line `/etc/passwd` entries. But you really want to find duplicate entries for the username field, so you only want to look at the first field from each line (recall that the leading characters of each line of `/etc/passwd` up to the colon are the username). This can't be done directly through an option to `uniq`, but can be accomplished by using `cut` to extract the username from each line of the password file before sending it to `uniq`.

```
$ sort /etc/passwd | cut -f1 -d: | uniq -d    Find duplicates
cem
harry
$
```

It turns out that there are multiple entries in `/etc/passwd` for `cem` and `harry`. If you wanted more information on the particular entries, you could now `grep` them from `/etc/passwd`:

```
$ grep -n 'cem' /etc/passwd
20:cem:*:91:91::/users/cem:
166:cem:*:91:91::/users/cem:
$ grep -n 'harry' /etc/passwd
29:harry:*:103:103:Harry Johnson:/users/harry:
79:harry:*:90:90:Harry Johnson:/users/harry:
$
```

The `-n` option was used to find out where the duplicate entries occur. In the case of `cem`, there are two entries on lines 20 and 166; in `harry`'s case, the two entries are on lines 29 and 79.

Other Options

The `-c` option to `uniq` adds an occurrence count, which can be tremendously useful in scripts:

```
$ sort names | uniq -c          Count line occurrences
      1 Charlie
      1 Emanuel
      1 Fred
      1 Lucy
      1 Ralph
      2 Tony
$
```

One common use of `uniq -c` is to figure out the most common words in a data file, easily done with a command like:

```
tr '[A-Z]' '[a-z]' datafile | sort | uniq -c | head
```

Two other options that we don't have space to describe more fully let you tell `uniq` to ignore leading characters/fields on a line. For more information, consult the man page for your particular implementation of `uniq` with the command `man  uniq`.

We would be remiss if we neglected to mention the programs `awk` and `perl`, which can be useful when writing shell programs too. They are both big, complicated programming environments unto themselves, however, so we're going to encourage you to check out *Awk—A Pattern Scanning and Processing Language*, by Aho, et al., in the *Unix Programmer's Manual, Volume II* for a description of `awk`, and *Learning Perl* and *Programming Perl*, both from O'Reilly and Associates, offering a good tutorial and reference on the language, respectively.

And Away We Go

Based on our discussions in Chapter 2, "What Is the Shell?," you should now realize that whenever you type something like

```
who | wc -l
```

you are actually programming in the shell. That's because the shell is interpreting the command line, recognizing the pipe symbol, connecting the output of the first command to the input of the second, and initiating execution of both commands.

In this chapter, you'll learn how to write your own commands and how to use shell *variables*.

Command Files

A shell program can be typed directly, as in

```
$ who | wc -l
```

or it can be typed into a file and then the file can be executed by the shell. For example, suppose that you need to find out the number of logged-in users several times throughout the day. It's not unreasonable to type in the preceding pipeline each time you want the information, but for the sake of example, let's type this pipeline into a file.

We'll call the file nu (for *n*umber of *u*sers), and its contents will be just the pipeline shown previously:

```
$ cat nu
who | wc -l
$
```

To execute the commands contained inside the file nu, all you now have to do is type nu as the command name to the shell:

```
$ nu
sh: nu: cannot execute
$
```

Oops! We forgot to mention one thing. Before you can execute a script from the command line, you must change the file's permission to make it *executable*. This is done with the change mode command, chmod. To add execute permission to the file nu, you simply type

```
chmod +x file(s)
```

The +x indicates that you want to make the *file(s)* that follow executable. The shell requires that a file be *both* readable and executable by you before you can invoke it directly on the command line.

```
$ ls -l nu
-rw-rw-r--    1 steve    steve      12 Jul 10 11:42 nu
$ chmod +x nu                        Make it executable
$ ls -l nu
-rwxrwxr-x    1 steve    steve      12 Jul 10 11:42 nu
$
```

Now that you've made it executable, try it again:

```
$ nu
     8
$
```

This time it worked.

> **Warning**
>
> If you fix the permission issue and still get an error "Command not found," try adding ./ before the command, like ./nu to ensure the shell looks in the current directory for commands as well as the usual system locations. To fix it long term, add . to the end of your PATH (typically within your .profile file).

You can put any commands inside a file, make the file executable, and then execute its contents simply by typing its name to the shell. It's that simple and that powerful, and everything you've learned about working on the command line therefore also applies to writing shell scripts too.

The standard shell mechanisms such as I/O redirection and pipes can be used on your own programs as well:

```
$ nu > tally
$ cat tally
     8
$
```

Suppose that you're working on a proposal called sys.caps and the following command sequence is needed every time you print the proposal:

```
tbl sys.caps | nroff -mm -Tlp | lp
```

You can save yourself some typing by placing this command sequence into a file—let's call it run—making it executable, and then just typing the name run whenever you want to print a new copy of the proposal:

```
$ cat run
tbl sys.caps | nroff -mm -Tlp | lp
$ chmod +x run
$ run
request id is laser1-15 (standard input)
$
```

(The request id message in the example is from the lp command.)

For the next example, suppose that you want to write a shell program called stats that prints the date and time, the number of users logged in, and your current working directory. The three command sequences you need to get this information are date, who | wc -l, and pwd:

```
$ cat stats
date
who | wc -l
pwd
$ chmod +x stats
$ stats                       Try it out
Wed Jul 10 11:55:50 EDT 2002
     13
/users/steve/documents/proposals
$
```

You can add some echo commands to stats to make the output a bit more informative:

```
$ cat stats
echo The current date and time is:
date
echo
echo The number of users on the system is:
who | wc -l
echo
echo Your current working directory is:
pwd
$ stats                       Execute it
The current date and time is:
Wed Jul 10 12:00:27 EDT 2002

The number of users on the system is:
     13

Your current working directory is:
/users/steve/documents/proposals
$
```

Recall that `echo` without any arguments produces a blank line. Shortly, you'll see how to have the message and command output displayed on the same line, like this:

```
The current date and time is: Wed Jul 10 12:00:27 EDT 2002
```

Comments

The shell programming language would not be complete without a *comment* statement. A comment is a way for you to insert remarks or comments inside the program that otherwise have no effect on its execution.

Whenever the shell encounters the special character #, it ignores whatever characters appear starting with the # through to the end of the line. If the # starts the line, the entire line is treated as a comment. Here are examples of valid comments:

```
# Here is an entire commentary line
who | wc -l        # count the number of users
#
#  Test to see if the correct arguments were supplied
#
```

Comments are useful for documenting commands or sequences of commands whose purposes may not be obvious or are sufficiently complex that you might forget why they're there or what they do. Judicious use of comments can also help make shell programs easier to debug and to maintain—both by you and by someone else who may have to support your programs.

Let's go back to the `stats` program and insert some comments and blank lines for legibility:

```
$ cat stats
#
# stats -- prints: date, number of users logged on,
#          and current working directory
#

echo The current date and time is:
date

echo
echo The number of users on the system is:
who | wc -l

echo
echo Your current working directory is:
pwd
$
```

The extra blank lines cost little in terms of program space yet add much in terms of program readability. They're simply ignored by the shell.

Variables

Like virtually all programming languages, the shell allows you to store values into *variables*. A shell variable begins with an alphabetic or underscore (_) character and is followed by zero or more alphanumeric or underscore characters.

> **Note**
>
> The regular expression for a shell variable name is therefore `[A-Za-z_]`
> `[a-zA-Z0-9_]*`, right?

To store a value inside a shell variable, you write the name of the variable, followed immediately by the equals sign =, followed immediately by the value you want to store in the variable:

`variable=value`

For example, to assign the value 1 to the shell variable count, you simply write

`count=1`

and to assign the value /users/steve/bin to the shell variable my_bin, you write

`my_bin=/users/steve/bin`

A few important points here. First, spaces are not permitted on either side of the equals sign. Keep that in mind, especially if you've worked in other programming languages and you're in the habit of inserting spaces around operators. In the shell language, you can't put those spaces in.

Second, unlike most other programming languages, the shell has no concept of *data types*. Whenever you assign a value to a shell variable, no matter what it is, the shell simply interprets that value as a string of characters. So when you assigned 1 to the variable count, the shell simply stored the *character* 1 inside the variable count, making no assumption that an integer value was being stored in the variable.

If you're used to programming in a language such as C, Perl, Swift, or Ruby where all variables must be *declared*, you're in for another adjustment: Because the shell has no concept of data types, variables are not declared before they're used; they're simply assigned values when you want to use them.

The shell does support integer operations on shell variables that contain strings that are also valid numbers through special built-in operations, but even then, the variable is continually evaluated to ensure it's a valid number.

Because the shell is an interpretive language, you can assign values to variables directly at your terminal:

```
$ count=1                    Assign character 1 to count
$ my_bin=/users/steve/bin    Assign /users/steve/bin to my_bin
$
```

So now that you know how to assign values to variables, what good is it? Glad you asked.

Displaying the Values of Variables

The echo command—which we've used already to print values such as strings received from standard input—is used to display the value stored inside a shell variable. To do this, you simply write

echo $*variable*

The $ character is a special character to the shell when followed by one or more alphanumeric characters. If a variable name follows the $, the shell takes this as an indication that the value stored inside that variable is to be substituted at that point. So, when you type

echo $count

the shell replaces $count with the value stored there; then it executes the echo command:

```
$ echo $count
1
$
```

Remember, the shell performs variable substitution *before* it executes the command (see Figure 4.1).

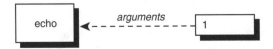

Figure 4.1   echo $count

You can have the value of more than one variable substituted at a time:

```
$ echo $my_bin
/users/steve/bin
$ echo $my_bin $count
/users/steve/bin 1
$
```

In the second example, the shell substitutes the values of my_bin and count and then executes the echo command (see Figure 4.2).

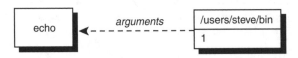

Figure 4.2   echo $my_bin $count

Variables can be used anywhere on any command line and will be replaced with their value by the shell prior to the specific command being invoked, as the next examples illustrate:

```
$ ls $my_bin
mon
nu
testx
$ pwd                        Where are we?
/users/steve/documents/memos
$ cd $my_bin                 Change to my bin directory
$ pwd
/users/steve/bin
$ number=99
$ echo There are $number bottles of beer on the wall
There are 99 bottles of beer on the wall
$
```

Here are some more examples:

```
$ command=sort
$ $command names
Charlie
Emanuel
Fred
Lucy
Ralph
Tony
Tony
$ command=wc
$ option=-l
$ file=names
$ $command $option $file
      7 names
$
```

So you see, even the name of a command can be stored inside a variable. Because the shell performs its substitution before determining the name of the program to execute and its arguments, it parses the line

```
$command $option $file
```

then makes all the substitutions requested, turning the command it actually invokes into

```
wc -l names
```

Then the shell executes wc, passing the two arguments -l and names.

Variables can even be assigned to other variables, as shown in the next example:

```
$ value1=10
$ value2=value1
$ echo $value2
```

```
value1                              Didn't do that right
$ value2=$value1
$ echo $value2
10                                  That's better
$
```

Remember that a dollar sign must always be placed before the variable name whenever you want to use the value stored in that variable.

Undefined Variables Have the Null Value

What do you think happens when you try to display the value of a variable that has no value assigned to it? Try it and see:

```
$ echo $nosuch                      Never assigned it a value
$
```

You don't get an error message. Did the echo command display anything at all? Let's see whether we can more precisely determine that:

```
$ echo :$nosuch:                    Surround its value with colons
::
$
```

So you see *no* characters were substituted by the shell for the unspecified value of nosuch.

A variable that contains no value is said to be undefined and contain the *null* value. It is the default case for variables that you never store values in. When the shell performs its variable substitution, any values that are null are effectively just removed from the command line (which makes sense if they have the null value):

```
$ wc  $nosuch -l $nosuch $nosuch names
      7 names
$
```

The shell scans the command line substituting the null value for the variable nosuch. After the scan is completed, the line effectively looks like this:

```
wc -l names
```

which explains why it works.

Sometimes you may want to initialize the value of a variable to be the value null. This can be done by simply assigning no value to the variable, as in

```
dataflag=
```

Alternatively, and as a better practice, you can list two adjacent pairs of quotes after the =. So

```
dataflag=""
```

and

```
dataflag=''
```

both have the same effect of assigning the null value to `dataflag` and have the added benefit that it looks like it's deliberate, rather than in the first instance where it might be perceived later as a mistake or typo.

Be advised that the assignment

```
dataflag=" "
```

is *not* equivalent to the three previous ones because it assigns a single space character to `dataflag`; that's different from assigning *no* characters to it.

Filename Substitution and Variables

Here's a puzzle for you: If you type

```
x=*
```

will the shell store the character * into the variable x, or will it store the names of all the files in your current directory into the variable x? Let's try it out and see:

```
$ ls                                    What files do we have?
addresses
intro
lotsaspaces
names
nu
numbers
phonebook
stat
$ x=*
$ echo $x
addresses intro lotsaSpaces names nu numbers phonebook stat
$
```

There's a lot to be learned from this simple example. Was the list of files stored into the variable x when

```
x=*
```

was executed, or did the shell do the substitution when

```
echo $x
```

was executed?

It turns out that the shell does not perform filename substitution when assigning values to variables. Therefore,

```
x=*
```

assigns the single character * to x. This means that given the output shown, the shell must have done the filename substitution when executing the `echo` command. In fact, the precise sequence of steps that occurred when

```
echo $x
```

was executed is as follows:

1. The shell scanned the line, substituting * as the value of x.

2. The shell rescanned the line, encountered the *, and then substituted the names of all files in the current directory.

3. The shell initiated execution of echo, passing it the file list as arguments (see Figure 4.3).

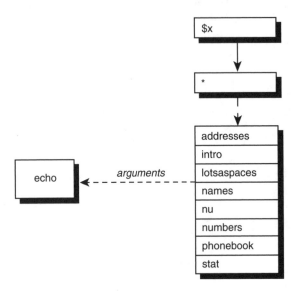

Figure 4.3 echo $x

This order of evaluation is important. Remember, first the shell does variable substitution, then does filename substitution, and then parses the line into arguments.

The ${variable} Construct

Suppose that you have the name of a file stored in the variable filename. If you wanted to rename that file so that the new name was the same as the old, except with an x added to the end, your first impulse would be to type

```
mv $filename $filenameX
```

When the shell scans this command line, however, it substitutes the value of the variable filename *and also the value of the variable* filenameX. The shell thinks filenameX is the full name of the variable because it's composed entirely of valid characters.

To avoid this problem, delimit the variable by enclosing the entire name (but not the leading dollar sign) in curly braces, as in

`${filename}X`

This removes any ambiguity, and the `mv` command then works as desired:

`mv $filename ${filename}X`

Remember that the braces are necessary only if the last character of the variable name is followed by an alphanumeric character or an underscore.

There are also quite a few functions applicable to variables within this curly brace notation, including extracting subsets, assigning values if the variable is currently unassigned, and more. Stay tuned for those!

Built-in Integer Arithmetic

The POSIX standard shell as included with all modern Unix and Linux variants (including Mac OS X's command shell) provides a mechanism for performing integer arithmetic on shell variables called *arithmetic expansion*. Note that some older shells do not support this feature.

The format for arithmetic expansion is

`$((expression))`

where `expression` is an arithmetic expression using shell variables and operators. Valid shell variables are those that contain numeric values (leading and trailing whitespace is allowed). Valid operators are taken from the C programming language and are listed in Appendix A, "Shell Summary."

`$(( ))` Operators

There is a surprisingly extensive list of operators, including the basic six: +, -, *, /, % and **, along with more sophisticated notations including +=, -=, *=, /=, easy increment and decrement with `variable++` and `variable--`, and more.

Our favorite? You can work with different numerical bases and even convert from one number base to another. For example, here are the answers to what 100 octal (base 8) and 101010101010101010 binary (base 2) are in decimal:

```
$ echo $(( 8#100 ))
64
$ echo $(( 2#101010101010101010 ))
174762
```

The result of computing `expression` is substituted on the command line. For example,

`echo $(i+1)`

adds one to the value in the shell variable `i` and prints the result. Notice that the variable i doesn't have to be preceded by a dollar sign because the shell knows that the only valid elements that can appear in arithmetic expansions are operators, numbers, and variables. If the variable is not defined or contains a NULL string, its value is assumed to be zero. So if we have not assigned any value yet to the variable a, we can still use it in an integer expression:

```
$ echo $a                         Variable a not set
$ echo $(( a = a + 1 ))              Equivalent to a = 0 + 1
$ 1
$ echo $a
1                        Now a contains 1
$
```

Note that assignment is a valid operator, and the value of the assignment is substituted in the second echo command in the preceding example.

Parentheses may be used freely inside expressions to force grouping, as in

```
echo $((i = (i + 10) * j))
```

If you want to perform an assignment without echo or some other command, you can move the assignment *before* the arithmetic expansion.

So to multiply the variable i by 5 and assign the result back to i you can write

```
i=$(( i * 5 ))
```

Note that spaces are optional inside the double parentheses, but are not allowed when the assignment is outside them.

A more succinct way to multiply $i by 5 is the following common notation, which would appear within another statement:

```
$(( i *= 5 ))
```

If you're just adding 1 to the value, you can be even more succinct:

```
$(( i++ ))
```

Finally, to test to see whether i is greater than or equal to 0 and less than or equal to 100, you can write

```
result=$(( i >= 0  &&  i <= 100 ))
```

which assigns result the value of 1 (true) if the expression is true or 0 (false) if it's false:

```
$ i=$(( 100 * 200 / 10 ))
$ j=$(( i < 1000 ))            If i is < 1000, set j = 0; otherwise 1
$ echo $i $j
2000 0                    i is 2000, so j was set to 0
$
```

That concludes our introduction to writing commands and using variables. The next chapter goes into detail on the various quoting mechanisms in the shell.

5

Can I Quote You on That?

This chapter teaches you about a unique feature of the shell programming language: the way it interprets quote characters. The shell recognizes four different types of quote characters:

- The single quote character '
- The double quote character "
- The backslash character \
- The back quote character `

The first two and the last characters in the preceding list must occur in pairs, while the backslash character can be used any number of times in a command as needed. Each of these quotes has a distinct meaning to the shell. We'll cover them in separate sections of this chapter.

The Single Quote

There are many reasons that you'll need to use quotes in the shell. One of the most common is to keep character sequences that include whitespace together as a single element.

Here's a file called phonebook that contains names and phone numbers:

```
$ cat phonebook
Alice Chebba      973-555-2015
Barbara Swingle   201-555-9257
Liz Stachiw       212-555-2298
Susan Goldberg    201-555-7776
Susan Topple      212-555-4932
Tony Iannino      973-555-1295
$
```

To look up someone in our phonebook file you could use grep:

```
$ grep Alice phonebook
Alice Chebba      973-555-2015
$
```

Look what happens when you look up `Susan`:

```
$ grep Susan phonebook
Susan Goldberg   201-555-7776
Susan Topple     212-555-4932
$
```

There are two Susans in the datafile, hence the two lines of output—but suppose you only wanted Susan Goldberg's information. One way to overcome this problem would be to further qualify the name. For example, you could specify the last name as well:

```
$ grep Susan Goldberg phonebook
grep: can't open Goldberg
Susan Goldberg   201-555-7776
Susan Topple     212-555-4932
$
```

But that's not going to work, as you can see.

Why? Because the shell uses whitespace characters to separate the command arguments, the preceding command line results in `grep` being passed three arguments: `Susan`, `Goldberg`, and `phonebook` (see Figure 5.1).

Figure 5.1 grep Susan Goldberg phonebook

When `grep` is executed, it interprets the first argument as the search pattern and the remaining arguments as the names of the files to search. In this case, `grep` thinks it's supposed to look for `Susan` in the files `Goldberg` and `phonebook`. It tries to open the file `Goldberg`, can't find it, and issues the error message:

```
grep: can't open Goldberg
```

Then it goes to the next file, `phonebook`, opens it, searches for the pattern `Susan`, and prints the two matching lines. Quite logical, really.

The problem is really about how to pass arguments that include whitespace characters to programs.

The solution: enclose the entire argument inside a pair of single quotes, as in

grep 'Susan Goldberg' phonebook

When the shell sees the first single quote, *it ignores any special characters that follow until it sees the matching closing quote.*

```
$ grep 'Susan Goldberg' phonebook
Susan Goldberg   201-555-7776
$
```

As soon as the shell encountered the first ' it stopped interpreting any special characters until it found the closing '. So the space between Susan and Goldberg, which would have normally delimited two separate arguments, was ignored by the shell. The shell then split the command line into *two* arguments, the first Susan Goldberg (which includes the space character) and the second phonebook. It then invoked grep, passing it these two arguments (see Figure 5.2).

Figure 5.2   grep 'Susan Goldberg' phonebook

grep interpreted the first argument, Susan Goldberg, as a pattern that included an embedded space and looked for it in the file specified by the second argument, phonebook. Note that the shell *removes* the quotes and does not pass them to the program.

No matter how many space characters are enclosed between quotes, they are all preserved by the shell.

```
$ echo   one            two       three     four
one two three four
$ echo 'one            two       three     four'
one            two       three     four
$
```

In the first case, the shell removes the extra whitespace characters from the line (no quotes!) and passes echo the four arguments one, two, three, and four (see Figure 5.3).

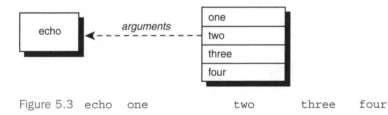

Figure 5.3   echo   one   two   three   four

In the second case, the extra spaces are preserved and the shell treats the entire string of characters enclosed in quotes as a single argument when executing echo (see Figure 5.4).

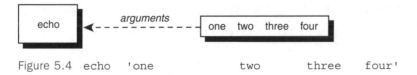

Figure 5.4   echo   'one   two   three   four'

Worth emphasizing is that *all* special characters are ignored by the shell if they appear within single quotes. That explains how the following works:

```
$ file=/users/steve/bin/prog1
$ echo $file
/users/steve/bin/prog1
$ echo '$file'                    $ not interpreted
$file
$ echo *
addresses intro lotsaspaces names nu numbers phonebook stat
$ echo '*'
*
$ echo '< > | ; ( ) { } >> " &'
< > | ; ( ) { } >> " &
$
```

Even the Enter key will be retained as part of the command argument if it's enclosed in single quotes:

```
$ echo 'How are you today,
> John'
How are you today,
John
$
```

After parsing the first line, the shell sees that the quote isn't matched, so it prompts the user (with >) to type in the closing quote. The > is known as the *secondary* prompt character and is displayed by the shell whenever it's waiting for you to finish typing a multi-line command.

Quotes are also needed when assigning values containing whitespace or special characters to shell variables, though there are nuances, as demonstrated:

```
$ message='I must say, this sure is fun'
$ echo $message
I must say, this sure is fun
$ text='* means all files in the directory'
$ echo $text
names nu numbers phonebook stat means all files in the directory
$
```

The quotes are needed in the first statement because the value being stored includes spaces.

The second sequence with the variable text highlights that the shell does filename substitution after variable name substitution, meaning that the * is replaced by the names of all the files in the current directory after the variable is expanded, but before the echo is executed. Annoying!

How do you fix these sort of problems? Through the use of double quotes.

The Double Quote

Double quotes work similarly to single quotes, except they're less protective of their content: single quotes tell the shell to ignore *all* enclosed characters, double quotes say to ignore *most*. In particular, the following three characters are not ignored inside double quotes:

- Dollar signs
- Back quotes
- Backslashes

The fact that dollar signs are not ignored means that variable name substitution is done by the shell inside double quotes.

```
$ filelist=*
$ echo $filelist
addresses intro lotsaspaces names nu numbers phonebook stat
$ echo '$filelist'
$filelist
$ echo "$filelist"
*
$
```

Here you see the major difference between no quotes, single quotes, and double quotes. In the first instance, the shell sees the asterisk and substitutes all the filenames from the current directory. In the second case, the shell leaves the characters enclosed within the single quotes completely alone, which results in the display of `$filelist`. In the final case, the double quotes indicate to the shell that variable name substitution is still to be performed inside the quotes. So the shell substitutes * for `$filelist`. But because filename substitution is *not* done inside double quotes, * is then safely passed to echo as the value to be displayed.

> ### Note
>
> While we're talking about single versus double quotes, you should also be aware that the shell has no idea what "smart quotes" are. Those are generated by word processors like Microsoft Word and curl "inward" towards the material they surround, making it much more attractive when printed. The problem is, that'll break your shell scripts, so be alert!

If you want to have the value of a variable substituted, but don't want the shell to then parse the substituted characters specially, enclose the variable inside double quotes.

Here's another example illustrating the difference between double quotes and no quotes:

```
$ address="39 East 12th Street
> New York, N. Y. 10003"
$ echo $address
39 East 12th Street New York, N. Y. 10003
$ echo "$address"
39 East 12th Street
New York, N. Y. 10003
$
```

Note that in this particular example, it makes no difference whether the value assigned to `address` is enclosed in single quotes or double quotes. The shell displays the secondary command prompt in either case to indicate it's waiting for the corresponding close quote.

After assigning the two-line address to `address`, the value of the variable is displayed by `echo`. Without the variable being quoted the address is displayed on a single line. The reason is the same as what caused

`echo one          two       three    four`

to be displayed as

`one two three four`

Because the shell removes spaces, tabs, and newlines (whitespace characters) from the command line and then cuts it up into arguments before giving it to the requested command, the invocation

`echo $address`

causes the shell to remove the embedded newline character, treating it as it would a space or tab: as an argument delimiter. Then the shell passes the *nine* arguments to `echo` for display. `echo` never sees that newline; the shell gets to it first (see Figure 5.5).

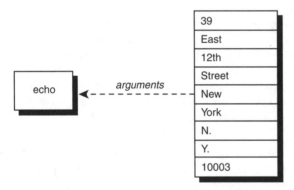

Figure 5.5 echo $address

When the command

`echo "$address"`

is used instead, the shell substitutes the value of `address` as before, except that the double quotes tell it to leave any embedded whitespace characters alone. So in this case, the shell passes a single argument to `echo`—an argument that contains an embedded newline. `echo` then displays its single argument. Figure 5.6 illustrates this, with the newline character depicted by the sequence \n.

Figure 5.6   `echo "$address"`

Where this gets a bit weird is that double quotes can be used to hide single quotes from the shell, and vice versa:

```
$ x="' Hello,' he said"
$ echo $x
'Hello,' he said
$ article=' "Keeping the Logins from Lagging," Bell Labs Record'
$ echo $article
"Keeping the Logins from Lagging," Bell Labs Record
$
```

The Backslash

Functionally, the backslash (used as a prefix) is equivalent to placing single quotes around a single character, though with a few minor exceptions. The backslash *escapes* the character that immediately follows it. The general format is

`\c`

where *c* is the character you want to quote. Any special meaning normally attached to that character is removed. Here is an example:

```
$ echo >
syntax error: 'newline or ;' unexpected
$ echo \>
>
$
```

In the first usage, the shell sees the > and thinks that you want to redirect echo's output to a file, so it expects a filename to follow. Because it doesn't, the shell issues the error message.

In the next usage, the backslash escapes the special meaning of the >, so it is passed along to echo as a character to be displayed.

```
$ x=*
$ echo \$x
$x
$
```

In this case, the shell ignores the $ that follows the backslash, and as a result, variable substitution is not performed.

Because a backslash removes the special meaning of the character that follows, can you guess what happens if that character is another backslash? It removes the special meaning of the backslash:

```
$ echo \\
\
$
```

You could have also used single quotes to accomplish this task:

```
$ echo '\'
\
$
```

Using the Backslash for Continuing Lines

As mentioned at the start of this section, \c is essentially equivalent to 'c'. The one exception to this rule is when the backslash is used as the very last character on the line:

```
$ lines=one'
> 'two                          Single quotes tell shell to ignore newline
$ echo "$lines"
one
two
$ lines=one\                    Try it with a \ instead
> two
$ echo "$lines"
onetwo
$
```

When a backslash is the last character of a line of input, the shell treats it as a line continuation character. It *removes* the newline character that follows and also does not treat the newline as an argument delimiter (it's as if it wasn't even typed). This construct is often used for entering long commands across multiple lines.

For example, the following is completely valid:

```
Longinput="The shell treats a backslash that's the \
last character of a line of input as a line \
continuation. It removes the newline too."
```

The Backslash Inside Double Quotes

We noted earlier that the backslash is one of the three characters interpreted by the shell inside double quotes. This means that you can use the backslash inside these quotes to remove the meaning of characters that otherwise *would* be interpreted inside double quotes (that is, other backslashes, dollar signs, back quotes, newlines, and other double quotes). If the backslash precedes any other character inside double quotes, the backslash is ignored by the shell and passed on to the program:

```
$ echo "\$x"
$x
$ echo "\ is the backslash character"
\ is the backslash character
$ x=5
$ echo "The value of x is \"$x\""
The value of x is "5"
$
```

In the first example, the backslash precedes the dollar sign so the shell ignores the dollar sign, removes the backslash, and hands the result to echo. In the second example, the backslash precedes a space, *not* interpreted by the shell inside double quotes. So the shell ignores the backslash and passes it on to the echo command. The last example shows the backslash used to enclose double quotes inside a double-quoted string.

As an exercise in the use of quotes, let's say that you want to display the following line at the terminal:

```
<<< echo $x >>> displays the value of x, which is $x
```

The intention here is to substitute the value of x in the second instance of $x, but not in the first. Let's first assign a value to x:

```
$ x=1
$
```

Now try displaying the line without using any quotes:

```
$ echo <<< echo $x >>> displays the value of x, which is $x
syntax error: '<' unexpected
$
```

The < signals input redirection to the shell, which lacks a subsequent filename, hence the resultant error message.

If you put the entire message inside single quotes, the value of x won't be substituted at the end. If you enclose the entire string in double quotes, both occurrences of $x will be substituted. Tricky!

Here are two different ways to properly quote the string so that everything works as desired:

```
$ echo "<<< echo \$x >>> displays the value of x, which is $x"
<<< echo $x >>> displays the value of x, which is 1
$ echo '<<< echo $x >>> displays the value of x, which is' $x
<<< echo $x >>> displays the value of x, which is 1
$
```

In the first case, everything is enclosed in double quotes, and the backslash is used to prevent the shell from performing variable substitution in the first instance of $x. In the second case, everything up to the last $x is enclosed in single quotes but the variable that *should* be substituted is added without quotes around it.

There's a slight danger to the latter solution, however: If the variable x contained filename substitution or whitespace characters, they would be interpreted. A safer way of writing the echo would have been

```
echo '<<< echo $x >>> displays the value of x, which is' "$x"
```

Command Substitution

Command substitution refers to the shell's capability to replace a specified command with the output of that command at any point in a command line. There are two ways in the shell to perform command substitution: by enclosing the command in back quotes or surrounding it with the `$(...)` construct.

The Back Quote

The back quote—often called "back tick"—is unlike any of the previously encountered types of quotes because its purpose is not to protect characters from the shell but to tell the shell to replace the enclosed command with its output. The general format for using back quotes is

```
`command`
```

where `command` is the name of the command to be executed and whose output is to be inserted at that point.

> **Note**
>
> Using the back quote for command substitution is no longer the preferred method; however, we cover it here because of the large number of older shell scripts that still use this construct. You should also know about back quotes in case you ever need to write shell programs that are portable to older Unix systems with shells that don't support the newer, preferred `$(...)` construct.

Here is an example:

```
$ echo The date and time is: `date`
The date and time is: Wed Aug 28 14:28:43 EDT 2002
$
```

When the shell does its initial scan of the command line, it recognizes the back quote and expects a command to follow. In this case, the shell finds the `date` command so it executes `date` and replaces the `` `date` `` sequence on the command line with the output from `date`. After that, the shell divides the resultant command line into arguments in the normal manner and then hands them all off to the `echo` command.

```
$ echo Your current working directory is `pwd`
Your current working directory is /users/steve/shell/ch6
$
```

Here the shell executes pwd, inserts its output on the command line, and then executes the echo. Note that in the following section, back quotes can be used in all the places where the $(...) construct is used and, of course, vice-versa with the examples in this section.

The $ (. . .) Construct

All modern Unix, Linux and any other POSIX-compliant shells support the newer and preferred $(...) construct for command substitution. The general format is

$(command)

where, just as with back quotes, command is the name of the command whose standard output is to be substituted on the command line. For example:

```
$ echo The date and time is: $(date)
The date and time is: Wed Aug 28 14:28:43 EDT 2002
$
```

This construct is better than back quotes for a couple of reasons. First, complex commands that use combinations of forward and back quotes can be difficult to read, particularly if the typeface you're using doesn't visually differentiate between single and back quotes; second, $(...) constructs can be easily nested, allowing command substitution *within* command substitution. Although nesting can also be performed with back quotes, it's trickier. You'll see an example of nested command substitution later in this section.

Let's emphasize something important: you aren't restricted to invoking a single command between the parentheses. Several commands can be executed if separated by semicolons; and, more commonly, you can also use command pipelines.

Here's a modified version of the nu program that displays the number of logged-in users:

```
$ cat nu
echo There are $(who | wc -1) users logged in
$ nu                          Execute it
There are 13 users logged in
$
```

Because single quotes protect everything, the following output should be clear:

```
$ echo '$(who | wc -1) tells how many users are logged in'
$(who | wc -1) tells how many users are logged in
$
```

But command substitution *is* interpreted inside double quotes:

```
$ echo "You have $(ls | wc -1) files in your directory"
You have       7 files in your directory
$
```

Remember that the shell is responsible for executing the command enclosed between the parentheses. The only thing the `echo` command sees is the output that has been inserted by the shell.

> **Note**
>
> Those leading spaces produced by the `wc` command in the above example are a constant source of annoyance for programmers. Can you think of a way to use `sed` to remove them?

Suppose that you're writing a shell program and want to assign the current date and time to a variable called `now`.

Command substitution can be used for this:

```
$ now=$(date)              Execute date and store the output in now
$ echo $now                See what got assigned
Wed Aug 28 14:47:26 EDT 2002
$
```

When you enter

```
now=$(date)
```

the shell understands that the entire output from `date` is to be assigned to `now`. Therefore, you don't need to enclose `$(date)` inside double quotes, though it's a common practice.

Even commands that produce more than a single line of output can be stored inside a variable:

```
$ filelist=$(ls)
$ echo $filelist
addresses intro lotsaspaces names nu numbers phonebook stat
$
```

What happened here? You end up with a horizontal listing of the files even though the newlines from `ls` were stored inside the `filelist` variable. The newlines got eaten up at display time when the value of `filelist` was substituted by the shell in processing the `echo` command line. Double quotes around the variable will preserve the newlines:

```
$ echo "$filelist"
addresses
intro
lotsaspaces
names
nu
numbers
phonebook
stat
$
```

Moving further into the world of shell scripting, let's see how this works with file redirection. For example, to store the contents of a file into a variable, you can use the handy `cat` command:

```
$ namelist=$(cat names)
$ echo "$namelist"
Charlie
Emanuel
Fred
Lucy
Ralph
Tony
Tony
$
```

If you want to mail the contents of the file `memo` to all the people listed in the `names` file, you can do the following:

```
$ mail $(cat names) < memo
$
```

Here the shell replaces the `cat` command with its output on the command line, so it looks like this:

```
mail Charlie Emanuel Fred Lucy Ralph Tony Tony < memo
```

Then the shell executes `mail`, redirecting its standard input from the file `memo` and passing it to the seven recipients specified.

Notice that `Tony` might receive the same mail twice because he's listed twice in the `names` file. You can remove any duplicate entries from the file by using `sort` with the `-u` option (remove duplicate lines) rather than `cat` to ensure that each person only receives mail once:

```
$ mail $(sort -u names) < memo
$
```

Remember that the shell does filename substitution *after* it substitutes the output from commands. Enclosing the commands inside double quotes prevents the shell from doing the filename substitution on the output.

Command substitution is often used to change the value stored in a shell variable. For example, if the shell variable `name` contains someone's name, and you want to convert every character in that variable to uppercase, you could use `echo` to send the variable to `tr`'s input, perform the translation, and then assign the result back to the variable:

```
$ name="Ralph Kramden"
$ name=$(echo $name | tr '[a-z]' '[A-Z]')          Translate to uppercase
$ echo $name
RALPH KRAMDEN
$
```

The technique of using echo in a pipeline to write data to the standard input of the subsequent command is simple but powerful, and is often used in shell programs.

The next example shows how cut can be used to extract the first character from the values stored in a variable called filename:

```
$ filename=/users/steve/memos
$ firstchar=$(echo $filename | cut -c1)
$ echo $firstchar
/
$
```

sed is also often used to "edit" the value stored in a variable. Here it is used to extract the last character from each line of the file specified by the variable file:

```
$ file=exec.o
$ lastchar=$(echo $file | sed 's/.*\(.\)$/\1/')
$ echo $lastchar
o
$
```

The sed command replaces all the characters on the line with the last one (remember that surrounding a pattern in parentheses causes it to be saved in a register[el] in this case register 1, which is then referenced as \1). The result of the sed substitution is stored in the variable lastchar. The single quotes around the sed command are important because they prevent the shell from trying to interpret the backslashes. (Question: would double quotes also have worked?)

Finally, command substitutions can be nested. Suppose that you want to change every occurrence of the first character in a variable to something else. In a previous example, firstchar=$(echo $filename | cut -c1) gets the first character from filename, but how would we use this character to change every occurrence of that character in filename? A two-step process is one way:

```
$ filename=/users/steve/memos
$ firstchar=$(echo $filename | cut -c1)
$ filename=$(echo $filename | tr "$firstchar" "^")      translate / to ^
$ echo $filename
^users^steve^memos
$
```

But a single, nested command substitution can perform the same operation:

```
$ filename=/users/steve/memos
$ filename=$(echo $filename | tr "$(echo $filename | cut -c1)" "^")
$ echo $filename
^users^steve^memos
$
```

If you have trouble understanding this example, compare it to the previous one: Note how the firstchar variable in the earlier example is replaced by the nested command substitution; otherwise, the two examples are the same.

The `expr` Command

Although the standard shell supports built-in integer arithmetic, older shells don't have this capability. In that situation, the mathematical equation solver `expr` can be used instead:

```
$ expr 1 + 2
3
$
```

It's easy to work with, but `expr` isn't very good at parsing equations, so each operator and operand given to `expr` must be separated by spaces to be properly understood. That explains the following:

```
$ expr 1+2
1+2
$
```

The usual arithmetic operators are recognized by `expr`: + for addition, - for subtraction, / for division, * for multiplication, and % for modulus (remainder).

```
$ expr 10 + 20 / 2
20
$
```

Multiplication, division, and modulus have higher precedence than addition and subtraction, as with standard mathematics. Thus, in the preceding example the division was performed before the addition.

But what about this example?

```
$ expr 17 * 6
expr: syntax error
$
```

The shell saw the * and substituted the names of all the files in your directory, which `expr` had no idea how to interpret! In the case of multiplication especially, the expression given to `expr` must be quoted to keep it away from the shell's interference—but not as a single argument, as in this example:

```
$ expr "17 * 6"
17 * 6
$
```

Remember that `expr` must see each operator and operand as a separate argument; the preceding example sends the whole expression in as a single argument, which doesn't give you the results you want.

This is a job for the backslash!

```
$ expr 17 \* 6
102
$
```

Naturally, one or more of the arguments to `expr` can be the value stored inside a shell variable because the shell takes care of the substitution first anyway:

```
$ i=1
$ expr $i + 1
2
$
```

This is the older method for performing arithmetic on shell variables and is less efficient than the shell built-in $ (...) construct. In the case of incrementing or otherwise modifying a variable, you can use the command substitution mechanism to assign the output from `expr` back to the variable:

```
$ i=1
$ i=$(expr $i + 1)          Add 1 to i
$ echo $i
2
$
```

In legacy shell programs, you're more likely to see `expr` used with the back quotes discussed earlier:

```
$ i=`expr $i + 1`           Add 1 to i
$ echo $i
3
$
```

Similar to the shell's built-in arithmetic, `expr` only evaluates integer arithmetic expressions. You can use `awk` or `bc` if you need to do floating point calculations. The difference? 17 is an integer, while 13.747 is a floating point (that is, number with a decimal point) value.

Also note that `expr` has other operators. One of the most frequently used is the : operator, which is used to match characters in the first operand against a regular expression given as the second operand. By default, it returns the number of characters matched.

For example, the `expr` command

```
expr "$file" : ".*"
```

returns the number of characters stored in the variable `file`, because the regular expression .* matches all the characters in the string. For more details on `expr` and the powerful colon construct, consult your *Unix User's Manual* or the man page for `expr` on your system.

Table A.5 in Appendix A summarizes the way quotes are handled by the shell.

6

Passing Arguments

Shell programs become far more useful after you learn how to process arguments passed to them. In this chapter, you'll learn how to write shell programs that take arguments typed on the command line. Recall the one-line program `run` that you wrote in Chapter 4 to run the file `sys.caps` through `tbl`, `nroff`, and `lp`:

```
$ cat run
tbl sys.caps | nroff -mm -Tlp | lp
$
```

Suppose that you need to run other files besides `sys.caps` through this same command sequence. You could make a separate version of `run` for each such file; or, you could modify the `run` program so that you could specify the name of the file to be run on the command line. That is, you could change `run` so that you could type

run new.hire

for example, to specify that the file `new.hire` is to be printed through this command sequence, or

run sys.caps

to specify the file `sys.caps`.

Whenever you execute a shell program, the shell automatically stores the first argument in the special shell variable 1, the second argument in the variable 2, and so on. (For convenience's sake, from now on we'll refer to these as $1, $2, and so on, even though the $ is actually part of the variable reference notation, not the variable name.) These special variables—more formally known as *positional parameters* because they're based on the position of the value in the command line—are assigned after the shell has done its normal command-line processing (that is, I/O redirection, variable substitution, filename substitution, and so on).

To modify the `run` program to accept the name of the file as an argument, all you do to the program is change the reference to the file `sys.caps` so that it instead references the first argument typed on the command line:

```
$ cat run
tbl $1 | nroff -mm -Tlp | lp
$
```

```
$ run new.hire                          Execute it with new.hire as the argument
request id is laserl-24 (standard input)
$
```

Each time you execute the `run` program, whatever word follows on the command line will be stored inside the first positional parameter by the shell and then handed to the program itself. In the first example, `new.hire` will be stored in this parameter.

Substitution of positional parameters is identical to substitution of other types of variables, so when the shell sees

```
tbl $1
```

it replaces the `$1` with the first argument supplied to the program: `new.hire`.

As another example, the following program, called `ison`, lets you know if a specified user is logged on:

```
$ cat ison
who | grep $1
$ who                                   See who's on
root       console Jul 7 08:37
barney     tty03 Jul 8 12:28
fred       tty04 Jul 8 13:40
joanne     tty07 Jul 8 09:35
tony       tty19 Jul 8 08:30
lulu       tty23 Jul 8 09:55
$ ison tony
tony       tty19 Jul 8 08:30
$ ison pat
$                                       Not logged on
```

The $# Variable

In addition to the positional variables, the special shell variable $# gets set to the number of arguments that were typed on the command line. As you'll see in the next chapter, this variable is often tested by programs to determine whether the correct number of arguments was specified by the user.

The next program, called `args`, was written just to get you more familiar with the way arguments are passed to shell programs. Study the output from each example and make sure that you understand it:

```
$ cat args                              Look at the program
echo $# arguments passed
echo arg 1 = :$1: arg 2 = :$2: arg 3 = :$3:
$ args a b c                            Execute it
3 arguments passed
arg 1 = :a: arg 2 = :b: arg 3 = :c:
$ args a b                              Try it with two arguments
```

```
2 arguments passed
arg 1 = :a: arg 2 = :b: arg 3 = ::          Unassigned args are null
$ args                            Try it with no arguments
0 arguments passed
arg 1 =:: arg 2 =:: arg 3 = ::
$ args "a b c"                    Try quotes
1 arguments passed
arg 1 = :a b c: arg 2 = :: arg 3 = ::
$ ls x*                          See what files start with x
xact
xtra
$ args x*                        Try filename substitution
2 arguments passed
arg 1 = :xact: arg 2 = :xtra: arg 3 = ::
$ my_bin=/users/steve/bin
$ args $my_bin                   And variable substitution
1 arguments passed
arg 1 = :/users/steve/bin: arg 2 = :: arg 3 = ::
$ args $(cat names)              Pass the contents of names
7 arguments passed
arg 1 = :Charlie: arg 2 = :Emanuel: arg3 = :Fred:
$
```

As you can see, the shell does its normal command-line processing even when it's executing your shell programs. This means that you can take advantage of the normal niceties, such as filename substitution and variable substitution, when specifying arguments to your programs.

The $* Variable

The special variable $* references *all* the arguments passed to the program. This is often useful in programs that take an indeterminate or *variable* number of arguments. You'll see some more practical examples later. Here's a program that illustrates its use:

```
$ cat args2
echo $# arguments passed
echo they are :$*:
$ args2 a b c
3 arguments passed
they are :a b c:
$ args2 one                two
2 arguments passed
they are :one two:
$ args2
0 arguments passed
they are ::
$ args2 *
8 arguments passed
they are :args args2 names nu phonebook stat xact xtra:
$
```

A Program to Look Up Someone in the Phone Book

Here's the phonebook file from previous examples:

```
$ cat phonebook
Alice Chebba      973-555-2015
Barbara Swingle   201-555-9257
Liz Stachiw       212-555-2298
Susan Goldberg    201-555-7776
Susan Topple      212-555-4932
Tony Iannino      973-555-1295
$
```

You know how to look up someone in the file by using grep:

```
$ grep Cheb phonebook
Alice Chebba      973-555-2015
$
```

And you know that if you want to look up someone by their full name, you need to put quotes around the words to keep the argument together:

```
$ grep "Susan T" phonebook
Susan Topple      212-555-4932
$
```

It would be nice to write a shell program that you could use to look up someone. Let's call the program lu and have it take as its argument the name of the person to seek:

```
$ cat lu
#
# Look someone up in the phone book
#

grep $1 phonebook
$
```

Here's a sample use of lu:

```
$ lu Alice
Alice Chebba      973-555-2015
$ lu Susan
Susan Goldberg    201-555-7776
Susan Topple      212-555-4932
$ lu "Susan T"
grep: can't open T
phonebook:Susan Goldberg  201-555-7776
phonebook:Susan Topple    212-555-4932
$
```

In the preceding example, you were careful to enclose Susan T in double quotes; so what happened? Look again at the grep invocation in the lu program:

```
grep $1 phonebook
```

See the problem? Enclosing `Susan T` inside double quotes results in its getting passed to `lu` as a single argument, but when the shell substitutes this value for `$1` on `grep`'s command line within the program itself, it then passes it as *two* arguments to `grep`.

You can fix this problem by enclosing `$1` inside double quotes in the `lu` program:

```
$ cat lu
#
# Look someone up in the phone book -- version 2
#

grep "$1" phonebook
$
```

Single quotes wouldn't work in this instance. Why not?

Now let's try that invocation again:

```
$ lu Tony
Tony Iannino    973-555-1295          This still works
$ lu "Susan T"                        Now try this again
Susan Topple    212-555-4932
$
```

A Program to Add Someone to the Phone Book

Let's continue with the development of programs that work with the `phonebook` file. You'll probably want to add someone to the file at some point, particularly because our `phonebook` file is so small, so let's write a program called `add` that takes two arguments: the name of the person to be added and their phone number.

The `add` program simply appends the name and number, separated by a tab character, onto the end of the `phonebook` file:

```
$ cat add
#
# Add someone to the phone book
#

echo "$1        $2" >> phonebook
$
```

Although you can't tell, there's a tab character that separates the `$1` from the `$2` in the preceding `echo` command. This tab must be quoted to make it to `echo` without getting gobbled up by the shell.

Let's try out the program:

```
$ add 'Stromboli Pizza' 973-555-9478
$ lu Pizza                            See if we can find the new entry
Stromboli Pizza 973-555-9478          So far, so good
```

```
$ cat phonebook                      See what happened
Alice Chebba      973-555-2015
Barbara Swingle 201-555-9257
Liz Stachiw       212-555-2298
Susan Goldberg 201-555-7776
Susan Topple      212-555-4932
Tony Iannino      973-555-1295
Stromboli Pizza 973-555-9478
$
```

Stromboli Pizza was quoted so that the shell passed it along to add as a single argument (what would have happened if it wasn't quoted?). After add finished executing, lu was run to see whether it could find the new entry, and it did. The cat command was executed to see what the modified phonebook file looked like. The new entry was added to the end, as intended.

Unfortunately, the new file is no longer sorted. This won't affect the operation of the lu program but it's a nice feature nonetheless. The solution? Add sorting to the program by using the sort command:

```
$ cat add
#
# Add someone to the phonebook file -- version 2
#

echo "$1        $2" >> phonebook
sort -o phonebook phonebook
$
```

Recall that the -o option to sort specifies where the sorted output is to be written, and that this can be the same as the input file:

```
$ add 'Billy Bach' 201-555-7618
$ cat phonebook
Alice Chebba      973-555-2015
Barbara Swingle 201-555-9257
Billy Bach        201-555-7618
Liz Stachiw       212-555-2298
Stromboli Pizza 973-555-9478
Susan Goldberg 201-555-7776
Susan Topple      212-555-4932
Tony Iannino      973-555-1295
$
```

Each time a new entry is added, the phonebook file will get re-sorted so that multi-line matches are always in alphabetical order.

A Program to Remove Someone from the Phone Book

No set of programs that enable you to look up or add someone to the phone book would be complete without a program to remove someone from the phone book too. We'll call this program rem and let the user specify the name of the person to be removed as a command argument.

What should the strategy be for developing the program? Essentially, you want to remove the line from the file that contains the specified name, which is a reverse pattern match. The -v option to grep can be used here because it does exactly what we want, printing all lines from a file that *don't* match a pattern:

```
$ cat rem
#
# Remove someone from the phone book
#

grep -v "$1" phonebook > /tmp/phonebook
mv /tmp/phonebook phonebook
$
```

The grep construct writes all lines that don't match into the file /tmp/phonebook. (Tip: /tmp is a directory designated in Unix systems for temporary files and is usually wiped clean every time the system restarts.) After the grep command is done, the old phonebook file is replaced by the new one from /tmp.

```
$ rem 'Stromboli Pizza'          Remove this entry
$ cat phonebook
Alice Chebba      973-555-2015
Barbara Swingle   201-555-9257
Billy Bach        201-555-7618
Liz Stachiw       212-555-2298
Susan Goldberg    201-555-7776
Susan Topple      212-555-4932
Tony Iannino      973-555-1295
$ rem Susan
$ cat phonebook
Alice Chebba      973-555-2015
Barbara Swingle   201-555-9257
Billy Bach        201-555-7618
Liz Stachiw       212-555-2298
Tony Iannino      973-555-1295
$
```

The first case, where Stromboli Pizza was removed, worked fine. In the second case, however, both Susan entries were removed because they both matched the pattern. Not good! You can use the add program to add them back to the phone book:

```
$ add 'Susan Goldberg' 201-555-7776
$ add 'Susan Topple' 212-555-4932
$
```

In Chapter 7, you'll learn how to test the action prior to taking it so the program can determine whether more than one matching entry is found. The program might want to alert the user that more than one match has been found, for example, rather than just blindly delete multiple entries. (This can be very helpful, because most implementations of grep will match *everything* if an empty string is passed as the pattern, which would effectively delete the phonebook entirely. Not good.)

Incidentally, note that sed could have also been used to delete the matching entry. In such a case, the grep could be replaced with

```
sed "/$1/d" phonebook > /tmp/phonebook
```

to achieve the same result. The double quotes are needed around the sed command's argument to ensure that the value of $1 is substituted, while at the same time ensuring that the shell doesn't see a command line like

```
sed /Stromboli Pizza/d phonebook > /tmp/phonebook
```

and pass three arguments to sed rather than two.

${*n*}

If you supply more than nine arguments to a program, you cannot access the tenth and greater arguments with $10, $11, and so on. If you try to access the tenth argument by writing

```
$10
```

the shell actually substitutes the value of $1 followed by a 0. Instead, the format

```
${n}
```

must be used. To directly access argument 10, you must write

```
${10}
```

in your program, and so on for arguments 11, 12, and so on.

The shift Command

The shift command allows you to effectively *left-shift* your positional parameters. If you execute the command

```
shift
```

whatever was previously stored inside $2 will be assigned to $1, whatever was previously stored in $3 will be assigned to $2, and so on. The old value of $1 will be irretrievably lost.

When this command is executed, $# (the number of arguments variable) is also automatically decremented by one:

```
$ cat tshift              Program to test the shift
echo $# $*
shift
echo $# $*
```

```
shift
echo $# $*
shift
echo $# $*
shift
echo $# $*
shift
echo $# $*
$ tshift a b c d e
5 a b c d e
4 b c d e
3 c d e
2 d e
1 e
0
$
```

If you try to shift when there are no variables to shift (that is, when $# already equals zero), you'll get an error message from the shell (the error will vary from one shell to the next):

prog: shift: bad number

where *prog* is the name of the program that executed the offending shift.

You can shift more than one "place" at once by writing a *count* immediately after shift, as in

shift 3

This command has the same effect as performing three separate shifts:

```
shift
shift
shift
```

The shift command is useful when processing a variable number of arguments. You'll see it put to use when you learn about loops in Chapter 8. For now, just remember that positional parameters can be moved along the chain by using shift.

## 7

Decisions, Decisions

This chapter introduces the conditional statement, a construct that is present in almost every programming language: `if`. It enables you to test a condition and then change the flow of program execution based on the result of the test.

The general format of the `if` command is

```
if command_t
then
        command
        command
        ...
fi
```

where *command_t* is executed and its *exit status* is tested. If the exit status is zero, the commands that follow between `then` and `fi` are executed; otherwise, they're skipped.

Exit Status

To understand how conditional tests work, it's important to know about how Unix works with what's called the *exit status*. Whenever any program completes execution, it returns an exit status code to the shell. This status is a numeric value that indicates whether the program ran successfully or failed. By convention, an exit status of zero indicates that a program succeeded, and non-zero indicates that it failed, with different values indicating different kinds of failures.

Failures can be caused by invalid arguments passed to the program, or by an error condition detected by the program. For example, the `cp` command returns a non-zero (fail) exit status if the copy fails (for example, if it can't find the source file or create the destination file), or if the arguments aren't correctly specified (for example, the wrong number of arguments, or more than two arguments and the last one isn't a directory).

What do we mean by non-zero? Simply, any integer value that isn't 0. Most command man pages list possible exit status values too, so possible error conditions for a file copy command could be 1 for file not found, 2 for file not readable, 3 for destination folder not found, 4 for destination folder not writeable, 5 for general error copying the file and, of course, 0 for success.

In the case of grep, an exit status of zero (success) is returned if it finds the specified pattern in at least one of the files specified; a non-zero value is returned if it can't find the pattern or if a different error occurs, like failure to open a specified source file.

In a pipeline, the exit status reflects the last command in the pipe. So in

```
who | grep fred
```

the grep exit status is used by the shell as the exit status for the whole pipeline. In this case, an exit status of zero (success) means that fred was found in who's output (that is, fred was logged on at the time that this command was executed).

The $? Variable

The shell variable $? is automatically set by the shell to the exit status of the last command executed. Naturally, you can use echo to display its value at the terminal.

```
$ cp phonebook phone2
$ echo $?
0                        Copy "succeeded"
$ cp nosuch backup
cp: cannot access nosuch
$ echo $?
2                        Copy "failed"
$ who                    See who's logged on
root     console Jul 8 10:06
wilma    tty03   Jul 8 12:36
barney   tty04   Jul 8 14:57
betty    tty15   Jul 8 15:03
$ who | grep barney
barney   tty04   Jul 8 14:57
$ echo $?                Print exit status of last command (grep)
0                        grep "succeeded"
$ who | grep fred
$ echo $?
1                        grep "failed"
$ echo $?
0                        Exit status of last echo
$
```

Note that the numeric result of a "failure" for some commands can vary from one version of Unix to the next, but success is always signified by a zero exit status.

Let's write a shell program called on that tells us whether a specified user is logged on to the system. The name of the user to check will be passed to the program on the command line. If the user is logged on, we'll print a message to that effect; otherwise we'll say nothing. Here is the program:

```
$ cat on
#
# determine if someone is logged on
#

user="$1"

if who | grep "$user"
then
    echo "$user is logged on"
fi
$
```

This first argument typed on the command line is stored in the shell variable user. Then the if command executes the pipeline

```
who | grep "$user"
```

and tests the exit status returned by grep. If the exit status is zero (success), grep found user in who's output. In that case, the echo command that follows is executed. If the exit status is non-zero (failure), the specified user is not logged on, and the echo command is skipped.

The echo command is indented from the left margin for aesthetic reasons only. In this case, just a single command is enclosed between the then and fi. When more commands are included, and when the nesting gets deeper, indentation can have a significant impact on the program's readability. Later examples will help illustrate this point.

Here are some sample uses of on:

```
$ who
root      console Jul 8 10:37
barney    tty03   Jul 8 12:38
fred      tty04   Jul 8 13:40
joanne    tty07   Jul 8 09:35
tony      tty19   Jul 8 08:30
lulu      tty23   Jul 8 09:55
$ on tony                       We know he's on
tony      tty19   Jul 8 08:30   Where did this come from?
tony is logged on
$ on steve                      We know he's not on
$ on ann                        Try this one
joanne    tty07   Jul 8 09:35
ann is logged on
$
```

There are a couple of problems with the program as written, however. When the specified user is logged on, the corresponding line from who's output is also displayed, courtesy of the call to grep. This may not be such a bad thing, but the program requirements called for only the informational "logged on" message to be displayed and nothing else.

This extra line is displayed because of the conditional test: not only does `grep` return an exit status in the pipeline

```
who | grep "$user"
```

but it also goes about its normal function of writing any matching lines to standard output, even though we're really not interested in that.

Since we're not interested in seeing the result of the command, just testing the exit code, we can dispose of `grep`'s output by redirecting it to the system's "garbage can," `/dev/null`. This is a special file on the system that anyone can read from (and get an immediate end of file) or write to. When you write to it, the bits vanish, as if it were a massive black hole!

```
who | grep "$user" > /dev/null
```

That'll solve the superfluous output problem.

The second problem with `on` appears when the program is executed with the argument `ann`. Even though `ann` is not logged on, `grep` matches the characters `ann` for the user `joanne`. What we need is a more restrictive pattern, which you learned how to do in Chapter 3 where we talked about regular expressions. Because `who` lists each username in column one of the output, we can anchor the pattern to match the beginning of the line by preceding the pattern with the character `^`:

```
who | grep "^$user" > /dev/null
```

But that's still not enough. Search for a pattern like `bob` and `grep` still matches a line like

```
bobby     tty07  Jul 8 09:35
```

What you need to do is also anchor the pattern on the right too. Realizing that `who` ends each username with one or more spaces, the further modified pattern

```
"^$user "
```

now only matches lines for the specified `user`. Problem two fixed!

Let's try the new and improved version of `on`:

```
$ cat on
#
# determine if someone is logged on -- version 2
#
user="$1"

if who | grep "^$user " > /dev/null
then
        echo "$user is logged on"
fi
$ who                          Who's on now?
root      console Jul 8 10:37
barney    tty03   Jul 8 12:38
fred      tty04   Jul 8 13:40
```

```
joanne     tty07    Jul 8 09:35
tony       tty19    Jul 8 08:30
lulu       tty23    Jul 8 09:55
$ on lulu
lulu is logged on
$ on ann                         Try this again
$ on                             What happens if we don't give any arguments?
$
```

If no arguments are specified, user will be null. grep will then look through who's output for lines that start with a blank (why?). It won't find any, and so just a command prompt will be returned. In the next section, you'll see how to test whether the correct number of arguments has been supplied to a program and, if not, take some action.

The `test` Command

Though the previous example program used a pipeline to test for the `if` statement, a built-in shell command called `test` is much more commonly used for testing one or more conditions. Its general format is

```
test expression
```

where *expression* represents the condition you're testing. test evaluates *expression*, and if the result is *true*, it returns an exit status of zero, otherwise the result is *false*, and it returns a nonzero exit status.

String Operators

As an example, the following command returns a zero exit status if the shell variable name contains the characters julio:

```
test "$name" = julio
```

The = operator is used to test whether two values are identical. In this case, we're testing to see whether the *contents* of the shell variable name are identical to the characters julio. If it is, test returns an exit status of zero; nonzero otherwise.

Note that test must see all operands ($name and julio) and operators (=) as separate arguments, meaning that they must be delimited by one or more whitespace characters.

Getting back to the `if` command, to echo the message "Would you like to play a game?" if name contains the characters julio, you would write your `if` command like this:

```
if test "$name" = julio
then
        echo "Would you like to play a game?"
fi
```

When the `if` command gets executed, the command that follows the `if` is executed, and its exit status is evaluated. The test command is passed the three arguments $name (with its value substituted, of course), =, and `julio`. `test` then evaluates whether the first argument is identical to the third argument and returns a zero exit status if it is and a nonzero exit status if it is not.

The `exit` status returned by `test` is then tested by the `if` statement. If it's zero, the commands between `then` and `fi` are executed; in this case, the single `echo` command is executed. If the exit status is nonzero, the `echo` command is skipped.

As demonstrated above, it's good programming practice to enclose shell variables that are arguments to `test` inside a pair of *double* quotes (to allow variable substitution). This ensures that `test` sees the argument in the even if its value is null. For example, consider the following example:

```
$ name=                        Set name null
$ test $name = julio
sh: test: argument expected
$
```

Because `name` was null, only two arguments were passed to `test`: `=` and `julio`—because the shell substituted the value of `name` *before* parsing the command line into arguments. In fact, after $name was substituted by the shell, it was as if you typed the following:

```
test = julio
```

When `test` executed, it saw only two arguments (see Figure 7.1) and therefore issued the error message.

Figure 7.1 `test $name = julio` with name null

By placing double quotes around the variable, you ensure that `test` sees the argument because quotes act as a "placeholder" when the argument is null.

```
$ test "$name" = julio
$ echo $?                      Print the exit status
1
$
```

Even if `name` is null, the shell still passes three arguments to `test`, the first one being a null value (see Figure 7.2).

Figure 7.2 `test "$name" = julio` with name null

Other operators can be used to test character strings. There are a number of them, as summarized in Table 7.1.

Table 7.1   test **String Operators**

Operator	Returns TRUE (exit status of 0) if
string₁ = *string₂*	*string₁* is identical to *string₂*
string₁ != *string₂*	*string₁* is *not* identical to *string₂*
string	*string* is not null
-n *string*	*string* is not null (and *string* must be seen by test)
-z *string*	*string* is null (and *string* must be seen by test)

You've seen how the = operator is used. The != operator is similar, except it tests two strings for inequality. That is, the exit status from test is zero if the two strings are not equal, and nonzero if they are.

Let's look at three similar examples.

```
$ day="monday"
$ test "$day" = monday
$ echo $?
0                              True
$
```

The test command returns an exit status of 0 because the value of day is equal to the characters monday. Now look at the following:

```
$ day="monday"
$ test "$day" = monday
$ echo $?
1                              False
$
```

Here we assigned the characters monday—*including the space character that immediately followed*—to day. Therefore, when the previous test was made, test returned FALSE because the characters "monday" were not identical to the characters "monday".

If you wanted these two values to be considered equal, omitting the double quotes around the variable reference would have caused the shell to "eat up" the trailing space character, and test would have never seen it:

```
$ day="monday"
$ test $day = monday
$ echo $?
0
$                              True
```

Although this seems to violate our rule about always quoting shell variables that are arguments to `test`, it's okay to omit the quotes if you're sure that the variable is not null (and not composed entirely of whitespace characters).

You can test to see whether a shell variable has a null value with the third operator listed in Table 7.1:

```
test "$day"
```

This returns TRUE if `day` is not null and FALSE if it is. Quotes are not necessary here because `test` doesn't care whether it sees an argument in this case. Nevertheless, you are better off using them here as well because if the variable consists entirely of whitespace characters, the shell will get rid of the argument if it's not enclosed in quotes.

```
$ blanks="    "
$ test $blanks            Is it not null?
$ echo $?
1                         False—it's null
$ test "$blanks"          And now?
$ echo $?
0                         True—it's not null
$
```

In the first case, `test` was not passed *any* arguments because the shell ate up the four spaces in `blanks`. In the second case, `test` got one argument consisting of four space characters which is not null.

In case we seem to be belaboring the point about blanks and quotes, realize that this is a frequent source of shell programming errors. It's good to really understand the principles here to save yourself a lot of programming headaches in the future.

There is another way to test whether a string is null, and that's with either of the last two operators listed previously in Table 7.1. The -n operator returns an exit status of zero if the argument that follows is not null. Think of this operator as testing for nonzero length.

The -z operator tests the argument that follows to see whether it is null and returns an exit status of zero if it is. Think of this operator as testing to see whether the following argument has zero length.

So the command

```
test -n "$day"
```

returns an exit status of 0 if `day` contains at least one character. The command

```
test -z "$dataflag"
```

returns an exit status of 0 if `dataflag` *doesn't* contain any characters. That is, -n and -z are the opposite of each other, and both exist just to make it easier to write clear, readable conditional statements.

Be warned that both of the preceding operators expect an argument to follow, so get into the habit of enclosing the argument within double quotes.

```
$ nullvar=
$ nonnullvar=abc
$ test -n "$nullvar"          Does nullvar have nonzero length?
$ echo $?
1                             No
$ test -n "$nonnullvar"       And what about nonnullvar?
$ echo $?
0                             Yes
$ test -z "$nullvar"          Does nullvar have zero length?
$ echo $?
0                             Yes
$ test -z "$nonnullvar"       And nonnullvar?
$ echo $?
1                             No
$
```

Note that test can also be picky about its arguments. For example, if the shell variable symbol contains an equals sign, look at what happens if you try to test it for zero length:

```
$ echo $symbol
=
$ test -z "$symbol"
sh: test: argument expected
$
```

The = operator has higher precedence than the -z operator, so test attempts to process the command as an equality test, and expects an argument to follow the =. To avoid this sort of problem, many shell programmers write their test commands as

```
test X"$symbol" = X
```

which will be true if symbol is null, and false if it's not. The X in front of symbol prevents test from interpreting the characters stored in symbol as an operator.

An Alternative Format for test

The test command is used so often by shell programmers that an alternative format of the command is available and can make your programs a lot neater: [. This format improves the readability of if statements and other conditional tests throughout your shell scripts.

You'll recall that the general format of the test command is

```
test expression
```

This can also be expressed in the alternative format as

```
[ expression ]
```

The [is actually the name of the command (who said anything about command names having to be alphanumeric characters?). It still initiates execution of the same `test` command, but when used this way it also expects to see a closing] at the end of the expression. Spaces must appear after the [and before the].

You can rewrite the `test` command shown in a previous example with this alternative format as shown:

```
$ [ -z "$nonnullvar" ]
$ echo $?
1
$
```

When used in an `if` command, the alternative format looks like this:

```
if [ "$name" = julio ]
then
        echo "Would you like to play a game?"
fi
```

Which format of the `if` command you use is up to you; we prefer the [...] format, which coaxes shell programming into a syntax much more similar to other popular programming languages, so that's what we'll use throughout the remainder of the book.

Integer Operators

`test` has a large assortment of operators for performing integer comparisons. Table 7.2 summarizes these operators.

Table 7.2 test **Integer Operators**

Operator	Returns TRUE (exit status of 0) if
int_1 -eq int_2	int_1 is equal to int_2
int_1 -ge int_2	int_1 is greater than or equal to int_2
int_1 -gt int_2	int_1 is greater than int_2
int_1 -le int_2	int_1 is less than or equal to int_2
int_1 -lt int_2	int_1 is less than int_2
int_1 -ne int_2	int_1 is not equal to int_2

For example, the operator -eq tests to see whether two integers are equal. So if you had a shell variable called count and you wanted to see whether its value was equal to zero, you would write

```
[ "$count" -eq 0 ]
```

Other integer operators behave similarly, so

```
[ "$choice" -lt 5 ]
```

tests to see whether the variable choice is less than 5.

The command

```
[ "$index" -ne "$max" ]
```

tests to see whether the value of index is not equal to the value of max.

Finally

```
[ "$#" -ne 0 ]
```

tests to see whether the number of arguments passed to the command is not equal to zero.

It's important to note that the test command, not the shell itself, interprets the variable's value as an integer when an integer operator is used, so these comparisons work regardless of the shell variable's type.

Let's have a closer look at the difference between test's string and integer operators with a few examples.

```
$ x1="005"
$ x2="  10"
$ [ "$x1" = 5 ]            String comparison
$ echo $?
1                         False
$ [ "$x1" -eq 5 ]         Integer comparison
$ echo $?
0                         True
$ [ "$x2" = 10 ]          String comparison
$ echo $?
1                         False
$ [ "$x2" -eq 10 ]        Integer comparison
$ echo $?
0                         True
$
```

The first test

```
[ "$x1" = 5 ]
```

uses the *string* comparison operator = to test whether the two strings are identical. They're not, because the first string is composed of the three characters 005, and the second the single character 5.

In the second test, the integer comparison operator -eq is used. Treating the two values as integers (numbers), 005 is equal to 5, as verified by the test exit status.

The third and fourth tests are similar, but in these cases you can see how even a leading space stored in the variable x2 can influence a test made with a string operator versus one made with an integer operator.

File Operators

Virtually every shell program deals with one or more files. For this reason, a wide assortment of operators are provided by test to enable you to ask various questions about files. Each of these operators is *unary* in nature, meaning that they expect a single argument to follow. In all cases, the second argument is the name of a file (and that includes a directory name, as appropriate).

Table 7.3 lists the common file operators.

Table 7.3 **Commonly Used** test **File Operators**

Operator	Returns TRUE (exit status of 0) if
-d *file*	*file* is a directory
-e *file*	*file* exists
-f *file*	*file* is an ordinary file
-r *file*	*file* is readable by the process
-s *file*	*file* has nonzero length
-w *file*	*file* is writable by the process
-x *file*	*file* is executable
-L *file*	*file* is a symbolic link

The command

```
[ -f /users/steve/phonebook ]
```

tests whether the file /users/steve/phonebook exists and is an ordinary file (that is, not a directory or special file).

The command

```
[ -r /users/steve/phonebook ]
```

tests whether the indicated file exists and is also readable by you.

The command

```
[ -s /users/steve/phonebook ]
```

tests whether the indicated file has non-zero content (that is, isn't an empty file). This is useful if you create an error log file and later want to see whether anything was written to it:

```
if [ -s $ERRFILE ]
then
```

```
        echo "Errors found:"
        cat $ERRFILE
fi
```

A few more test operators, when combined with the previously described operators, enable you to specify more complicated conditional expressions.

The Logical Negation Operator !

The unary logical negation operator ! can be placed in front of any other test expression to *negate* the result of the evaluation of that expression. For example,

```
[ ! -r /users/steve/phonebook ]
```

returns a zero exit status (true) if /users/steve/phonebook is *not* readable; and

```
[ ! -f "$mailfile" ]
```

returns true if the file specified by $mailfile does *not* exist or is *not* an ordinary file. Finally,

```
[ ! "$x1" = "$x2" ]
```

returns true if $x1 is not identical to $x2 and is obviously equivalent to (and the more confusing cousin of) the clearer conditional expression

```
[ "$x1" != "$x2" ]
```

The Logical AND Operator -a

The operator -a performs a logical *AND* of two expressions and returns TRUE only if the two joined expressions are both true. So

```
[ -f "$mailfile"   -a   -r "$mailfile" ]
```

returns TRUE if the file specified by $mailfile is an ordinary file and is readable by you. (An extra space was placed around the -a operator to aid in the expression's readability and obviously has no effect on its execution.)

The command

```
[ "$count" -ge 0   -a   "$count" -lt 10 ]
```

will be true if the variable count contains an integer value greater than or equal to zero but less than 10. The -a operator has lower *precedence* than the integer comparison operators (and the string and file operators, for that matter), meaning that the preceding expression gets evaluated as

```
("$count" -ge 0) -a ("$count" -lt 10)
```

as you would expect.

In some cases, it's important to know that test immediately stops evaluating an AND expression as soon as something is proven to be false, so a statement like

```
[ ! -f "$file" -a $(who > $file) ]
```

will not run in the subshell with the who invocation if the ! -f (non-existence) test fails, because test already knows that the AND (-a) expression is false. Subtle, but something that can trip up shell programmers if they try to jam too much into conditional expressions with the assumption that everything is run prior to the conditional tests being applied.

Parentheses

You *can* use parentheses in a test expression to alter the order of evaluation as needed; just make sure that the parentheses themselves are quoted because they have a special meaning to the shell. So to translate the earlier example into a test command, you would write

```
[ \( "$count" -ge 0 \) -a \( "$count" -lt 10 \) ]
```

As is typical, spaces must surround the parentheses because test expects to see every element in the conditional statement as a separate argument.

The Logical OR Operator -o

The -o operator is similar to the -a operator, only it forms a logical *OR* of two expressions. That is, evaluation of the expression will be true if *either* the first expression is true *or* the second expression is true *or* both expressions are true.

```
[ -n "$mailopt" -o -r $HOME/mailfile ]
```

This command will be true if the variable mailopt is not null *or* if the file $HOME/mailfile is readable by you.

The -o operator has lower precedence than the -a operator, meaning that the expression

```
"$a" -eq 0   -o   "$b" -eq 2   -a   "$c" -eq 10
```

gets evaluated by test as

```
"$a" -eq 0   -o   ("$b" -eq 2   -a   "$c" -eq 10)
```

Naturally, you can use parentheses to change this order if necessary:

```
\( "$a" -eq 0   -o   "$b" -eq 2 \) -a "$c" -eq 10
```

Since precedence is critically important in complex conditional statements, you'll find that a lot of shell programmers have nested if statements to side-step any issues, while others use explicit parentheses to clarify order of interpretation. Certainly just assuming things are interpreted left-to-right is dangerous!

You will see many uses of the test command throughout the book because it's almost impossible to write even simple shell programs without some sort of conditional statements involved. Table A.11 in Appendix A summarizes all available test operators.

The else Construct

A construct known as else can be added to the if command, with the general format as shown:

```
if command_t
then
        command
        command
        . . .
else
        command
        command
. . .
fi
```

In the above, *command_t* is executed and its exit status evaluated. If it's true (zero), the then code block (all the statements between then and else) is executed and the else block is ignored. If the exit status is false (non-zero), the then code block is ignored and the else code block (everything between else and fi) is executed. In either case, only one set of commands gets executed: the first set if the exit status is zero, and the second set if it's nonzero.

This can be more succinctly explained:

```
if condition then statements-if-true else statements-if-false fi
```

Let's now write a modified version of on. Instead of having no output if the requested user is not logged on, we'll have the program report that fact to the user.

Here is version 3 of the program:

```
$ cat on
#
# determine if someone is logged on -- version 3
#

user="$1"

if who | grep "^$user " > /dev/null
then
        echo "$user is logged on"
else
        echo "$user is not logged on"
fi
$
```

If the user specified as the first argument to on is logged on, the grep will succeed and the message *user* is logged on will be displayed; otherwise, the message *user* is not logged on will be displayed.

```
$ who                           Who's on?
root       console Jul 8 10:37
barney     tty03   Jul 8 12:38
fred       tty04   Jul 8 13:40
joanne     tty07   Jul 8 09:35
tony       tty19   Jul 8 08:30
lulu       tty23   Jul 8 09:55
$ on pat
pat is not logged on
$ on tony
tony is logged on
$
```

To turn a quick prototype into a useful program for the long term, it's a good practice to make sure that the correct number of arguments is passed to the program. If the user specifies the wrong number of arguments, an appropriate error message can be issued, along with a usage message. Like this:

```
$ cat on
#
# determine if someone is logged on -- version 4
#

#
# see if the correct number of arguments were supplied
#
if [ "$#" -ne 1 ]
then
        echo "Incorrect number of arguments"
        echo "Usage: on user"
else
        user="$1"

        if who | grep "^$user " > /dev/null
        then
                echo "$user is logged on"
        else
                echo "$user is not logged on"
        fi
fi
$
```

It seems like a lot of changes, but other than wrapping all the previous code within an else-fi pair, the primary addition is an if command to evaluate whether the correct number of arguments was supplied. If $# is not equal to 1, the required number of arguments, the program prints two error messages; otherwise, the commands after the else clause are executed. Note that two fi commands are required because two if commands are used.

As you can see, indentation goes a long way toward making the program easy to read and understand. Get into the habit of setting and following indentation rules in your own programs and you'll definitely thank us later on as your programs become increasingly complicated.

The sophistication of the user experience is clearly improved over previous versions of the program:

```
$ on                            No arguments
Incorrect number of arguments
Usage:  on user
$ on priscilla                  One argument
priscilla is not logged on
$ on jo anne                    Two arguments
Incorrect number of arguments
Usage:  on user
$
```

The exit Command

A built-in shell command called exit enables you' to immediately terminate execution of your shell program. The general format of this command is

```
exit n
```

where n is the exit status that you want returned. If none is specified, the exit status used is that of the last command executed prior to the exit (that is, it's effectively exit $?).

Be advised that executing the exit command directly from your terminal will log you off the system because it will have the effect of terminating execution of your login shell.

A Second Look at the rem Program

exit is frequently used as a convenient way to terminate execution of a shell program. For example; let's take another look at the rem program, which removes an entry from the phonebook file:

```
$ cat rem
#
# Remove someone from the phone book
#

grep -v "$1" phonebook > /tmp/phonebook
mv /tmp/phonebook phonebook
$
```

As written, this program has the potential to create problems if unexpected situations arise, potentially even corrupting or wiping out the entire phonebook file.

For example, suppose that you type in

```
rem Susan Topple
```

The shell will pass two arguments to `rem` because of the missing quotes. The `rem` program will then remove all `Susan` entries, as specified by `$1`, without ever seeing that there were too many arguments specified by the user in the first place.

As a result, it's always best to take precautions with any potentially destructive program and to be certain that the action intended by the user is consistent with the action that the program is poised to take.

One of the first checks that can be made in `rem` is for the correct number of arguments, as was done earlier with the `on` program. This time, we'll use the `exit` command to terminate the program if the correct number of arguments isn't supplied:

```
$ cat rem
#
# Remove someone from the phone book -- version 2
#

if [ "$#" -ne 1 ]
then
        echo "Incorrect number of arguments."
        echo "Usage: rem name"
        exit 1
fi

grep -v "$1" phonebook > /tmp/phonebook
mv /tmp/phonebook phonebook
$ rem Susan Goldberg                         Try it out
Incorrect number of arguments.
Usage: rem name
$
```

The `exit` command returns an exit status of 1, to signal failure, in case some other program wants to check it in a conditional expression. How could you have written the preceding program with an `if-else` instead of using the `exit`?

Whether you use the `exit` or an `if-else` is up to you. Sometimes the `exit` is a more convenient way to get out of the program quickly, particularly if it's done early in the program, and it has the additional benefit of avoiding the need for deeply nested conditionals.

The `elif` Construct

As your programs become more complex, you may find yourself stuck writing nested `if` statements like this:

```
if command₁
then
```

```
        command
        command
        ...
else
        if command₂
        then
                command
                command
                ...
        else
                ...
                if commandₙ
                then
                        command
                        command
                        ...
                else
                        command
                        command
                        ...
                fi
                ...
        fi
fi
```

This type of command sequence can be useful when you need to make more than just a two-choice decision. In this case, a multiway decision is made, with the last else clause executed if none of the preceding conditions is satisfied.

As a relatively simple example, let's write a program called greetings that prints a friendly Good morning, Good afternoon, or Good evening based on time of day. For purposes of the example, consider any time from midnight to noon to be the morning, noon to 6 pm the afternoon, and 6 pm to midnight the evening.

To write this program, you have to find out what time it is. date serves just fine for this purpose. Take another look at the output from this command:

```
$ date
Wed Aug 29 10:42:01 EDT 2002
$
```

The format of date's output is fixed, a fact that you can use to your advantage because the time will always appear in character positions 12 through 19. In fact, you really only need the hour value in positions 12 and 13:

```
$ date | cut -c12-13
10
$
```

Now the task of writing the `greetings` program is straightforward:

```
$ cat greetings
#
# Program to print a greeting
#

hour=$(date | cut -c12-13)

if [ "$hour" -ge 0 -a "$hour" -le 11 ]
then
        echo "Good morning"
else
        if [ "$hour" -ge 12 -a "$hour" -le 17 ]
        then
                echo "Good afternoon"
        else
                echo "Good evening"
        fi
fi
$
```

If `hour` is greater than or equal to 0 (midnight) and less than or equal to 11 (up to 11:59:59), `Good morning` is displayed. If `hour` is greater than or equal to 12 (noon) and less than or equal to 17 (up to 5:59:59 pm), `Good afternoon` is displayed. If neither of the preceding conditions is satisfied, `Good evening` is displayed.

```
$ greetings
Good morning
$
```

Look at the program again, however, and you'll realize that the nested `if` command sequence used in `greetings` is rather clumsy. To streamline these sorts of `if-then-else` sequences, the shell also supports a special `elif` element that acts somewhat like `else if` *condition*, except it doesn't increase your nesting level. The general format is

```
if command₁
then
        command
        command
        . . .
elif command₂
then
        command
        command
        . . .
else
        command
        command
        . . .
fi
```

command₁, *command₂*, ..., *command_n* are executed in turn and their exit statuses tested. As soon as one returns an exit status of TRUE (zero), the commands listed after the then that follows are executed, up to another elif, else, or fi. If none of the conditional expressions is true, the commands listed after the optional else are executed.

Now you can rewrite the greetings program using this new format as shown:

```
$ cat greetings
#
# Program to print a greeting -- version 2
#

hour=$(date | cut -c12-13)

if [ "$hour" -ge 0 -a "$hour" -le 11 ]
then
        echo "Good morning"
elif [ "$hour" -ge 12 -a "$hour" -le 17 ]
then
        echo "Good afternoon"
else
        echo "Good evening"
fi
$
```

A definite improvement. The program is easier to read, and it doesn't have the tendency to wander off the right margin due to progressively increasing indentation.

Incidentally, it's very rare to see date | cut as a pipe because the date command itself has a rich and complex set of output formats you can utilize to get just the information or value you want. For example, to output just the current hour in 0–23 format, use %H with the necessary + prefix to indicate it's a formatting string:

```
$ date +%H
10
$
```

As an exercise, you should change greetings to make use of this more streamlined way to identify the current hour of the day.

Yet Another Version of rem

Let's jump back to the phone number removal program rem. Earlier we mentioned that it was dangerous because without checking the validity of its actions, it could blindly delete more than the user desired.

One way to address this problem is to check the *number* of entries that match the user specified pattern before doing the removal: If there's more than one match, issue a message to that effect and terminate execution of the program. But how do you determine the number of matching entries?

One easy way is to do a `grep` on the `phonebook` file and count the number of resulting matches with `wc`. If the number of matches is greater than one, the appropriate message can be issued. That logic can be coded like this:

```
$ cat rem
#
# Remove someone from the phone book -- version 3
#

if [ "$#" -ne 1 ]
then
        echo "Incorrect number of arguments."
        echo "Usage: rem name"
        exit 1
fi

name=$1

#
# Find number of matching entries
#

matches=$(grep "$name" phonebook | wc -1)

#
# If more than one match, issue message, else remove it
#

if [ "$matches" -gt 1 ]
then
        echo "More than one match; please qualify further"
elif [ "$matches" -eq 1 ]
then
        grep -v "$name" phonebook > /tmp/phonebook
        mv /tmp/phonebook phonebook
else
        echo "I couldn't find $name in the phone book"
fi
$
```

To improve readability, the positional parameter $1 is assigned to the variable `name` after the number of arguments is checked.

Assigning the output of a command sequence to a variable is very common in shell programs, as demonstrated on the line

```
matches=$(grep "$name" phonebook | wc -1)
```

With `matches` calculated, it's easy to step through the if...elif...else command sequence and see that it first tests to see whether the number of matches is greater than one. If it is, the "more than one match" message is printed. If it's not, a test is made to see whether the number of matches is equal to one. If it is, the entry is removed from the phone book. If it's not one or greater than one, the number of matches must be zero, in which case a message is displayed to alert the user to this fact.

Note that the grep command is used twice in this program: first to determine the number of matches, then with the -v option to remove the matching entry after ensuring that only one line matches.

Here are some sample runs of this version of rem:

```
$ rem
Incorrect number of arguments.
Usage: rem name
$ rem Susan
More than one match; please qualify further
$ rem 'Susan Topple'
$ rem 'Susan Topple'
I couldn't find Susan Topple in the phone book     She's history
$
```

Now you have a fairly robust rem program: it checks for the correct number of arguments, printing the proper usage if the correct number isn't supplied; it also checks to make sure that precisely one entry is removed from the phonebook file.

In typical Unix fashion, also note that the rem script has no output when the requested action succeeds.

The case Command

The case command allows you to compare a single value against a set of other values or expressions and to execute one or more commands when a match is found. The general format of this command is

```
case value in
pattern₁)    command
             command
             ...
             command;;
pattern₂)    command
             command
             ...
             command;;
...
patternₙ)    command
             command
             ...
             command;;
esac
```

The word *value* is successively compared against the values *pattern₁*, *pattern₂*, ..., *patternₙ*, until a match is found. When a match is found, the commands listed after the matching value are executed, up to the double semicolons, which serve as a "break" statement that shows you've finished specifying commands for that particular conditional. After the double semicolons are reached, the execution of the case is terminated. If a match is not found, none of the commands listed in the case is executed.

As an example of the use of the case statement, the following program called number takes a single digit and translates it to its English equivalent:

```
$ cat number
#
# Translate a digit to English
#

if [ "$#" -ne 1 ]
then
        echo "Usage: number digit"
        exit 1
fi

case "$1"
in
        0) echo zero;;
        1) echo one;;
        2) echo two;;
        3) echo three;;
        4) echo four;;
        5) echo five;;
        6) echo six;;
        7) echo seven;;
        8) echo eight;;
        9) echo nine;;
esac
$
```

Now to test it:

```
$ number 0
zero
$ number 3
three
$ number                    Try no arguments
Usage: number digit
$ number 17                 Try a two-digit number
$
```

The last case shows what happens when you type in more than one digit: $1 doesn't match any of the values listed in the case, so none of the echo commands is executed.

Special Pattern-Matching Characters

The case statement is quite powerful because instead of just specifying sequences of letters, you can create complex regular expressions in the shell notation. That is, you can use the same special characters for specifying the patterns in a case as you can with filename substitution. For example, ? can be used to specify any single character; * can be used to specify zero or more occurrences of any character; and [...] can be used to specify any single character enclosed between the brackets.

Because the pattern * matches *anything* (just like how echo * matches all files in the current directory), it's frequently used at the end of the case as the "catch-all" or default value: if none of the previous values in the case match, this one's guaranteed to be a match.

With that in mind, here's a second version of the number program that has such a catch-all case statement.

```
$ cat number
#
# Translate a digit to English -- version 2
#

if [ "$#" -ne 1 ]
then
        echo "Usage: number digit"
        exit 1
fi

case "$1"
in
        0) echo zero;;
        1) echo one;;
        2) echo two;;
        3) echo three;;
        4) echo four;;
        5) echo five;;
        6) echo six;;
        7) echo seven;;
        8) echo eight;;
        9) echo nine;;
        *) echo "Bad argument; please specify a single digit";;
esac
$ number 9
nine
$ number 99
Bad argument; please specify a single digit
$
```

Let's switch to another program, ctype, that identifies and prints the class of the single character given as an argument. Character types recognized are digits, uppercase letters, lowercase letters, and special characters (anything not in the first three categories). As an added check, the program also ensures that only a single character is given as the argument.

```
$ cat ctype
#
# Classify character given as argument
#

if [ $# -ne 1 ]
then
        echo Usage: ctype char
        exit 1
fi


#
# Ensure that only one character was typed
#

char="$1"
numchars=$(echo "$char" | wc -c)

if [ "$numchars" -ne 1 ]
then
        echo Please type a single character
        exit 1
fi


#
# Now classify it
#

case "$char"
in
        [0-9]    ) echo digit;;
        [a-z]    ) echo lowercase letter;;
        [A-Z]    ) echo uppercase letter;;
        *        ) echo special character;;
esac
$
```

But when we try a few sample runs, something's not right:

```
$ ctype a
Please type a single character
$ ctype 7
Please type a single character
$
```

The -x Option for Debugging Programs

A bug. Not uncommon at all in the process of developing programs, whether they're 5 lines or 500 lines long. In this instance, it appears that the letter counting portion of our program isn't working properly. But how do you figure out what's not working?

This is a good point to introduce the shell's -x option. To debug any shell program—or !earn more about how it works—trace the sequence of its execution by typing in sh -x followed by the regular invocation (name and arguments). This starts up a new shell to execute the indicated program with the -x option enabled.

In this mode, commands are printed at the terminal as they are executed, preceded by a plus sign. Let's try it out!

```
$ sh -x ctype a            Trace execution
+ [ 1 -ne 1 ]              $# equals 1
+ char=a                   Assignment of $1 to char
+ echo a
+ wc -c
+ numchars=       2        wc returned 2???
+ [       2 -ne 1 ]        That's why this test succeeded
+ echo please type a single character
please type a single character
+ exit 1
$
```

The trace output indicates that wc returned 2 when this command was executed:

```
echo "$char" | wc -c
```

But why the value 2 if the command was given the single letter a? It turns out that two characters were actually given to wc: the single character a and the "invisible" newline character that echo automatically prints at the end of each line. Oops. So instead of testing for a single character by comparing it to 1, the conditional expressions should be comparing the user input to 2: the character typed plus the newline added by echo.

Go back to the ctype program and update the if command that reads

```
if [ "$numchars" -ne 1 ]
then
        echo Please type a single character
        exit 1
fi
```

to look like this

```
if [ "$numchars" -ne 2 ]
then
        echo Please type a single character
        exit 1
fi
```

and try it again.

```
$ ctype a
lowercase letter
$ ctype abc
Please type a single character
$ ctype 9
digit
$ ctype K
uppercase letter
$ ctype :
special character
$ ctype
Usage: ctype char
$
```

Now it seems to work just fine.

In Chapter 11 you'll learn how you can turn this trace feature on and off at will from *inside* your program too; but for now, we encourage you to try using sh -x on the various scripts we've created so far.

Before leaving the ctype program, here's a version that avoids the use of wc and handles all possible conditions with case statements:

```
$ cat ctype
#
# Classify character given as argument -- version 2
#

if [ $# -ne 1 ]
then
        echo Usage: ctype char
        exit 1
fi


#
# Now classify char, making sure only one was typed
#

char=$1

case "$char"
in
        [0-9] ) echo digit;;
        [a-z] ) echo lowercase letter;;
        [A-Z] ) echo uppercase letter;;
        ?     ) echo special character;;
        *     ) echo Please type a single character;;
esac
$
```

Remember, the ? matches any single character. Since we already have tested the character against digits, and lowercase and uppercase letters, if this pattern is matched, the character must be a special character. Finally, if this pattern *isn't* matched, more than one character must have been typed, so the catch-all case prints the appropriate error message.

```
$ ctype u
lowercase letter
$ ctype '>'
special character
$ ctype xx
Please type a single character
$
```

Back to the case

The symbol | has the effect of a logical OR when used between two patterns. That is, the pattern

pat_1 | pat_2

specifies that either pat_1 or pat_2 is to be matched. For example,

-l | -list

matches either the value -l or -list, and

dmd | 5620 | tty5620

matches any of dmd or 5620 or tty5620.

Knowing about the case statement, there are a number of different programmatic flow structures that can be more neatly and efficiently rewritten as case sequences.

For example, the greetings program that you saw earlier in this chapter can be rewritten to use a case statement rather than the clunkier if-elif. This time, let's take advantage of the fact that date with the +%H option writes a two-digit hour to standard output.

```
$ cat greetings
#
# Program to print a greeting -- case version
#

hour=$(date +%H)


case "$hour"
in
        0? | 1[01] ) echo "Good morning";;
        1[2-7]     ) echo "Good afternoon";;
        *          ) echo "Good evening";;
esac
$
```

The two-digit hour obtained from date is assigned to the shell variable hour, then the case statement is executed. The value of hour is compared against the first pattern:

```
0? | 1[01]
```

which matches any value that starts with a zero followed by any character (midnight through 9 am), or any value that starts with a one and is followed by a zero or one (10 or 11 am).

The second pattern

```
1[2-7]
```

matches a value that starts with a one and is followed by any one of the digits two through seven (noon through 5 pm).

The last case, the catch-all, matches anything else (6 pm through 11 pm).

```
$ date
Wed Aug 28 15:45:12 EDT 2002
$ greetings
Good afternoon
$
```

The Null Command :

Every matching case statement needs a resulting command, and every if-then conditional needs a resultant command too—but sometimes you don't want to execute anything, just "eat" the result. How do you do that? With the shell's built-in *null* command. The format of this command is simply

```
:
```

and the purpose of it is—you guessed it—to do nothing.

In most cases it's used to satisfy the requirement that a command appear, particularly in if statements. Suppose that you want to make sure that the value stored in the variable system exists in the file /users/steve/mail/systems, and if it doesn't, you want to issue an error message and exit from the program. So you start by writing something like

```
if grep "^$system" /users/steve/mail/systems > /dev/null
then
```

but you don't know what to write after the then because you want to test for the nonexistence of the system in the file and don't want to do anything special if the grep succeeds. The shell requires that you write a command after the then, so here's where the null command comes to the rescue:

```
if grep "^$system" /users/steve/mail/systems > /dev/null
then
        :
else
        echo "$system is not a valid system"
        exit 1
fi
```

If the conditional test is valid, nothing is done. If it's not valid, the error message is issued and the program exited.

To be fair, this particular example could be reversed by restructuring the `grep` statement (remember the '!' argument to `test`?) but sometimes it's easier to test for a positive condition and do nothing than a negative. In either case, this is where a well placed comment can do wonders when the code is read weeks or months later.

The && and || Constructs

The shell has two special constructs that enable you to execute a command based on whether the preceding command succeeds or fails. In case you think this sounds similar to the `if` command, well it is. Sort of. It's a shorthand form of the `if`.

If you write

```
command₁ && command₂
```

anywhere that the shell expects to see a command, $command_1$ will be executed, and if it returns an exit status of zero (success), $command_2$ will be executed. If $command_1$ returns a non-zero exit status (fail), $command_2$ is *not* invoked but is ignored.

For example, if you write

```
sort bigdata > /tmp/sortout && mv /tmp/sortout bigdata
```

then the `mv` command will be executed only if the `sort` is successful. Note that this is equivalent to writing

```
if sort bigdata > /tmp/sortout
then
        mv /tmp/sortout bigdata
fi
```

The command

```
[ -z "$EDITOR" ] && EDITOR=/bin/ed
```

tests the value of the variable EDITOR. If it's null, `/bin/ed` is assigned to it.

The || construct works similarly, except that the second command gets executed only if the exit status of the first is nonzero. So if you write

```
grep "$name" phonebook || echo "Couldn't find $name"
```

the `echo` command will get executed only if the `grep` fails (that is, if it can't find $name in phonebook, or if it can't open the file phonebook). In this case, the equivalent `if` command would look like

```
if grep "$name" phonebook
then
    :
```

```
else
        echo "Couldn't find $name"
fi
```

You can use a complex sequence of commands on either or both the left- or right-hand side of these constructs. On the left, the exit status tested is that of the last command in the pipeline; thus

```
who | grep "^$name " > /dev/null || echo "$name's not logged on"
```

causes execution of the echo if the grep fails.

The && and || can also be combined on the same command line:

```
who | grep "^$name " > /dev/null && echo "$name's not logged on" \
     || echo "$name is logged on"
```

(Recall that when \ is used at the end of the line it signals line continuation to the shell.) The first echo gets executed if the grep succeeds; the second if it fails.

These constructs are also often used in if commands, as demonstrated in this snippet from a system shell program (don't worry if you don't understand every command invoked):

```
if validsys "$sys" && timeok
then
        sendmail "$user@$sys" < $message
fi
```

If validsys returns an exit status of zero, timeok is executed and its exit status is then tested for the if. If that status is zero, then sendmail is executed. If validsys returns a nonzero exit status, however, timeok is not executed, and the failed exit status is then tested by the if, and sendmail ends up not being executed.

The use of the && operator in the preceding case is a *logical AND;* both programs must return an exit status of zero for the sendmail program to be executed. In fact, you could have written the above if conditional as

```
validsys "$sys" && timeok && sendmail "$user@$sys" < $message
```

By comparison, when the || is used in an if, the effect is like a *logical OR:*

```
if endofmonth || specialrequest
then
        sendreports
fi
```

If endofmonth returns a zero exit status, sendreports is executed; otherwise specialrequest is executed and if its exit status is zero, sendreports is executed. The net effect is that sendreports is executed if either endofmonth or specialrequest returns an exit status of zero.

In Chapter 8 you'll learn about how to write complex flow control loops in your programs. But before you get there, try the exercises that follow using the if, case, && and || notations explained in this chapter.

'Round and 'Round She Goes

In this chapter you'll learn how to set up program loops. These loops will enable you to execute a set of commands either a specified number of times or until a specific end condition is met.

The three built-in looping commands for shell programming are

- `for`
- `while`
- `until`

You'll learn about each one of these loops in separate sections of this chapter.

The `for` Command

The `for` command is used to execute one or more commands a specified number of times. Its basic format is as shown:

```
for var in word₁ word₂ ... wordₙ
do
        command
        command
        ...
done
```

The commands enclosed between the `do` and the `done` are what's known as the *body* of the loop and are executed for as many items as are listed after the `in`. When the loop is executed, the first word, $word_1$, is assigned to the variable `var`, and the body of the loop is then executed. Next, the second word in the list, $word_2$, is assigned to `var`, and the body of the loop is executed again.

This process continues with successive words in the list being assigned to *var* and the commands in the loop body being executed until the last word in the list, *word_n*, is assigned to *var* and the body of the loop executed. At that point, no words are left in the list, and execution of the for command is then complete. Execution then continues with the command that immediately follows the done.

If there are *n* words listed after the in, the body of the loop will have been executed a total of *n* times when the loop has finished.

Here's a loop that will be executed three times:

```
for i in 1 2 3
do
        echo $i
done
```

To try it out, type this in directly at the terminal, just like any other shell command:

```
$ for i in 1 2 3
> do
>            echo $i
> done
1
2
3
$
```

While the shell is waiting for the done to be typed to complete the for command, it keeps showing the secondary command prompt. When the user enters done, the shell then proceeds to execute the loop. Because three items are listed after the in (1, 2, and 3), the body of the loop—in this case a single echo command—will be executed a total of three times.

The first time through the loop, the first value in the list, 1, is assigned to the variable i. Then the body of the loop is executed. This displays the value of i at the terminal. Then the next word in the list, 2, is assigned to i and the echo command re-executed, resulting in the display of 2 at the terminal. The third word in the list, 3, is assigned to i the third time through the loop and the echo command executed. This results in 3 being displayed at the terminal. At that point, no more words are left in the list, so execution of the for command is complete, and the shell displays the command prompt to let you know it's done.

Now let's back up to Chapter 6 and recall the run program that enabled you to run a file through tbl, nroff, and lp:

```
$ cat run
tbl $1 | nroff -mm -Tlp | lp
$
```

If you wanted to run the files memo1 through memo4, you could type the following at the terminal:

```
$ for file in memo1 memo2 memo3 memo4
> do
```

```
>            run $file
> done
request id is laser1-33 (standard input)
request id is laser1-34 (standard input)
request id is laser1-35 (standard input)
request id is laser1-36 (standard input)
$
```

The four values memo1, memo2, memo3, and memo4 will be assigned in turn to the variable file and the run program will be executed with that value as the argument. Execution will be just as if you typed in four commands:

```
$ run memo1
request id is laser1-33 (standard input)
$ run memo2
request id is laser1-34 (standard input)
$ run memo3
request id is laser1-35 (standard input)
$ run memo4
request id is laser1-36 (standard input)
$
```

The shell permits filename substitution in the list of words in the for statement, so the previous loop could have also been written this way:

```
for file in memo[1-4]
do
      run $file
done
```

If you wanted to print all the files in your current directory using the run program, you could type

```
for file in *
do
      run $file
done
```

To do something more sophisticated, imagine filelist contains a list of the files that you want to run through run. You can type

```
files=$(cat filelist)

for file in $files
do
      run $file
done
```

to run each of the files, or, more succinctly,

```
for file in $(cat filelist)
do
      run $file
done
```

The better way to address this is to actually improve the run script itself, however, and it turns out that the for statement is perfect for the job:

```
$ cat run
#
# process files through nroff -- version 2
#
for file in $*
do
        tbl $file | nroff -rom -Tlp | lp
done
$
```

Recall that the special shell variable $* stands for *all* the arguments typed on the command line. If you executed the new version of run by typing

```
run memo1 memo2 memo3 memo4
```

the $* in the for's list would be replaced by the four arguments memo1, memo2, memo3, and memo4. Of course, you could also type

```
run memo[1-4]
```

to achieve the same results.

The $@ Variable

While we're utilizing $*, let's have a closer look at how it and its cousin $@ work. To do that, let's write a program called args that displays all the arguments typed on the command line, one per line.

```
$ cat args
echo Number of arguments passed is $#

for arg in $*
do
        echo $arg
done
$
```

Now to try it:

```
$ args a b c
Number of arguments passed is 3
a
b
c
$ args 'a b' c
```

```
Number of arguments passed is 2
a
b
c
$
```

Look closely at the second example: even though `'a b'` was passed as a single argument to `args`, it was split into two values within the `for` loop. That's because the `$*` in the `for` command was replaced by the shell with `a b c` and the quotes were lost. Thus the loop was executed three times.

The shell replaces the value of `$*` with `$1`, `$2`, … , but if you instead use the special shell variable `"$@"` the values will be passed with `"$1"`, `"$2"`, … . The key difference is the double quotes around the `$@`: without them this variable behaves just like `$*`.

Go back to the `args` program and replace the unquoted `$*` with `"$@"`:

```
$ cat args
echo Number of arguments passed is $#

for arg in "$@"
do
        echo $arg
done
$
```

Now try it:

```
$ args a b c
Number of arguments passed is 3
a
b
c
$ args 'a b' c
Number of arguments passed is 2
a b
c
$ args                          Try it with no arguments
Number of arguments passed is 0
$
```

In the last case, no arguments were passed to the program so the variable `"$@"` was replaced by *nothing*. The net result is that the body of the loop was not executed at all.

The `for` Without the List

A special notation is recognized by the shell when writing `for` commands. If you omit the `in` element and its subsequent list

```
for var
do
        command
        command
        ...
done
```

the shell automatically sequences through all the arguments typed on the command line, just as if you had written

```
for var in "$@"
do
        command
        command
        ...
done
```

With that in mind, here's the third and last version of the args program:

```
$ cat args
echo Number of arguments passed is $#

for arg
do
        echo $arg
done
$ args a b c
Number of arguments passed is 3
a
b
c
$ args 'a b' c
Number of arguments passed is 2
a b
c
$
```

The while Command

The second type of looping command is the while statement. The format of this command is

```
while command_t
do
        command
        command
        ...
done
```

$command_t$ is executed and its exit status tested. If it's zero, the commands enclosed between the do and done are executed once. Then $command_t$ is executed again and its exit status tested.

If it's zero, the commands enclosed between the do and done are once again executed. This continues until command$_t$ returns a nonzero exit status. At that point, execution of the loop is terminated. Execution then proceeds with the command that follows the done.

Note that the commands between the do and done might never be executed if command$_t$ returns a nonzero exit status the first time it's executed.

Here's a program called twhile that simply counts to 5:

```
$ cat twhile
i=1

while [ "$i" -le 5 ]
do
        echo $i
        i=$((i + 1))
done
$ twhile                    Run it
1
2
3
4
5
$
```

The variable i is initially set to the value 1. Then the while loop is entered, succeeding on the conditional test so the code block is executed. The shell continues execution as long as i is less than or equal to 5. Inside the loop, the value of i is displayed at the terminal, then incremented by one.

The while loop is often used in conjunction with the shift command to process an unknown number of arguments typed on the command line.

Consider the next program, called prargs, which prints each of the command-line arguments out, one per line.

```
$ cat prargs
#
# Print command line arguments one per line
#

while [ "$#" -ne 0 ]
do
        echo "$1"
        shift
done
$ prargs a b c
a
b
c
```

```
$ prargs 'a b' c
a b
c
$ prargs *
addresses
intro
lotsaspaces
names
nu
numbers
phonebook
stat
$ prargs          No arguments
$
```

While the number of arguments is not equal to zero, the value of $1 is displayed and then a shift is invoked to shift down the variables (that is, $2 to $1, $3 to $2, and so on) and also decrement $#. When the last argument has been displayed and shifted out, $# will equal zero, at which point execution of the while will be terminated.

Note that if no arguments are given to prargs (as was done in the last case), the echo and shift are never executed because $# is equal to zero as soon as the loop is entered.

The until Command

The while command continues execution as long as the test expression continues to return a TRUE (zero) exit status. The until command is the opposite: It continues executing the code block until the test expression returns a *nonzero* exit status and stops once a zero status is produced.

Here is the general format of the until:

```
until command_t
do
        command
        command
        . . .
done
```

Like the while, the commands between the do and done might never be executed if command_t returns a zero exit status the first time it's executed.

While the two commands are quite similar, the until command is useful for writing programs that wait for a particular event to occur. For example, suppose that you want to see whether sandy is logged on because you have to give her something important. You could send her electronic mail, but you know that she usually doesn't get around to reading her mail until late in the day. You could use the on program from Chapter 7 to see whether sandy's logged on:

```
$ on sandy
sandy is not logged on
$
```

Simple, but ineffective because it runs once and is done. You could run the program periodically throughout the day (rather tedious), or, better, you could write your own program to continually check until she does log in!

Let's call the program waitfor and have it take a single argument: the name of the user you want to monitor. Instead of having the program continually check for that user logging on, however, let's have it check only once every minute. To do this, we'll have to use a command called sleep, which suspends execution of a program for a specified number of seconds. The command

```
sleep n
```

suspends execution of the program for n seconds. At the end of that interval, the program resumes execution where it left off—with the command that immediately follows sleep.

```
$ cat waitfor
#
# Wait until a specified user logs on
#

if [ "$#" -ne 1 ]
then
        echo "Usage: waitfor user"
        exit 1
fi

user="$1"

#
# Check every 60 seconds for user logging on
#

until who | grep "^$user " > /dev/null
do
        sleep 60
done

#
# When we reach this point, the user has logged on
#
echo "$user has logged on"
$
```

After checking that exactly one argument was provided, the program assigns $1 to user. Then an until loop is entered that will be executed until the grep exit status is zero; that is, until the specified user logs on. As long as the user isn't logged on, the body of the loop—the sleep command—is executed to suspend execution for 60 seconds. At the end of the minute, the pipeline listed after the until is re-invoked and the process is repeated.

When the `until` loop is exited—signaling that the monitored user has logged on—a message is displayed at the terminal to that effect and the script is done.

```
$ waitfor sandy          Time passes
sandy has logged on
$
```

Of course, running the program as shown here is not very practical because it ties up your terminal until `sandy` logs on. A better idea is to run `waitfor` in the background so that you can use your terminal for other work:

```
$ waitfor sandy &              Run it in the background
[1] 4392                       Job number and process id
$ nroff newmemo                Do other work
    . . .
sandy has logged on            Happens sometime later
```

Now you can do other work and the `waitfor` program continues executing in the background until `sandy` logs on, or until you log off the system.

> **Note**
>
> By default, all your processes are automatically terminated when you log off the system. If you want a program to continue running after you've logged off, you can run it with the `nohup` command, or schedule it to run with `at` or from `cron`. Consult your Unix User's Manual for more details.

Because `waitfor` only checks once per minute for the user logging on, it won't consume many system resources while it's running (an important consideration when running programs in the background).

Unfortunately, after the specified `user` logs on, there's a chance you might miss the one-line notification message. If you're editing a file with a screen editor such as `vi`, the notification message could turn your screen into a mess, and you still might not be able to read it!

A better alternative might be to mail it to yourself instead. Heck, you can let the user choose which they'd prefer by adding an option to the program that, if selected, indicates that the message is to be mailed. If not selected, the message is then displayed at the terminal.

In the version of `waitfor` that follows, a `-m` option has been added for this purpose:

```
$ cat waitfor
#
# Wait until a specified user logs on -- version 2
#

if [ "$1" = -m ]
then
        mailopt=TRUE
        shift
```

```
else
        mailopt=FALSE
fi


if [ "$#" -eq 0  -o  "$#" -gt 1 ]
then
        echo "Usage: waitfor [-m] user"
        echo"    -m means to be informed by mail"
        exit 1
fi


user="$1"


#
# Check every minute for user logging on
#

until who | grep "^$user " > /dev/null
do
        sleep 60
done


#
# When we reach this point, the user has logged on
#

if [ "$mailopt" = FALSE ]
then
     .  echo "$user has logged on"
else
        echo "$user has logged on" | mail steve
fi
$
```

The first test checks to see whether the -m option was specified. If it was, mailopt is assigned the value TRUE, and shift is executed to "shift out" the first argument (moving the name of the user to be monitored to $1 and decrementing $#). If the -m option wasn't specified, mailopt is set to FALSE.

Execution then proceeds as in the previous version, except this time when the main block of code completes, the mailopt variable is tested to determine whether to output the notification via email or as an echo statement.

```
$ waitfor sandy -m
Usage: waitfor [-m] user
        -m means to be informed by mail
$ waitfor -m sandy &
[1] 5435
```

```
$ vi newmemo              Work continues
   ...
you have mail
$ mail
From steve Wed Aug 28 17:44:46 EDT 2002
sandy has logged on

?d
$
```

Of course, we could have written `waitfor` to accept the `-m` option as either the first or second argument, but that's not how traditional Unix syntax works: all options are expected to precede any other types of arguments on the command line.

Also note that the old version of `waitfor` could have been executed as follows:

```
$ waitfor sandy | mail steve &
[1] 5522
$
```

to achieve the same result as adding the `-m` option, but it's considerably less elegant.

The program always sends mail to `steve` as it's written now, which isn't particularly useful if someone else wants to run it. A better way is to determine the user running the program and then send them the mail if they specify the `-m` option. But how do you do that? One way is to execute the `who` command with the `am i` options and get the user name that comes back. You can then use `cut` to extract the username from the `who` output and use that name as the recipient of the mail.

All of this can be done in the last `if` command of `waitfor` if it's changed to read as shown:

```
if [ "$#" -eq 1 ]
then
        echo "$user has logged on"
else
        runner=$(who am i | cut -c1-8)
        echo "$user has logged on" | mail $recipient
fi
```

Now the program can be run by anyone, and the mail notification will be sent to the correct recipient.

More on Loops

Breaking Out of a Loop

Sometimes program logic dictates an immediate exit from a loop statement. To exit from the loop but not from the program, use the `break` command:

```
break
```

When the `break` is executed, control is immediately moved outside of the loop, where execution then continues as normal.

One common way this is used is with an infinite loop, a block of code that is intended to go around and around executing the same commands until `break` stops it.

In these situations the command `true` can be used to return an exit status of zero. The command `false` can be used in the opposite situation too, as it returns a nonzero exit status. If you write

```
while true
do
     ...
done
```

the `while` loop will be executed forever, because `true` always returns a zero exit status.

Because `false` always returns a nonzero exit status, the loop

```
until false
do
     ...
done
```

will also execute forever.

The `break` command is therefore used to exit from these sorts of infinite loops, usually when an error condition or the end of processing is detected:

```
while true
do
     cmd=$(getcmd)

     if [ "$cmd" = quit ]
     then
          break
     else
          processcmd "$cmd"
     fi
done
```

Here the `while` loop will continue to execute the `getcmd` and `processcmd` programs until `cmd` is equal to `quit`. At that point, the `break` command will be executed, causing the loop to be exited.

If the `break` command is used in the form

```
break n
```

the *n* innermost loops are immediately exited, so in

```
for file
do
     ...
```

```
        while [ "$count" -lt 10 ]
        do
                . . .
                if [ -n "$error" ]
                then
                        break 2
                fi
                . . .
        done
        . . .
done
```

both the `while` *and* the `for` loops will be exited if `error` is nonnull.

Skipping the Remaining Commands in a Loop

The `continue` command is similar to `break`, only it doesn't cause the loop to be exited, just the remaining commands in the current iteration of the loop to be skipped. The program moves immediately to the next iteration of the loop and continues as normal. Like the `break`, an optional number can follow the `continue`, so

```
continue n
```

causes the commands in the innermost *n* loops to be skipped, after which execution of the program continues as normal.

```
for file
do
        if [ ! -e "$file" ]
        then
                echo "$file not found!"
                continue
        fi

        #
        # Process the file
        #

        . . .
done
```

Each value of `file` is checked to make sure that the file exists. If it doesn't, a message is printed, and further processing of the file within the `for` loop is skipped. Execution continues with the next value in the list.

The preceding example is equivalent to writing

```
for file
do
        if [ ! -e "$file" ]
        then
```

```
              echo "$file not found!"
       else
              #
              # Process the file
              #

              ...
       fi
done
```

Executing a Loop in the Background

An entire loop can be sent to the background for execution simply by placing an ampersand after the done statement:

```
$ for file in memo[1-4]
> do
>          run $file
> done &                              Send it to the background
[1] 9932
$
request id is laser1-85 (standard input)
request id is laser1-87 (standard input)
request id is laser1-88 (standard input)
request id is laser1-92 (standard input)
```

This—and subsequent examples—work because the shell treats loops as if they were mini-programs of their own, so whatever appears after block closing statements like done, fi and esac can have redirects, be put into background with the ampersand or even form part of a pipeline of commands.

I/O Redirection on a Loop

You can also perform I/O redirection on a loop. Input redirected into the loop applies to all commands in the loop that read their data from standard input. Output redirected from the loop to a file applies to all commands in the loop that write to standard output. And it all happens at the loop closing statement done:

```
$ for i in 1 2 3 4
> do
>          echo $i
> done > loopout              Redirect loop's output to loopout
$ cat loopout
1
2
3
4
$
```

Individual statements can override block redirection, just as any other statements in your shell programs can explicitly read from a specified source or send output to a specified destination.

To force input or output to come from or go to the terminal, utilize /dev/tty, which always refers to your terminal program, whether you're on a Mac, Linux, or Unix system.

In the following loop, all output is redirected to the file output except the echo command's output, which is explicitly redirected to the terminal:

```
for file
do
        echo "Processing file $file" > /dev/tty
        ...
done > output
```

You can also redirect the standard error output from a loop, simply by tacking on a 2> *file* after the done:

```
while [ "$endofdata" -ne TRUE ]
do
        ...
done 2> errors
```

Here output from all commands in the loop writing to standard error will be redirected to the file errors.

A variation of the 2> format is commonly used to ensure that error messages go to the terminal even when a script might have its output redirected into a file or pipe:

```
echo "Error: no file" 1>&2
```

By default, echo sends its output to standard output (file descriptor 1), while file descriptor 2 remains standard error and is not redirected on file redirection or pipes by default. So the notation above means that the error message from echo should have its "file #1" output redirected to "file #2", that is, standard error. You can test this with code like this:

```
for i in "once"
do
  echo "Standard output message"
  echo "Error message" 1>&2
done > /dev/null
```

Try it yourself and see what happens.

Piping Data into and out of a Loop

A command's output can be piped into a loop (by having the commands prior to the loop command end with a pipe symbol), and the output from a loop can be piped into another command too. Here's an example of the output from a for command piped into wc:

```
$ for i in 1 2 3 4
> do
```

```
>         echo $i
> done | wc -l
      4
$
```

Typing a Loop on One Line

If you find yourself frequently typing in loops directly at the command line, you might want to try the following shorthand notation to type in an entire command on a single line: Put a semicolon after the last item in the list and one after each command in the loop (but not after the do).

Using this shorthand, the loop

```
for i in 1 2 3 4
do
        echo $i
done
```

can be written

```
for i in 1 2 3 4; do echo $i; done
```

You can type it in directly on the command line this way:

```
$ for i in 1 2 3 4; do echo $i; done
1
2
3
4
$
```

The same rules apply to `while` and `until` loops.

`if` commands can also be typed on the same line using a similar format:

```
$ if [ 1 = 1 ]; then echo yes; fi
yes
$ if [ 1 = 2 ]; then echo yes; else echo no; fi
no
$
```

Note that no semicolons appear after the `then` and the `else`.

Many shell programmers use a hybrid structure where if statements are structured thusly:

```
if [ condition ] ; then
    command
fi
```

This simple usage of the semicolon can help increase the readability of your shell programs and is worth considering as part of your own code formatting.

The `getopts` **Command**

Let's extend the `waitfor` program further by adding a `-t` option that specifies how frequently, in seconds, to perform the check. Now `waitfor` takes both `-m` and `-t` options. We'll allow these options to be specified in any order on the command line, as long as they appear before the name of the user that we're monitoring. So valid `waitfor` command lines look like this:

```
waitfor ann
waitfor -m ann
waitfor -t 600 ann
waitfor -m -t 600 ann
waitfor -t 600 -m ann
```

and invalid ones look like this:

```
waitfor                     Missing user name
waitfor -t600 ann           Need a space after –t
waitfor ann -m              Options must appear first
waitfor -t ann              Missing argument after –t
```

As you start writing code to allow this sort of flexibility on the command line, you will soon discover that it can become quite complicated!

Don't fret, though; the shell provides a built-in command called `getopts` that makes it easy to process command line arguments. The general format of the command is

`getopts options variable`

We'll dig into the options string shortly. For now, just know that letter-only options are specified as such and options that have a required argument have a trailing colon, so "ab:c" means that -a and -c are allowed, as is -b, but -b requires an additional parameter to be specified.

The `getopts` command is designed to be executed within a loop, however, because it makes it easy to take whatever actions are required for each of the user specified options. Each time through the loop, `getopts` examines the next command line argument and determines whether it is a valid option by checking to see whether the argument begins with a minus sign and is followed by any of the letters specified as *options*. If it does, `getopts` stores the matching option letter inside the specified *variable* and returns a zero exit status. You'll see what I mean in just a few lines ...

If the letter that follows the minus sign is *not* listed in *options*, `getopts` stores a question mark inside *variable* before returning with a zero exit status. It also writes an error message to standard error about the bad parameter that the user specified.

If no more arguments are left on the command line or if the current argument doesn't begin with a minus sign, `getopts` returns a nonzero exit status, allowing the script to then process any subsequent arguments. Think of the command `ls -C /bin` in this context: -C is a flag that could be parsed and processed by `getopts`, while /bin is an argument to the the `ls` command itself, processed after all the starting arguments are dealt with.

Don't get too anxious if this seems really confusing. The fact is, it is all very complicated, so let's look at an example so you can see how getopts works. Suppose for a script you're writing you want to use getopts to recognize the options -a, -i, and -r. Your getopts call might look like this:

```
getopts "air" option
```

Here the first argument—air—specifies the three acceptable command flags (-a, -i, and -r) and option is the name of the variable that getopts will use to store each matching value encountered.

The getopts command also allows options to be clustered or grouped together on the command line. This is done by following a single minus sign with more than one consecutive option. For example, our foo command can be executed like this:

```
foo -a -r -i
```

or like this:

```
foo -ari
```

using this simple grouping feature.

But wait, getopts is far more powerful than what we've explained so far! For example, it can also handle the case where an option requires an additional argument. For example, the new -t option to be added to the waitfor command requires an argument too.

To properly parse arguments subsequent to a user-specified option, getopts requires that the command be invoked with at least one space separating the option from the argument. In this instance, options cannot be grouped together.

To indicate to getopts that an option has a required argument, add a colon character after the option letter on the getopts command line. So the waitfor program, which allows both -m and -t options, the latter of which has a required additional argument, should call getopts like this:

```
getopts mt: option
```

If getopts doesn't find an argument after an option that requires one, it stores a question mark inside the variable and outputs an error message to standard error. Otherwise, it stores the character in the variable and the user specified argument inside a special variable called OPTARG.

One final note about getopts: Another special variable called OPTIND is initially set to 1 and is updated each time getopts returns to reflect the number of the *next* command line argument to be processed.

To make this clearer, here is the third version of waitfor that uses the getopts command to process the command line arguments. It also incorporates the previously noted change to send mail to the user running the program.

```
$ cat waitfor
#
# Wait until a specified user logs on -- version 3
#

# Set up default values

mailopt=FALSE
interval=60

# process command options

while getopts mt: option
do
        case "$option"
        in
                m)  mailopt=TRUE;;
                t)  interval=$OPTARG;;
                \?) echo "Usage: waitfor [-m] [-t n] user"
                    echo "    -m means to be informed by mail"
                    echo "    -t means check every n secs."
                    exit 1;;
        esac
done

# Make sure a user name was specified

if [ "$OPTIND" -gt "$#" ]
then
        echo "Missing user name!"
        exit 2
fi

shiftcount=$((OPTIND - 1))
shift $shiftcount
user=$1

#
# Check for user logging on
#

until who | grep "^$user " > /dev/null
do
        sleep $interval
done

#
# When we reach this point, the user has logged on
#
```

```
if [ "$mailopt" = FALSE]
then
        echo "$user has logged on"
else
        runner=$(who am i | cut -cl-8)
        echo "$user has logged on" | mail $runner
fi
```

```
$ waitfor -m
Missing user name!
$ waitfor -x fred                           Illegal option
waitfor: illegal option -- x
Usage: waitfor [-m] [-t n] user
   -m means to be informed by mail
   -t means check every n secs.
$ waitfor -m -t 600 ann &                    Check every 10 min. for ann
[1] 5792
$
```

Let's look at the last line more closely. When the line

```
waitfor -m -t 600 ann &
```

is executed, the following occurs inside the while loop: getopts is invoked and stores the character m inside the variable option, sets OPTIND to 2, and returns a zero exit status.

The case command then determines what was stored inside option. A match on the character m indicates that the "send mail" option was selected, so mailopt is set to TRUE. (Note that the ? inside the case is quoted. This is to remove its special meaning as a pattern matching character from the shell.)

The second time getopts is executed, getopts stores the character t inside option, stores the next command line argument (600) inside OPTARG, sets OPTIND to 3, and returns a zero exit status. The case command then matches the character t stored inside option. Then the code associated with that case copies the value of 600 that was stored in OPTARG into the variable interval.

The third time getopts is executed, getopts returns a nonzero exit status, indicating that it's reached the end of the user-specified command options.

The program then checks the value of OPTIND against $# to make sure that a username was typed on the command line. If OPTIND is greater than $#, then no more arguments remain and the user forgot the user name argument. Otherwise, the shift command is used to move the user name argument into $1. The actual number of places to shift is one less than the value of OPTIND.

The rest of the `waitfor` program remains as before; the only change is the use of the `interval` variable to specify the number of seconds to sleep.

If your head's a bit awhirl with `getopts` and its use, don't worry, it'll keep showing up in subsequent shell programs, and you'll get the hang of it with more exposure. It is worth studying for advanced shell programming too, because manually parsing anything more than a single command flag is prohibitively inefficient otherwise.

9

Reading and Printing Data

In this chapter you'll learn how to read data from the terminal or from a file using the `read` command and how to write formatted data to standard output using the `printf` command.

The `read` Command

The general format of the `read` command is

```
read variables
```

When this command is executed, the shell reads a line from standard input and assigns the first word to the first variable listed in *variables*, the second word to the second variable, and so on. If there are more words on the line than there are variables listed, the excess words get assigned to the last variable. For example, the command

```
read x y
```

reads a line from standard input, storing the first word in variable x, and the remainder of the line in variable y. It follows from this that the command

```
read text
```

reads and stores an entire line into the shell variable text.

A Program to Copy Files

Let's put the `read` command to work by writing a simplified version of the `cp` command. We'll call it mycp, and we'll have it take two arguments: the source file and the destination file. If the destination file already exists, the program will warn the user and ask them if they want to proceed with the copy. If the answer is "yes," we'll proceed; otherwise the program will quit.

```
$ cat mycp
#
# Copy a file
#
```

```
if [ "$#" -ne 2 ] ; then
        echo "Usage: mycp from to"
        exit 1
fi

from="$1"
to="$2"

#
# See if the destination file already exists
#

if [ -e "$to" ] ; then
        echo "$to already exists; overwrite (yes/no)?"
        read answer

        if [ "$answer" != yes ] ; then
                echo "Copy not performed"
                exit 0
        fi
fi

#
# Either destination doesn't exist or "yes" was typed
#

cp $from $to        # proceed with the copy
$
```

Now let's give the program a quick test:

```
$ ls -C                      What files? -C forces multicolumn output too
Addresses       intro       lotsaspaces        mycp
names           nu          numbers            phonebook
stat
$ mycp                       No arguments
Usage: mycp from to
$ mycp names names2          Make a copy of names
$ ls -l names*               Did it work?
-rw-r--r--  1 steve   steve       43 Jul  20 11:12 names
-rw-r--r--  1 steve   steve       43 Jul  21 14:16 names2
$ mycp names numbers         Try to overwrite an existing file
numbers already exists; overwrite (yes/no)?
no
Copy not performed
$
```

Notice that if the file already exists, the echo command that prompts for the yes/no response is executed. The read command that follows causes the shell to wait for the user to type a response. What this shows is that the shell doesn't prompt the user when it's waiting for data; it's up to the programmer to add a useful prompt to the program.

The data that is typed is stored in the variable answer and is then tested against the characters yes to determine whether the copy process should proceed. The quotes around the reference to the variable answer in the test

```
[ "$answer" != yes]
```

are necessary in case the user just presses the Enter key without typing any data. In that case, the shell would store a null value in answer and, without the quotes, test would issue an error message.

Also note the use of the semicolon to move the then statements onto the same line as the if statement. This is a common shell programmer notational trick, as mentioned in the previous chapter.

Special echo **Escape Characters**

A slight annoyance with mycp is that after the echo command is run, the response typed by the user appears on the next line. This happens because the echo command automatically adds a terminating newline character after the last argument.

Fortunately, this can be suppressed if the last two characters given to echo are the special *escape* characters \c. This tells echo to omit the newline after displaying the last argument. If you changed the echo command in mycp to read like this:

```
echo "$to already exists; overwrite (yes/no)? \c"
```

The user's input would be typed right after the message on the same line. Bear in mind that the \c is interpreted by echo and not by the shell, meaning that it must be quoted so that the backslash makes it to echo.

> **Note**
>
> Some Linux and Mac OS X systems have shells that don't interpret these echo escape characters, so the above would be shown as
>
> ```
> newfile.txt already exists; overwrite (yes/no)? \c
> ```
>
> If testing reveals that your shell works like that, change those specific invocations of echo to the separate program /bin/echo and they'll work fine. All your other echo statements can remain as just regular echo commands, of course.

The echo command can also interpret other special characters (see note if yours doesn't work as expected). These must each be preceded by a backslash and are summarized in Table 9.1.

Table 9.1   echo **Escape Characters**

Character	Prints
\b	Backspace
\c	The line without a terminating newline
\f	Formfeed
\n	Newline
\r	Carriage return
\t	Tab character
\\	Backslash character
\0nnn	The character whose ASCII value is *nnn*, where *nnn* is a one- to three-digit octal number

An Improved Version of mycp

Suppose that you have a program called prog1 in your current directory and you want to copy it into your bin directory. With the regular cp program, you could use the shortcut of just specifying the destination directory to have the file copied there with its existing filename. But take another look at the mycp program and determine what happens if you type in

```
mycp prog1 bin
```

The -e test on bin will succeed (because –e tests for existence of a file), and mycp will display the "already exists" message and wait for a yes/no answer. That's a dangerous mistake, particularly if the user types yes!

If the second argument is a *directory*, mycp should instead check to see whether the from file exists *inside* the specified directory.

The next version of mycp performs this check. It also has the modified echo command that includes the \c to suppress the terminating newline.

```
$ cat mycp
#
# Copy a file -- version 2
#

if [ "$#" -ne 2 ] ; then
        echo "Usage: mycp from to"
        exit 1
fi

from="$1"
to="$2"
```

```
#
# See if destination file is a directory
#

if [ -d "$to" ] ; then
        to="$to/$(basename $from)"
fi


#
# See if the destination file already exists
#

if [ -e "$to" ] ; then
        echo "$to already exists; overwrite (yes/no)? \c"
        read answer

        if [ "$answer" != yes ] ; then
                echo "Copy not performed"
                exit 0
        fi
fi
#
# Either destination doesn't exist or "yes" was typed
#

cp $from $to        # proceed with the copy
$
```

If the destination file is a directory, the program changes the variable to to more precisely identify the destination filename by including the directory name: $to/$(basename $from). This ensures that the subsequent test for the existence of the ordinary file $to will be done on the file in the directory, not on the directory itself.

The basename command gives the base filename of its argument with all directory components stripped away (for example, basename /usr/bin/troff produces troff; basename troff also produces troff). This extra step ensures that the copy is made from and to the correct place. (As an example, if mycp /tmp/data bin is typed, where bin is a directory, you want to copy /tmp/data into bin/data and not into bin/tmp/data.)

Here's some sample output. Note the effect of the \c escape characters.

```
$ ls                    Check out current directory
bin
prog1
$ ls bin                Look inside bin
lu
nu
prog1
```

```
$ mycp prog1 prog2     Simple case
$ mycp prog1 bin       Copy into directory
bin/prog1 already exists; overwrite (yes/no)? yes
$
```

A Final Version of mycp

The last modification to mycp makes the program virtually equivalent to the standard Linux cp command by allowing a variable number of arguments. Recall that with the standard command any number of files can precede the name of a directory, as in

```
cp prog1 prog2 greetings bin
```

To modify mycp to accept any number of files in a similar format, you can use this approach:

1. Get each argument but the last from the command line and store it in the shell variable filelist.

2. Store the last argument in the variable to.

3. If $to is not a directory, test the argument count as there must be exactly two arguments.

4. If $to is a directory, for each file in $filelist, check whether the file already exists in the destination directory. If it doesn't, add the filename to the variable copylist. If it does exist, ask the user whether the file should be overwritten. If the answer is yes, add the filename to copylist.

5. If copylist is non-null, copy the files in it to $to.

If this algorithm seems a bit fuzzy, the program and a detailed explanation will help clear things up. Note the modified command usage message.

```
$ cat mycp
#
# Copy a file -- final version
#

numargs=$#                    # save this for later use
filelist=
copylist=


#
# Process the arguments, storing all but the last in filelist
#

while [ "$#" -gt 1 ] ; do
        filelist="$filelist $1"
        shift
done
```

```
to="$1"

#
# If less than two args, or if more than two args and last arg
# is not a directory, then issue an error message
#

if [ "$numargs" -lt 2  -o  "$numargs" -gt 2  -a  ! -d "$to" ] ; then
    echo "Usage: mycp file1 file2"
    echo "       mycp file(s) dir"
    exit 1
fi

#
# Sequence through each file in filelist
#

for from in $filelist ; do
    #
    # See if destination file is a directory
    #

    if [ -d "$to" ] ; then
        tofile="$to/$(basename $from)"
    else
        tofile="$to"
    fi

    #
    # Add file to copylist if file doesn't already exist
    # or if user says it's okay to overwrite
    #

    if [ -e "$tofile" ] ; then
        echo "$tofile already exists; overwrite (yes/no)? \c"
        read answer

        if [ "$answer" = yes ] ; then
            copylist="$copylist $from"
        fi
    else
        copylist="$copylist $from"
    fi
done
```

```
#
# Now do the copy -- first make sure there's something to copy
#
if [ -n "$copylist" ] ; then
        cp $copylist $to          # proceed with the copy
fi
$
```

Let's look at some sample output before delving into the code itself.

```
$ ls -C                          See what's around
bin        lu        names      prog1
prog2
$ ls bin                         And what's in bin?
lu
nu
prog1
$ mycp                           No arguments
Usage: mycp file1 file2
       mycp file(s) dir
$ mycp names prog1 prog2         Last arg isn't a directory
Usage: mycp file1 file2
       mycp file(s) dir
$ mycp names prog1 prog2 lu bin   Legitimate use
bin/prog1 already exists; overwrite (yes/no)? yes
bin/lu already exists; overwrite (yes/no)? no
$ ls -l bin                      See what happened
total 5
-rw-r--r--   1 steve    steve     543 Jul 19 14:10 lu
-rw-r--r--   1 steve    steve     949 Jul 21 17:11 names
-rw-r--r--   1 steve    steve      38 Jul 19 09:55 nu
-rw-r--r--   1 steve    steve     498 Jul 21 17:11 prog1
-rw-r--r--   1 steve    steve     498 Jul 21 17:11 prog2
$
```

In the last case, prog1 was overwritten and lu wasn't, as per the user's request.

When the program starts execution, it saves the number of arguments in the variable numargs. This is done because the argument variables are changed later in the program by the shift command.

Next a loop is entered that is executed as long as the number of arguments is greater than one. The purpose of this loop is to get the last argument on the line. While doing this, the loop stashes away the other arguments into the shell variable filelist, which ultimately will contain a list of all the files to be copied. The statement

```
filelist="$filelist $1"
```

says to take the previous value of filelist, add on a space followed by the value of $1, and then store the result back into filelist. Then the shift command is executed to "move" all the arguments over by one. Eventually, $# will be equal to one, and the loop will be exited.

At that point, filelist will contain a space-delimited list of all the files to be copied, and $1 will contain the last argument, which is either the destination filename or destination directory.

To see how this works, consider execution of the while loop when the command is executed as

```
mycp names prog1 prog2 lu bin
```

Figure 9.1 depicts the changing values of the variables through each iteration of the loop. The first line shows the state of the variables before the loop is entered.

$#	$1	$2	$3	$4	$5	filelist
5	names	prog1	prog2	lu	bin	null
4	prog1	prog2	lu	bin		names
3	prog2	lu	bin			names prog1
2	lu	bin				names prog1 prog2
1	bin					names prog1 prog2 lu

Figure 9.1   Processing command line arguments

After the loop is exited, the last argument contained in $1 is stored in the variable to. Next a test is made to ensure that at least two arguments were typed on the command line and, if more than two were typed, that the last argument is a directory. If either condition is not satisfied, usage information is displayed to the user, and the program exits with a status of 1.

Following this, the for loop examines each file in the list to see whether it already exists in the destination directory. If it does, the user is prompted as before. If the user wants to overwrite the file—or if the file doesn't exist—the file is added to the shell variable copylist. The technique used here is the same used to accumulate the arguments inside filelist.

When the for loop is exited, copylist contains a list of all the files to be copied. In an extreme case, notice that this list can be null if the user decided not to overwrite any files and every file specified already existed in the destination directory too. Therefore a test is made to ensure copylist is non-null, and if it is, the copy is performed.

Take some time to review the logic of the final version of mycp; it illustrates many of the features you've learned so far in this book. Some exercises at the end of this chapter will also test your understanding of this program.

A Menu-Driven Phone Program

One useful thing about the read command is that it enables you to write menu-driven shell programs. As an example, let's return to the three phone book programs we wrote earlier, add, lu, and rem, and create what's known as a *wrapper*, a program that makes other programs easier to use. This time we'll create the wrapper program rolo ("rolo" short for Rolodex, just in case you remember what a Rolodex is!).

When invoked, rolo will display a list of choices to the user and then execute the appropriate program depending on the selection after prompting for the necessary arguments:

```
$ cat rolo
#
# rolo - rolodex program to look up, add, and
#           remove people from the phone book
#

#
# Display menu
#

echo '
      Would you like to:

            1. Look someone up
            2. Add someone to the phone book
            3. Remove someone from the phone book

      Please select one of the above (1-3): \c'

#
# Read and process selection
#

read choice
echo ""
case "$choice"
in
      1) echo "Enter name to look up: \c"
         read name
         lu "$name";;
      2) echo "Enter name to be added: \c"
         read name
         echo "Enter number: \c"
         read number
         add "$name" "$number";;
      3) echo "Enter name to be removed: \c"
         read name
         rem "$name";;
      *) echo "Bad choice";;
esac
$
```

Notice how a single echo command is used to display the full multi-line menu, taking advantage of the fact that the quotes preserve formatting and embedded newlines. Then read gets the selection from the user and stores it in the variable choice.

A case statement determines what choice was made. If choice 1 was selected, the user wants to look up someone in the phone book. In that case, the user is asked to enter the desired name, and the lu program is called with the specified argument. Note also that the double quotes around name in

```
lu "$name"
```

are necessary to ensure that two or more words typed in by the user are handed to lu as a single argument.

A similar sequence occurs if the user selects menu items 2 or 3.

The programs lu, rem, and add are from earlier chapters.

Here are some sample runs of rolo:

```
$ rolo

        Would you like to:

                1.   Look someone up
                2.   Add someone to the phone book
                3.   Remove someone from the phone book


Please select one of the above (1-3): 2
Enter name to be added: El Coyote
Enter number: 212-567-3232
$ rolo                          Try it again

        Would you like to:

                1. Look someone up
                2. Add someone to the phone book
                3. Remove someone from the phone book


Please select one of the above (1-3): 1

Enter name to look up: Coyote
El Coyote         212-567-3232
$ rolo                          Once again

        Would you like to:

                1. Look someone up
                2. Add someone to the phone book
                3. Remove someone from the phone book
```

```
        Please select one of the above (1-3): 4
Bad choice
$
```

When an invalid choice is entered, the program displays Bad choice and then terminates.
A friendlier approach would be to loop around and again prompt the user until a proper choice
is made. This can be done by enclosing the entire program inside an until loop that will be
executed until a valid selection is made.

Another change to rolo reflects its most likely usage: Because the most common operation will
be looking someone up, there will be a tendency to avoid typing rolo, then making selection
1, then typing the desired name. Instead, it's a lot easier to just type in

lu *name*

directly. Given this, let's give rolo some useful command line arguments so it can also be
used as efficiently. By default if any arguments are specified, rolo will assume that a lookup is
requested and call lu directly, handing all the arguments along. If the user wants to perform
a quick lookup, they can type rolo followed by the name. If they want to get the full menu
interface, typing just rolo offers just that alternative too.

The preceding two changes (looping until a valid choice is selected and doing a quick lookup)
are added to version 2 of rolo:

```
$ cat rolo
#
# rolo - rolodex program to look up, add, and
#    remove people from the phone book -- version 2
#


#
# If arguments are supplied, then do a lookup
#

if [ "$#" -ne 0 ] ; then
        lu "$@"
        exit
fi

validchoice=""          # set it null

#
# Loop until a valid selection is made
#

until [ -n "$validchoice" ]
do
        #
        # Display menu
        #
```

```
        echo '

Would you like to:

        1. Look someone up
        2. Add someone to the phone book
        3. Remove someone from the phone book

Please select one of the above (1-3): \c'

        #
        # Read and process selection
        #
        read choice
        echo

        case "$choice"
        in
            1) echo "Enter name to look up: \c"
                read name
                lu "$name"
                validchoice=TRUE;;
            2) echo "Enter name to be added: \c"
                read name
                echo "Enter number: \c"
                read number
                add "$name" "$number"
                validchoice=TRUE;;
            3) echo "Enter name to be removed: \c"
                read name
                rem "$name"
                validchoice=TRUE;;
            *) echo "Bad choice";;
        esac
done
$
```

If $# is non-zero, lu is called directly with the arguments typed on the command line, then the program exits. Otherwise, the until loop is executed until the variable validchoice is non-null. Remember that the only way it will be assigned a value is if the command

```
validchoice=TRUE
```

is executed inside the case of either choice 1, 2, or 3. Otherwise, the program continues to loop.

```
$ rolo Bill                    Quick lookup
Billy Bach      201-331-7618
$ rolo                         Let's have the menu this time
```

```
        Would you like to:

            1. Look someone up
            2. Add someone to the phone book
            3. Remove someone from the phone book

Please select one of the above (1-3): 4
Bad choice


        Would you like to:

            1. Look someone up
            2. Add someone to the phone book
            3. Remove someone from the phone book

        Please select one of the above (1-3): 0
Bad choice


        Would you like to:

            1. Look someone up
            2. Add someone to the phone book
            3. Remove someone from the phone book

        Please select one of the above (1-3): 1

Enter name to look up: Tony
Tony Iannino    973-386-1295
$
```

The $$ Variable and Temporary Files

If two or more people on your system use the rolo program at the same time, a potential
problem may occur. Look at the rem program and see whether you can spot it. The problem
occurs with the temporary file /tmp/phonebook that is used to create a new version of the
phone book file.

The specific statements in the rem program look like this:

```
grep -v "$name" phonebook > /tmp/phonebook
mv /tmp/phonebook phonebook
```

But here's the problem: If more than one person uses rolo at the same time to remove an
entry, there's a chance that the phone book file can get messed up because the same temporary
file will be simultaneously used more than once. To be fair the chance of this happening is
rather small, but it's non-zero and that means it's a problem.

There are two important concepts that this code raises, actually. The first is to do with how computers actually implement multitasking, by swapping individual programs in and out of the processor. The result is that at any point during execution, a program can be swapped out, even half-way through a series of commands. Now you can see the problem with the above code: because it's two statements, what happens if the program loses its place in line between the two statements and another instantiation of the program happens to run the exact same two lines of code? The second program overwrites the result of the first program's grep invocation. Not good for either user!

The second point relates to what's known as a *race condition*, a situation where more than one simultaneous invocation of a program can cause trouble. Most often that's related to temporary files, but it can also occur with sub-processes and lock files, as we'll discuss later in the book.

For now, just keep in mind that when writing shell programs that can be run by more than one person, make sure that each user's temporary files are unique.

One solution is to create temporary files in the user's home directory instead of /tmp. Another way is to choose a temporary filename that will be unique and different for each invocation of the program. A neat way to do this is to embed the unique process ID (PID) of the specific invocation into the filename. This is easily accomplished by referring to the special $$ shell variable:

```
$ echo $$
4668
$ ps
  PID  TTY TIME COMMAND
  4668 co  0:09 sh
  6470 co  0:03 ps
$
```

When substituted by the shell, $$ becomes the process ID number of the login shell itself. Because each process on the system is given a unique process ID, using the value of $$ in the name of a file eliminates the possibility of a different process using the same name. To fix the problem highlighted earlier, replace the two lines from rem with this improved sequence:

```
grep -v "$name" phonebook > /tmp/phonebook$$
mv /tmp/phonebook$$ phonebook
```

to side-step any potential race conditions. Each person using rolo will run it as a different process, so the temporary file used in each instance will be different. Problem solved.

The Exit Status from read

read returns an exit status of zero unless an end-of-file condition is encountered. If the data is coming from the terminal, this means that the user has pressed *Ctrl+d*. If the data is coming from a file, it means that there's no more data to read from the file.

This makes it easy to write a loop that will read lines of data from either a file or the terminal.

The next program, called `addi`, reads in lines containing pairs of numbers, which are added together; their sums are then written to standard output:

```
$ cat addi
#
# add pairs of integers on standard input
#

while read n1 n2
do
        echo $(( $n1 + $n2))
done
$
```

The `while` loop is executed as long as the `read` command returns an exit status of zero, which occurs as long as there's still data to be read. Inside the loop, the two values read from the line (presumably integers—no error checking is done here) are added up and the result written to standard output by `echo`.

```
$ addi
10 25
35
-5 12
7
123 3
126
Ctrl+d
$
```

Standard input for `addi` can be redirected from a file, and standard output can be another file (or a pipe, of course):

```
$ cat data
1234 7960
593 -595
395 304
3234 999
-394 -493
$ addi < data > sums
$ cat sums
9194
-2
699
4233
-887
$
```

The following program, called `number`, is a simplified version of the standard Unix `nl` command: it accepts one or more files as arguments and displays their contents with each line preceded by its line number. If no arguments are supplied, it reads standard input instead.

```
$ cat number
#
# Number lines from files given as argument or from
# standard input if none supplied
#

lineno=1

cat $* |
while read line
do
        echo "$lineno: $line"
        lineno=$((lineno + 1))
done
$
```

The variable `lineno`—the line number count—is initially set to 1. Then the arguments typed to `number` are given to `cat` to be collectively written to standard output. If no arguments are supplied, `$*` will be null, and `cat` will be passed no arguments. This will cause it to read from standard input. The output from `cat` is piped into the `while` loop.

Each line encountered by `read` is echoed at the terminal, prefaced by the current value of `lineno`, whose value is then incremented by one.

```
$ number phonebook
1: Alice Chebba      973-555-2015
2: Barbara Swingle   201-555-9257
3: Billy Bach        201-555-7618
4: El Coyote         212-555-3232
5: Liz Stachiw       212-555-2298
6: Susan Goldberg    201-555-7776
7: Teri Zak          201-555-6000
8: Tony Iannino      973-555-1295
$ who | number                          Try from standard input
1: root      console  Jul 25 07:55
2: pat       tty03    Jul 25 09:26
3: steve     tty04    Jul 25 10:58
4: george    tty13    Jul 25 08:05
$
```

Note that `number` won't work too well for lines that contain backslashes or leading whitespace characters. The following example illustrates this point.

```
$ number
            Here are some backslashes: \ \*
1: Here are some backslashes: *
$
```

Leading whitespace characters are removed from any line that's read. The backslash characters are also interpreted by the shell when it reads the line. You can use the -r option of read to prevent it from interpreting the backslash character. If we change the

```
while read line
```

in number to

```
while read -r line
```

the output will look better:

```
$ number
            Here are some backslashes: \ \*
1: Here are some backslashes: \ \*
$
```

In Chapter 11 you'll learn how to preserve the leading whitespace characters and also how to have some control over the parsing of the input data.

The `printf` Command

Although echo is quite adequate for displaying simple messages, sometimes you'll want to print *formatted* output: for example, lining up columns of data. Unix systems provide the printf command for these tasks. Those of you familiar with the C or C++ programming language will notice many similarities with their function of the same name.

The general format of the printf command is

```
printf "format" arg1 arg2 ...
```

where *format* is a string that details how the subsequent values are to be displayed. Since the format string is a single argument and is likely to contain special characters and spaces, it's always a good idea to enclose it in quotes.

Characters in the format string that are not preceded by a percent sign (%) are written directly to standard output. At its most simple, then, printf can work like echo (as long as you remember to end each line with \n for a newline, as shown):

```
$ printf "Hello world!\n"
Hello world!
$
```

Characters preceded by a percent sign are called *format specifications* and tell printf how the corresponding argument should be displayed. For each percent sign in the format string there should be a corresponding argument, except for the special specification %%, which causes a single percent sign to be displayed.

Let's start with a simple example of printf:

```
$ printf "This is a number: %d\n" 10
This is a number: 10
$
```

printf doesn't automatically add a newline character to the end of its output like echo but it does understand the same escape sequences (refer to Table 9.1 earlier in this chapter), so adding \n to the end of the format string causes the newline character sequence to also be printed and the command prompt to appear on the next line as expected.

Although the preceding is a simple example that could also be handled by echo, it helps to illustrate how the conversion specification (%d) is interpreted by printf: the format string is scanned and outputs each character in the string until it sees the percent sign. Then it reads the d and tries to replace the %d with the next argument given to printf, which must be an integer. After that argument (10) is sent to standard output, printf continues scanning the format string, sees the \n, and outputs a newline.

Table 9.2 summarizes the different format specification characters.

Table 9.2   printf **Format Specification Characters**

Character	Use for Printing
%d	Integers
%u	Unsigned integers
%o	Octal integers
%x	Hexadecimal integers, using a-f
%X	Hexadecimal integers, using A-F
%c	Single characters
%s	Literal strings
%b	Strings containing backslash escape characters
%%	Percent signs

The first five conversion specification characters are all used for displaying integers. %d displays signed integers, and %u displays unsigned integers; %u can also be used to display the positive representation of a negative number. By default, integers displayed as octal or hexadecimal numbers do not have a leading 0 or 0x, but you can fix that if needed, as we'll show later in this section.

Strings are printed using %s or %b. %s is used to print strings literally, without any processing of backslash escape characters; %b is used to force interpretation of the backslash escape characters in the string argument.

Here are a few printf examples to clarify:

```
$ printf "The octal value for %d is %o\n" 20 20
The octal value for 20 is 24
$ printf "The hexadecimal value for %d is %x\n" 30 30
The hexadecimal value for 30 is 1e
```

```
$ printf "The unsigned value for %d is %u\n" -1000 -1000
The unsigned value for -1000 is 4294966296
$ printf "This string contains a backslash escape: %s\n" "test\nstring"
This string contains a backslash escape: test\nstring
$ printf "This string contains an interpreted
➥backslash escape: %b\n" "test\nstring"
This string contains an interpreted backslash escape: test string
$ printf "A string: %s and a character: %c\n" hello A
A string: hello and a character: A
$
```

In the last printf, %c is used to display a single character. If the corresponding argument is longer than one character, only the first is displayed:

```
$ printf "Just the first character: %c\n" abc
a
$
```

The general format of a conversion specification is

```
%[flags][width][.precision]type
```

The type is the conversion specification character from Table 9.2. As you can see, only the percent sign and type are required; the other parameters are called *modifiers* and are optional. Valid flags are -, +, #, and the space character.

– left-justifies the value being printed, which will make more sense when we discuss the width modifier.

+ causes printf to precede integers with a + or – sign (by default, only negative integers are printed with a sign).

causes printf to precede octal integers with 0 and hexadecimal integers with 0x or 0X, specified as %#x or %#X, respectively.

The space character causes printf to precede positive integers with a space and negative integers with a – for alignment purposes.

A few more examples. Pay close attention to the format strings!

```
$ printf "%+d\n%+d\n%+d\n" 10 -10 20
+10
-10
+20
$ printf "% d\n% d\n% d\n" 10 -10 20
 10
-10
 20
$ printf "%#o %#x\n" 100 200
0144 0xc8
$
```

As you can see, using + or space as the flag causes a column of positive and negative numbers to align nicely.

The *width* modifier is a positive number that specifies the minimum *field width* for printing an argument. The argument is right-justified within this field unless the – flag is used:

```
$ printf "%20s%20s\n" string1 string2
            string1             string2
$ printf "%-20s%-20s\n" string1 string2
string1             string2
$ printf "%5d%5d%5d\n" 1 10 100
    1   10  100
$ printf "%5d%5d%5d\n" -1 -10 -100
   -1  -10 -100
$ printf "%-5d%-5d%-5d\n" 1 10 100
1    10   100
$
```

The *width* modifier can be useful for lining up columns of text or numbers (Tip: signs for numbers and leading 0, 0x, and 0X characters are counted as part of the argument width). The *width* specifies a *minimum* size for the field, but if the width of an argument exceeds *width*, it can overflow or not be output at all. An easy way to test:

```
printf "%-15.15s\n" "this is more than 15 chars long"
```

What happens on your system when you try that command?

The *.precision* modifier is a positive number that specifies a minimum number of digits to be displayed for %d, %u, %o, %x, and %X. This results in *zero-padding* on the left of the value:

```
$ printf "%.5d %.4X\n" 10 27
00010 001B
$
```

For strings, the *.precision* modifier specifies the maximum number of characters to be printed from the string. If the string is longer than *precision* characters, it is truncated on the right. That's important to realize as it lets you line up text across multiple lines, but with some data missing if any individual value is wider than the specified field:

```
$ printf "%.6s\n" "Ann Smith"
Ann Sm
$
```

A *width* can be combined with *.precision* to specify both a field width and zero padding (for numbers) or truncation (for strings):

```
$ printf ":%#10.5x:%5.4x:%5.4d\n" 1 10 100
:   0x00001: 000a: 0100
$ printf ":%9.5s:\n" abcdefg
:    abcde:
$ printf ":%-9.5s:\n" abcdefg
:abcde    :
$
```

Finally, in case all of this isn't confusing enough, if a * is used in place of a number for *width* or *precision*, the argument *preceding* the value to be printed must be a number and will be used as the width or precision, respectively. If a * is used in place of both, two integer arguments must precede the value being printed and are used for the width and precision:

```
$ printf "%*s%*.*s\n" 12 "test one" 10 2 "test two"
    test one         te
$ printf "%12s%10.2s\n" "test one" "test two"
    test one         te
$
```

As you can see, the two printfs in this example produce the same result. In the first printf, 12 is used as the width for the first string, 10 as the width for the second string, and 2 as the precision for the second string. In the second printf, these numbers are specified as part of the format specification.

While the format specification for printf is unquestionably complex, its power and capabilities to turn the relatively unstructured output of echo into exactly what you want from your own shell programs is darn helpful. It's a command well worth studying more closely so you know how to use it as you develop your own more sophisticated programs.

Table 9.3 summarizes the various format specification modifiers.

Table 9.3 printf **Format Specification Modifiers**

Modifier	Meaning
Flags	
-	Left-justify value.
+	Precede integer with + or -.
(space)	Precede positive integer with space character.
#	Precede octal integer with 0, hexadecimal integer with 0x or 0X.
width	Minimum width of field; * means use next argument as width.
precision	Minimum number of digits to display for integers; maximum number of characters to display for strings; * means use next argument as precision.

Let's keep exploring printf. Here's a simple example that uses printf to align two columns of numbers from a file:

```
$ cat align
#
# Align two columns of numbers
# (works for numbers up to 12 digits long, including sign)
```

```
cat $* |
while read number1 number2
do
      printf "%12d %12d\n" $number1 $number2
done
```
$ cat data
```
1234 7960
593 -595
395 304
3234 999
-394 -493
```
$ align data
```
        1234           7960
         593           -595
         395            304
        3234            999
        -394           -493
```
$

In Chapters 11, 13, and 14 you'll see more examples of different uses for printf.

Your Environment

When you log on to your system, whether it's a shiny new Mac OS X Terminal app, a clean Linux install, or a Unix server in the back office, you're effectively given your own copy of the shell program. This login shell maintains what's known as your *environment*—a configuration that is distinct from other users on the system. This environment is maintained from the moment you log on until the moment you log off. In this chapter you'll learn about the shell environment and you'll see how it relates to writing and running programs.

Local Variables

Type the following program called `vartest` into your computer:

```
$ cat vartest
echo :$x:
$
```

`vartest` consists of a single `echo` command that displays the value of the variable `x` surrounded by colons.

Assign any value you want to the variable x from your terminal:

```
$ x=100
```

Question: What do you think will be displayed when `vartest` is now executed? Answer:

```
$ vartest
::
$
```

`vartest` doesn't know about the value of x. Therefore, its value is the default: null. The variable x that was assigned the value `100` in the login shell is known as a *local* variable. The reason why it has this name will become clear shortly.

Here's another example called `vartest2`:

```
$ cat vartest2
x=50
echo :$x:
$ x=100
$ vartest2                    Execute it
:50:
$
```

Since the script changed the value of x from 100 to 50, the question is: What's the value of x after the script completes?

```
$ echo $x
100
$
```

You can see that `vartest2` didn't change the value of x, previously set to `100` in the interactive shell.

Subshells

The seemingly weird behavior exhibited by `vartest` and `vartest2` is due to the fact that these programs are run within *subshells* by your login shell. A subshell is essentially an entirely new shell just to run the desired program.

When you ask the login shell to execute `vartest`, it starts up a new shell to execute the program. Whenever a new shell runs, it runs in its own environment, with its own set of local variables. A subshell has no knowledge of local variables that were assigned values by the login shell (the *parent* shell). Furthermore, a subshell cannot change the value of a variable in the parent shell, as evidenced by `vartest2`.

Let's review the process that goes on here so you can better understand what's called the *scoping* of variables in shell programs: Before executing `vartest2`, your shell has a variable called x that has been assigned the value `100`. This is depicted in Figure 10.1.

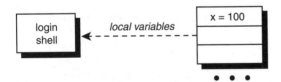

Figure 10.1   Login shell with x=100

When you invoke `vartest2`, your shell starts up a subshell to run it, giving it an *empty* list of local variables to start with (see Figure 10.2).

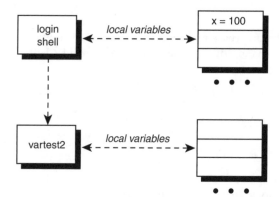

Figure 10.2   Login shell executes `vartest2`

After the first command in `vartest2` is executed, assigning 50 to x, the local variable x *that exists in the subshell's environment* will have the value 50 (see Figure 10.3) but the value of x in the parent shell will be unchanged.

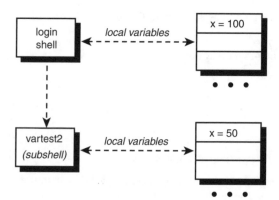

Figure 10.3   `vartest2` executes `x=50`

When `vartest2` finishes execution, the subshell goes away, *together with any variables assigned values by the program.*

This is less of a problem than it might seem. You just need to understand that the login shell environment and the environment of subshells and their shell programs are very different.

Exported Variables

There *is* a way to make the value of a variable known to a subshell, and that's by *exporting* it with the `export` command. The format of this command is simply export *variables*

where *variables* is the list of variable names that you want exported. For any subshells that get executed subsequent to the export command, the value of the exported variables will be passed to the subshell.

Here's a program called vartest3 to help illustrate the difference between local and exported variables:

```
$ cat vartest3
echo x = $x
echo y = $y
$
```

Assign values to the variables x and y in the login shell, and then run vartest3:

```
$ x=100
$ y=10
$ vartest3
x =
y =
$
```

x and y are both local variables, so their values aren't passed down to the subshell that runs vartest3. That's as expected.

But now let's export the variable y and try the program again:

```
$ export y                Make y known to subshells
$ vartest3
x =
y = 10
$
```

This time vartest3 knew about y because it is an exported variable.

Conceptually, whenever a subshell is executed the exported variables get "copied down" to the subshell, whereas the local variables do not (see Figure 10.4).

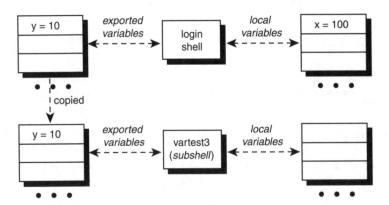

Figure 10.4 Execution of vartest3

Now it's time for another question: What do you think happens if a subshell changes the value of an exported variable? That is, will the parent shell know about it after the subshell has finished?

To answer this question, here's a program called vartest4:

```
$ cat vartest4
x=50
y=5
$
```

We'll assume that you haven't changed the values of x and y, and that y is still exported from the previous example.

```
$ vartest4
$ echo $x $y
100 10
$
```

The subshell couldn't change the value of either the local variable x (no surprise!) or the exported variable y, it merely changed its local subshell copy of y that was instantiated when it was executed (see Figure 10.5). Just as with local variables, when a subshell goes away, so do the values of the exported variables. In fact, once they get to the subshell, they *are* local variables.

That's why this is true: *There is no way to change the value of a variable in a parent shell from within a subshell.*

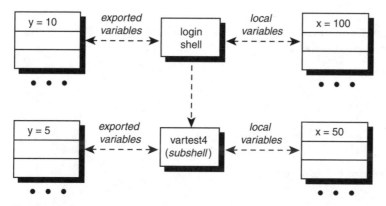

Figure 10.5   Execution of vartest4

In the case of a shell program invoking another shell program (for example, the rolo program calling the lu program), the process is repeated: the exported variables from the subshell are copied to the new subshell. These exported variables may have been exported from the login shell, or newly exported from within the subshell.

After a variable is exported, it remains exported to all subshells subsequently executed.

Consider a modified version of vartest4:

```
$ cat vartest4
x=50
y=5
z=1
export z
vartest5
$
```

and vartest5:

```
$ cat vartest5
echo x = $x
echo y = $y
echo z = $z
$
```

When vartest4 gets executed, the exported variable y will be copied into the subshell's environment. vartest4 sets the value of x to 50, changes the value of y to 5, and sets the value of z to 1. Then it exports z which makes the value of z accessible to any subsequent subshell.

vartest5 is such a subshell and when it is executed the shell copies into its environment the exported variables from vartest4: y and z.

This explains the following output:

```
$ vartest4
x =
y = 5
z = 1
$
```

This entire process is depicted in Figure 10.6.

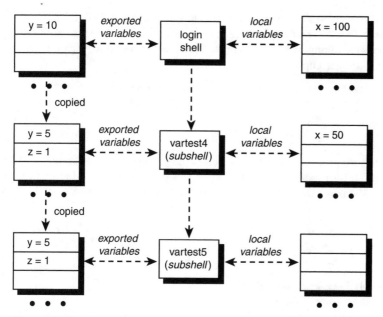

Figure 10.6   Subshell execution

To summarize the way local and exported variables work:

1. Any variable that is not exported is a local variable whose existence will not be known to subshells.

2. Exported variables and their values are copied into a subshell's environment, where they may be accessed and changed. However, such changes have no effect on the variables in the parent shell.

3. Exported variables retain this characteristic not only for directly spawned subshells, but also for subshells spawned by those subshells (and so on down the line).

4. A variable can be exported any time before or after it is assigned a value but takes on its value at the moment of export; subsequent changes aren't tracked.

export -p

If you type export -p, you'll get a list of the variables and their values exported by your shell:

```
$ export -p
export LOGNAME=steve
export PATH=/bin:/usr/bin:.
export TIMEOUT=600
export TZ=EST5EDT
export y=10
$
```

As you can see, there are actually lots of exported variables in a typical login shell. On the Mac, `export -p` produces a list of 22 variables. Note that in the example y shows up from our earlier export experimentation, along with other variables that were exported when you logged on and your login shell was started up.

But what are these all-capital-letter exported variables? Let's have a closer look.

PS1 **and** PS2

The sequence of characters that the shell uses as your command prompt are stored in the environment variable PS1. It turns out that you can change this to be anything you want and as soon as you change it, the new value will be used by the shell from that point on.

```
$ echo :$PS1:
:$ :
$ PS1="==> "
==> pwd
/users/steve
==> PS1="I await your next command, master: "
I await your next command, master: date
Wed Sep 18 14:46:28 EDT 2002
I await your next command, master: PS1="$ "
$                               Back to normal
```

Your secondary command prompt, used when a command requires more than a single line of input, defaults to > and is kept in the variable PS2. This too you can change to your heart's content:

```
$ echo :$PS2:
:> :
$ PS2="=======> "
$ for x in 1 2 3
=======> do
=======> echo $x
=======> done
1
2
3
$
```

Once you log off the system, all the changes will vanish, just like modifications to any other shell variables. If you change PS1, the shell will use the new value for the remainder of your login session. Next time you log in, however, you'll get the old prompt unless you save the new PS1 value by adding it to your .profile file (discussed later in this chapter).

> **Tip**
> The PS1 prompt has a language all its own with special sequences that produce the command count, current directory, time of day, and much more. Learn about it by reading the "Prompting" section of the Bash or Sh man page!

HOME

Your home directory is where you're placed whenever you log on to the system. A special shell variable called HOME is also automatically set to this directory when you log on:

```
$ echo $HOME
/users/steve
$
```

This variable can be used by your programs to identify your home directory and is widely used by other programs in Unix for just this purpose. It's also used by the cd command as the desired destination when you type cd with no arguments:

```
$ pwd                        Where am I?
/usr/src/lib/libc/port/stdio
$ cd
$ pwd
/users/steve                 There's no place like home
$
```

You can change your HOME variable to anything you want, but be warned that doing so may affect the operation of any programs that rely on it:

```
$ HOME=/users/steve/book          Change it
$ pwd
/users/steve
$ cd
$ pwd                             See what happened
/users/steve/book
$
```

You can change your HOME, but you really shouldn't unless you're prepared to have a lot of things go wonky rather quickly.

PATH

Let's return to the rolo program from Chapter 9:

```
$ rolo Liz
Liz Stachiw    212-775-2298
$
```

To keep things neat and organized, the program was created in steve's /bin subdirectory, as shown:

```
$ pwd
/users/steve/bin
$
```

Change directory to anywhere else on the system:

```
$ cd                          Go home
$
```

And try to look up Liz in the phone book:

```
$ rolo Liz
sh: rolo: not found
$
```

Uh oh, that's not good. What happened?

Whenever you type in the name of a program, the shell searches a list of directories until it finds the requested program. When found, the program is started up. This list of directories to search for user commands is stored in a shell variable called PATH and it's automatically set when you log on. To see what it's set to at any point, use echo:

```
$ echo $PATH
/bin:/usr/bin:.
$
```

Chances are that your PATH has a somewhat different value, but don't worry about that—it's just variations in system configuration. The important thing to notice is that directories are separated by a colon (:) and that the shell searches them in order, left to right, to find requested commands or programs.

In the preceding example, three directories are listed: /bin, /usr/bin, and ., (which, you'll recall, stands for the current directory). So whenever you type in the name of a program, the shell searches the directories listed in PATH until it finds a matching executable file. Type in rolo and the shell first looks for /bin/rolo, then /usr/bin/rolo, then, finally, ./rolo in the current directory. As soon as it finds a match the shell executes it, but if the shell doesn't find rolo in any of the directories specified in PATH, it issues a "not found" error.

To have the current directory searched before anything else, put the period at the start of PATH:

```
.:/bin:/usr/bin
```

Warning! For security reasons, it's not a good idea to have your current directory searched before the system ones.

This is to avoid a *Trojan horse* attack: Imagine that someone creates their own version of a command like su (which allows you to switch to root or superuser status by prompting for the admin password) in a directory then waits for another user to change to that directory and run the command. If PATH specifies that the current directory be searched first, then the modified version of su will be executed. The problem is, this version prompts for the password, emails it to the malicious user, deletes itself, and prints out an innocuous error message. Reinvoked, password retyped, it all works fine and the administrator account has just been compromised without the user realizing anything has occurred! Sneaky, eh?

The period . for specifying the current directory is optional but useful as a visible reminder. For example, a PATH of

```
:/bin:/usr/bin
```

is equivalent to the previous one; however, throughout this text we'll specify the current directory with a period for clarity.

Worried about Trojan horses now? Don't fret, you can always override the search specified by PATH by specifying an explicit path to the program to be executed. For example, if you type

```
/bin/date
```

the shell goes directly to /bin to execute date. PATH in this case is ignored, as it is if you type in

```
../bin/lu
```

or

```
./rolo
```

This last case says to execute the program rolo in the current directory and is commonly used while developing shell programs because it lets programmers omit . from their PATH.

Now you understand why you couldn't execute rolo from your HOME directory: /users/steve/bin wasn't included in PATH so the shell couldn't find rolo. A simple matter to rectify: You can simply add this directory to PATH:

```
$ PATH=/bin:/usr/bin:/users/steve/bin:.
$
```

Now *any* program in /users/steve/bin can be executed regardless of your current directory in the file system:

```
$ pwd                          Where am I?
/users/steve
$ rolo Liz
grep: can't open phonebook
$
```

Oops. The shell finds rolo and executes it correctly, but the grep command can't find the phonebook data file.

Look more closely at the rolo program and you'll see that the grep error message must be coming from lu. Here's lu, as it exists currently:

```
$ cat /users/steve/bin/lu
#
# Look someone up in the phone book -- version 3
#
```

```
if [ "$#" -ne 1 ]
then
        echo "Incorrect number of arguments"
        echo "Usage: lu name"
        exit 1
fi

grep "$name" phonebook
$
```

grep is trying to open the phonebook file in the current directory—which is /users/steve—and that's the problem: where the program is being executed from has no relation to the directory in which the program and its data file reside.

PATH only specifies the directories to be searched for programs invoked on the command line, and not for any other types of files. So phonebook must be precisely located for lu to make it more useful.

There are several ways to fix this problem, which also exists with the rem and add programs. One approach is to have the lu program change directory to /users/steve/bin before it invokes grep. That way, grep finds phonebook because it exists in the new current directory:

```
    . . .
cd /users/steve/bin
grep "$1" phonebook
```

This approach is a good one to take when you're doing a lot of work with different files in a particular directory. Simply cd to the directory first and then you can directly reference all the files you need.

A second, more common approach is to list a full path to phonebook in the grep command:

```
    . . .
grep "$1" /users/steve/bin/phonebook
```

Suppose that you want to let others use your rolo program (and associated lu, add, and rem helper programs). You can give them each their own copy, but then you'll have several copies on the system and what happens if you make a small change? Are you going to update all their copies as well? Tedious.

A better solution is to have a single copy of rolo but to give other users access to it.

The problem should be obvious at this point: If you change all the references of phonebook to explicitly reference *your* phone book, everyone else will be using *your* phone book too. A smarter way to solve the problem is to require that everyone have a phonebook file in their home directory and refer to the file as $HOME/phonebook.

To use a very common shell programming convention, define a variable inside rolo called PHONEBOOK and set it to the multi-user friendly value $HOME/phonebook. If you export this variable, lu, rem, and add (which are executed as subshells by rolo) can also use the value of PHONEBOOK to reference the individual user's version of the file.

One advantage of this approach is that if you change the location of the phonebook file, all you'll have to do is change this one variable in rolo; the other three programs will continue to work without a glitch.

With that in mind, here is the new rolo program, followed by modified lu, add, and rem programs.

```
$ cd /users/steve/bin
$ cat rolo
#
# rolo - rolodex program to look up, add, and
#        remove people from the phone book
#

#
# Set PHONEBOOK to point to the phone book file
# and export it so other progs know about it
#

PHONEBOOK=$HOME/phonebook
export PHONEBOOK

if [ ! -f "$PHONEBOOK" ] ; then
      echo "No phone book file in $HOME!"
      exit 1
fi

#
# If arguments are supplied, then do a lookup
#

if [ "$#" -ne 0 ] ; then
      lu "$@"
      exit
fi
validchoice=""          # set it null

#
# Loop until a valid selection is made
#

until [ -n "$validchoice" ]
do
      #
      # Display menu
      #
```

```
          echo '
          Would you like to:

          1. Look someone up
          2. Add someone to the phone book
          3. Remove someone from the phone book

Please select one of the above (1-3): \c'

#
# Read and process selection
#

read choice
echo

case "$choice"
in
          1) echo "Enter name to look up: \c"
             read name
             lu "$name"
             validchoice=TRUE;;
          2) echo "Enter name to be added: \c"
             read name
             echo "Enter number: \c"
             read number
             add "$name" "$number"
             validchoice=TRUE;;
          3) echo "Enter name to be removed: \c"
             read name
             rem "$name"
             validchoice=TRUE;;
          *) echo "Bad choice";;
        esac
done
$ cat add
#
# Program to add someone to the phone book file
#

if [ "$#"_ -ne 2 ] ;then
        echo "Incorrect number of arguments"
        echo "Usage: add name number"
        exit 1
fi

echo "$1      $2" >> $PHONEBOOK
```

```
sort -o $PHONEBOOK $PHONEBOOK
$ cat lu
#
# Look someone up in the phone book
#

if [ "$#" -ne 1 ] ; then
        echo "Incorrect number of arguments"
        echo "Usage: lu name"
        exit 1
fi

name=$1
grep "$name" $PHONEBOOK

if [ $? -ne 0 ] ; then
        echo "I couldn't find $name in the phone book"
fi
$ cat rem
#
# Remove someone from the phone book
#

if [ "$#" -ne 1 ] ; then
        echo "Incorrect number of arguments"
        echo "Usage: rem name"
        exit 1
fi

name=$1

#
# Find number of matching entries
#

matches=$(grep "$name" $PHONEBOOK | wc -1)

#
# If more than one match, issue message, else remove it
#

if [ "$matches" -gt 1 ] ; then
        echo "More than one match; please qualify further"
elif [ "$matches" -eq 1 ] ; then
        grep -v "$name" $PHONEBOOK > /tmp/phonebook$$
        mv /tmp/phonebook$$ $PHONEBOOK
else
```

```
        echo "I couldn't find $name in the phone book"
fi
$
```

Note that we added one more tweak: In an effort to be more user-friendly, a test was added to the end of lu to see whether the grep succeeded or not, and a fail message is now displayed if the search doesn't produce any results.

Now to test it:

`$ cd`	*Return home*
`$ rolo Liz`	*Quick lookup*
`No phonebook file in /users/steve!`	*Forgot to move it*
`$ mv /users/steve/bin/phonebook .`	
`$ rolo Liz`	*Try again*
`Liz Stachiw    212-775-2298`	
`$ rolo`	*Try menu selection*

```
     Would you like to:

        1. Look someone up
        2. Add someone to the phone book
        3. Remove someone from the phone book

     Please select one of the above (1-3): 2

Enter name to be added: Teri Zak
Enter number: 201-393-6000
$ rolo Teri
Teri Zak       201-393-6000
$
```

rolo, lu, and add are working fine. rem should also be tested to make sure that it's okay as well.

If you still want to run lu, rem, or add standalone, you can do it provided that you first define PHONEBOOK and export it:

```
$ PHONEBOOK=$HOME/phonebook
$ export PHONEBOOK
$ lu Harmon
I couldn't find Harmon in the phone book
$
```

If you do intend to run these programs standalone, you'd better put checks in the individual programs to ensure that PHONEBOOK is set to the correct value.

Your Current Directory

Your current directory is also part of your shell environment. Consider this small shell program called `cdtest`:

```
$ cat cdtest
cd /users/steve/bin
pwd
$
```

The program uses `cd` to move to `/users/steve/bin` and then invokes `pwd` to verify that the change was made. Let's run it:

```
$ pwd                          Get my bearings
/users/steve
$ cdtest
/users/steve/bin
$
```

Now for the $64,000 question: If you invoke `pwd`, will you be in `/users/steve` or `/users/steve/bin`?

```
$ pwd
/users/steve
$
```

It turns out that the `cd` in `cdtest` had no effect on your current directory. Because the current directory is part of the environment, when a `cd` is executed from a subshell, it only affects the directory of the subshell. *There is no way* to *change the current directory of a parent shell from a subshell.*

When `cd` is invoked, it changes your current directory and also sets the `PWD` variable to the full pathname of the new current directory. As a result, the command

```
echo $PWD
```

produces the same output as the `pwd` command:

```
$ pwd
/users/steve
$ echo $PWD
/users/steve
$ cd bin
$ echo $PWD
/users/steve/bin
$
```

`cd` also sets `OLDPWD` to the full pathname of the previous current directory, which can be useful in certain situations too.

CDPATH

The CDPATH variable works like the PATH variable: it specifies a list of directories to be searched by the shell whenever you execute a cd command. This search is done only if the specified directory is not given by a full pathname and if CDPATH is not null. If you type in

```
cd /users/steve
```

the shell changes your directory directly to /users/steve; but if you type

```
cd memos
```

the shell looks at your CDPATH variable to find the memos directory. And if your CDPATH looks like this:

```
$ echo $CDPATH
.:/users/steve:/users/steve/docs
$
```

the shell first looks in your current directory for a memos directory, and if not found then looks in /users/steve for a memos directory, and if not found there tries /users/steve/docs in a last ditch effort to find the directory. If the directory that it finds is not relative to your current one, the cd command prints the full path to the directory to let you know where it's taking you:

```
$ cd /users/steve
$ cd memos
/users/steve/docs/memos
$ cd bin
/users/steve/bin
$ pwd
/users/steve/bin
$
```

Like the PATH variable, use of the period for specifying the current directory is optional, so

```
:/users/steve:/users/steve/docs
```

is equivalent to

```
.:/users/steve:/users/steve/docs
```

Judicious use of the CDPATH variable can save you a lot of typing, especially if your directory hierarchy is fairly deep and you find yourself frequently moving around in it (or if you're frequently moving into other directory hierarchies as well).

Unlike PATH, you'll probably want to put your current directory first in the CDPATH list. This gives you the most natural use of CDPATH; if the current directory isn't listed first, you may end up in an unexpected directory!

Oh, and one more thing: CDPATH isn't set when you log in; you need to explicitly set it to the sequences of directories you'd like the shell to use when searching for the specified name.

More on Subshells

You know that a subshell can't change the value of a variable in a parent shell, nor can it change its current directory. Suppose that you want to write a program to set values for some variables that you like to use whenever you log on. For example, assume that you have the following file called `vars`:

```
$ cat vars
BOOK=/users/steve/book
UUPUB=/usr/spool/uucppublic
DOCS=/users/steve/docs/memos
DB=/usr2/data
$
```

If you invoke `vars`, the values assigned to these variables will essentially vanish after the program has finished executing because `vars` is run in a subshell:

```
$ vars
$ echo $BOOK

$
```

No surprise there.

The . Command

To address this dilemma, there's a built-in shell command called . (pronounced "dot") whose general format is

```
. file
```

and whose purpose is to execute the contents of `file` in the *current* shell. That is, commands from `file` are executed by the current shell just as if they were typed, not within a subshell. The shell uses your PATH variable to find `file`, just like it does when executing other programs.

```
$ . vars              Execute vars in the current shell
$ echo $BOOK
/users/steve/book     Hoorah!
$
```

Because a subshell isn't spawned to execute the program, any variable that gets assigned a value is retained even after the program completes.

If you have a program called `db` that has the following commands:

```
$ cat db
DATA=/usr2/data
RPTS=$DATA/rpts
BIN=$DATA/bin

cd $DATA
$
```

executing db with the "dot" command will do something interesting:

```
$ pwd
/users/steve
$ . db
$
```

This time the shell program defines the three variables DATA, RPTS, and BIN in the current shell and moves to the $DATA directory.

```
$ pwd
/usr2/data
$
```

If you work on multiple projects, you can create programs like db to customize your environment as needed. In that program, you can also include definitions for other variables, change prompts, and more. For example, you might want to change your PS1 prompt to DB—to let you know that your database variables have been set up. You could change your PATH to include a directory that has programs related to the database and your CDPATH so that the related directories will be easily accessed with the cd command.

On the other hand, if you make these sorts of changes, you might want to execute db in a subshell rather than the current shell because doing the latter leaves all the modified variables around after you've finished your work.

The best solution is to start a *new* shell from inside the subshell, with all the modified variables and updated environment settings. Then, when you're finished working, you can "log out" the new shell by pressing *Ctrl+d*.

Let's take a look at how this works with a new version of db:

```
$ cat db
#
# Set up and export variables related to the data base
#

HOME=/usr2/data
BIN=$HOME/bin
RPTS=$HOME/rpts
DATA=$HOME/rawdata

PATH=$PATH$BIN
CDPATH=:$HOME:$RPTS

PS1="DB: "

export HOME BIN RPTS DATA PATH CDPATH PS1

#
```

```
# Start up a new shell
#

/bin/sh
$
```

The HOME directory is set to /usr2/data, and then the variables BIN, RPTS, and DATA are defined relative to this HOME (a good idea in case you ever have to move the directory structure somewhere else: all you'd have to change in the program is the variable HOME).

Next, PATH is modified to include the database bin directory and the CDPATH variable is set to search the current directory, the HOME directory, and the RPTS directory (which presumably contains subdirectories).

After exporting these variables, the standard shell, /bin/sh, is invoked. From that point on, this new shell processes any user-entered commands until either the user types exit or uses the *Ctrl+d* sequence. Upon exit, control returns to db, which in turn returns control to your login shell.

```
$ db                                    Run it
DB: echo $HOME
/usr2/data
DB: cd rpts                             Try out CDPATH
/usr2/data/rpts                         It works
DB: ps                                  See what processes are running
PID TTY TIME COMMAND
123 13  0:40 sh                         Your login shell
761 13  0:01 sh                         Subshell running db
765 13  0:01 sh                         New shell run from db
769 13  0:03 ps
DB:  exit                               Done for now
$ echo $HOME
/users/steve                            Back to normal
$
```

The execution of db is depicted in Figure 10.7 (where we've shown only the exported variables of interest for simplicity's sake, not all that exist in the environment).

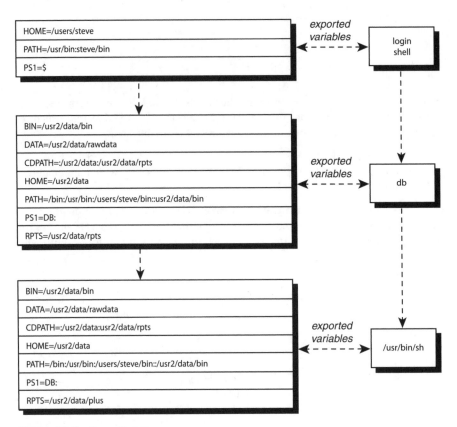

Figure 10.7   Executing db

The exec Command

Within the db program, once the shell process completed, you were done with everything, as demonstrated by the fact that no commands followed /bin/sh in the program. Instead of having db wait around for the subshell to finish, you can use the exec command to *replace the current program* (db) *with the new one* (/bin/sh).

The general format of exec is

```
exec program
```

Because the exec'ed program replaces the current one, there's one less process hanging around, which helps the system run quickly. The startup time of an exec'ed program is quicker too, due to how Unix systems execute processes.

To use exec in the db program, you simply replace the last line with

```
exec /bin/sh
```

After this statement is executed, db will be replaced by /bin/sh. This means that it would now be pointless to have any commands follow the exec because they'll never be executed.

exec can also be used to close standard input and reopen it with any file that you want to read. To change standard input to *infile*, for example, use the exec command in the form

```
exec < infile
```

Any commands that subsequently read data from standard input will read from *infile*.

Redirection of standard output is done similarly. The command

```
exec > report
```

redirects all subsequent output written to standard output to the file report. Note in both of the previous examples that exec is not used to start up execution of a new program, just used to reassign standard input or standard output.

If you use exec to reassign standard input and later want to reassign it someplace else, you can simply invoke exec again. To reassign standard input back to the terminal, you would write

```
exec < /dev/tty
```

The same concept also applies to reassignment of standard output.

The (...) and { ...; } Constructs

Sometimes you want to group a set of commands together. For example, you may want to push a sort followed by your plotdata program into the background. Not connected with a pipe; just two commands one after the other.

It turns out that you can group a set of commands together by enclosing them in parentheses or braces. The first form causes the commands to be executed by a subshell, the latter form by the current shell.

Here are some examples to illustrate how they work:

```
$ x=50
$ (x=100)                           Execute this in a subshell
$ echo $x
50                                  Didn't change
$ { x=100; }                        Execute this in the current shell
$ echo $x
100
$ pwd                               Where am I?
/users/steve
$ (cd bin; ls)                      Change to bin and do an ls
add
greetings
lu
number
```

```
phonebook
rem
rolo
$ pwd
/users/steve                    No change
$ { cd bin; }                   This should change me
$ pwd
/users/steve/bin
$
```

If the commands enclosed in the braces are all going to be on the same line, a space must follow the left brace, and a semicolon must appear after the last command. Look closely at the statement above—{ cd bin; }—for an example.

Parentheses work differently. As the example

```
(cd bin; ls)
```

demonstrates, parentheses are useful for executing commands without affecting the current environment.

You can also use them for other purposes like pushing a set of commands into the background:

```
$ (sort 2016data -0 2016data; plotdata 2016data) &
[1]    3421
$
```

The parentheses group the sort and plotdata commands together so that they can be sent to the background with their order of execution preserved.

Input and output can also be piped to and from these constructs, and I/O can be redirected too, which makes them darn helpful to shell programmers.

In the next example, a dot-prefaced nroff command—.ls 2— is effectively prepended to the beginning of the file memo before being sent to nroff for processing.

```
$ { echo ".ls 2"; cat memo; } | nroff -Tlp | lp
```

In the command sequence

```
$ { prog1; prog2; prog3; } 2> errors
```

all messages written to standard error by the three programs are collected into the file errors.

As a final example, let's return to the waitfor program from Chapter 8. As you'll recall, this program periodically checks for a user logging on to the system. You'll recall that it would be nice if the program could somehow automatically "send itself" to the background. Now you know how to do it: Simply enclose the until loop and the commands that follow within parentheses and send the entire grouping into the background:

```
$ cat waitfor
#
# Wait until a specified user logs on -- version 4
#
```

```
# Set up default values
mailopt=FALSE
interval=60

# process command options

while getopts mt: option
do
      case "$option"
      in
                  m)    mailopt=TRUE;;
                  t)    interval=$OPTARG;;
                  \?)   echo "Usage: mon [-m] [-t n] user"
                        echo" -m means to be informed by mail"
                        echo" -t means check every n secs."
                        exit 1;;
      esac
done

# Make sure a user name was specified

if [ "$OPTIND" -gt "$#" ] ; then
      echo "Missing user name!"
      exit 2
fi

shiftcount=$(( OPTIND - 1 ))
shift $shiftcount
user=$1

#
# Send everything that follows into the background
#

(
   #
   # Check for user logging on
   #

   until who | grep "^$user " > /dev/null
   do
           sleep $interval
   done

   #
   # When we reach this point, the user has logged on
   #
```

```
    if [ "$mailopt" = FALSE] ; then
          echo "$user has logged on"
    else
          runner=$(who am i | cut -cl-8)
          echo "$user has logged on" | mail $runner
    fi
) &
$
```

The entire program could have been enclosed in parentheses, but we decided to do the argument checking and parsing prior to moving the program into the background.

```
$ waitfor fred
$                               Prompt comes back so you can continue working
  ...
fred has logged on
```

Note that a process ID is not printed by the shell when a command is sent to the background within a shell program.

Another Way to Pass Variables to a Subshell

If you want to send the value of a variable to a subshell, there's another way to do it besides exporting the variable. On the command line, precede the command with the assignment of one or more variables. For example,

```
DBHOME=/uxn2/data DBID=452 dbrun
```

places the variables DBHOME and DBID, and their indicated values, into the environment of dbrun, then dbrun gets executed. These variables will not be known to the current shell, however, because they're only created for the execution of dbrun.

In fact, the preceding command behaves identically to typing

```
(DBHOME=/uxn2/data; DBID=452; export DBHOME DBID; dbrun)
```

Here's a short example:

```
$ cat foo1
echo :$x:
foo2
$ cat foo2
echo :$x:
$ foo1
::
::                              x not known to foo1 or foo2
$ x=100 foo1                    Try it this way
:100:                           x is known to foo1
:100:                           and to its subshells
$ echo :$x:
::                              Still not known to current shell
$
```

Variables defined this way otherwise behave as normal exported variables to the subshell but don't exist for the invoking shell once that line of code is executed.

Your `.profile` File

In Chapter 2 you learned about the login sequence completed before the shell displays your command prompt, ready for you to type your first command. Before the prompt, the login shell looks for and reads two special files on the system.

The first is `/etc/profile`, set up by the system administrator. It generally checks to see whether you have mail (it's where the "You have mail" message comes from), sets your default file creation mask (your *umask*), establishes a default PATH, and anything else that the administrator wants to have happen whenever a user logs in.

More interestingly, the second file that gets automatically executed is `.profile` in your home directory. Most Unix systems set up a default `.profile` file when the account is created, so let's start by seeing what's in it:

```
$ cat $HOME/.profile
PATH="/bin:/usr/bin:/usr/lbin:.:"
export PATH
$
```

This is a pretty modest `.profile` that simply sets the PATH and exports it.

You can change your `.profile` file to include any commands that you want executed whenever you log in, including indicating which directory you start out in, a check of who's logged in, and the instantiation of any system aliases you prefer. You can even put commands in your `.profile` that override settings (usually environment variables) established in `/etc/profile`.

Since we've said you can change your current working directory within the `.profile`, it should be no surprise that the login shell actually executes these files as if you typed in

```
$ . /etc/profile
$ . .profile
$
```

as soon as you logged in. This also means that changes to your environment made within the `.profile` remain until you log out of the shell.

Most Unix users dabble with their `.profile` to change lots of aspects of their command line environment. For example, here's a sample `.profile` that sets PATH to include your own `bin`, sets CDPATH, changes the primary and secondary command prompts, changes the erase character to a backspace (*Ctrl+h*) with the `stty` command, and prints a friendly message using the `greetings` program from Chapter 7:

```
$ cat $HOME/.profile
PATH=/bin:/usr/bin:/usr/lbin:$HOME/bin:.:
CDPATH=.:$HOME:$HOME/misc:$HOME/documents
```

```
PS1="=> "
PS2="====> "

export PATH CDPATH PS1 PS2

stty echoe erase CTRL-h

echo
greetings
$
```

Here's what a login sequence would look like with this `.profile`:

```
login: steve
Password:

Good morning                        Output from greetings
=>                                  New PS1
```

The `TERM` Variable

Though many of the programs in Unix are command-line based (like `ls` and `echo`), there are a number of full-screen commands (like the `vi` editor) that require a detailed knowledge of your terminal settings and capabilities. The environment variable that holds that information is `TERM` and usually it's nothing you need to worry about: your Terminal or SSH program usually sets it automatically to be the optimal value for things to work seamlessly.

However, some old-school users might find that `TERM` needs to have a specific value like `ansi` or `vt100` or `xterm` for the full-screen programs to behave properly. In those instances, setting the value within `.profile` is recommended.

You can even prompt for a `TERM` value during the login sequence by having a simple code block like this:

```
echo "What terminal are you using (xterm is the default)? \c"
read TERM
if [ -z "$TERM" ]
then
        TERM=xterm
fi
export TERM
```

Based on the terminal type entered, you may also want to do things such as set up the function keys or the tabs on the terminal.

Even if you always use the same terminal type, you should set the `TERM` variable in your `.profile` file.

As a point of interest, Mac OS X and Ubuntu Linux users will find that the TERM type for the Terminal program is xterm-256color, and Solaris Unix users have vt100 as their default TERM. Many third party telnet/SSH (terminal) programs use ansi as their TERM value.

The TZ Variable

The TZ variable is used by the date command and some Standard C library functions to determine the current time zone. Indeed, since users can log in remotely through the Internet, it's entirely possible that different users on a system are in different time zones. The simplest setting for TZ is a time zone name of three or more alphabetic characters followed by a number that specifies the number of hours that must be added to the local time to arrive at *Coordinated Universal Time*, also known as Greenwich Mean Time. This number can be positive (local time zone is west of 0 longitude) or negative (local time zone is east of 0 longitude). For example, Eastern Standard Time can be specified as

```
TZ=EST5
```

The date command calculates the correct time based on this information and uses the time zone name in its output, as necessary:

```
$ TZ=EST5 date
Wed Feb 17 15:24:09 EST 2016
$ TZ=xyz3 date
Wed Feb 17 17:46:28 xyz 2016
$
```

A second time zone name can follow the number and if this is specified, daylight saving time is assumed to apply (date then automatically adjusts the time when daylight saving is in effect) and is assumed to be one hour ahead of the standard time. If a number follows the daylight saving time zone name, this value is used to compute the daylight saving time from the Coordinated Universal Time in the same way as the number previously described.

Most commonly, you'll see a time zone specified as EST5EDT or MST7MDT, though since some areas of the world don't actually switch for DST, that can be specified too, of course.

The TZ variable is usually set in either the /etc/profile file or your .profile file. If not set, an implementation-specific default time zone is used, typically Coordinated Universal Time.

Also note that on many modern Linux systems the time zone can be set by specifying a geographic region, so

```
TZ="America/Tijuana" date
```

will show the current time in Tijuana, Mexico.

More on Parameters

In this chapter, you'll learn more about variables and parameters. Technically, parameters include the arguments passed to a program (the *positional* parameters), the special shell variables such as $# and $?, and ordinary variables, also known as *keyword* parameters.

Positional parameters cannot be assigned values directly but they can be reassigned values with the `set` command. As you know, variables are assigned values simply by writing

variable=value

The format is a bit more general than that shown, actually, because you can assign several variables at once using the format

variable=value variable=value . . .

The following example illustrates:

```
$ x=100  y=200  z=50
$ echo $x $y $z
100 200 50
$
```

Parameter Substitution

In the simplest form, to have the value of a parameter substituted, precede the parameter with a dollar sign, as in $i or $9.

${parameter}

If there's a potential conflict caused by the characters that follow the parameter name, you can enclose the name inside curly braces, as in

```
mv $file ${file}x
```

This command would add an x to the end of the filename specified by $file. It could not be written as

```
mv $file $filex
```

because the shell would try to substitute the value of a variable named `filex` for the second argument, not `file` plus the letter x.

As mentioned in Chapter 6, to access positional parameters 10 and above, you also must enclose the number inside curly braces using the same notational format: `${11}`.

But it turns out that once you wrap a variable name with curly braces, there's quite a bit more you can do...

${parameter:-value}

This construct says to use the value of *parameter* if it is not null, and to substitute *value* otherwise. For example, in the command line

```
echo Using editor ${EDITOR:-/bin/vi}
```

the shell will use the value of `EDITOR` if it's not null and the value `/bin/vi` otherwise. It has the same effect as writing

```
if [ -n "$EDITOR" ]
then
        echo Using editor $EDITOR
else
        echo Using editor /bin/vi
fi
```

The command line

```
${EDITOR:-/bin/ed} /tmp/edfile
```

starts up the program stored in the variable `EDITOR` (presumably a text editor), or `/bin/ed` if `EDITOR` is null.

Important to note is that this doesn't change the value of the variable, so even after the above statement, if `EDITOR` started out as null, it would continue to have the null value.

Here's a simple demonstration of this construct:

```
$ EDITOR=/bin/ed
$ echo ${EDITOR:-/bin/vi}
/bin/ed
$ EDITOR=                        Set it null
$ echo ${EDITOR:-/bin/vi}
/bin/vi
$
```

${parameter:=value}

This version is similar to the previous, but if *parameter* is null not only is *value* used, but it is also assigned to *parameter* as well (note the = in the construct). You can't assign values to positional parameters this way, however, so that means that *parameter* can't be a number.

A typical use of this construct would be in testing to see whether an exported variable has been set and, if not, assigning it a default value:

${PHONEBOOK:=$HOME/phonebook}

This says that if PHONEBOOK already has an assigned value, leave it alone, otherwise set it to $HOME/phonebook.

Note that the preceding example could not stand alone as a command because after the substitution is performed the shell would attempt to execute the result:

```
$ PHONEBOOK=
$ ${PHONEBOOK:=$HOME/phonebook}
sh: /users/steve/phonebook: cannot execute
$
```

To use this construct as a stand-alone command, the null command can be employed. If you write

: ${PHONEBOOK:=$HOME/phonebook}

the shell still does the substitution (it evaluates the rest of the command line), yet executes nothing (the null command).

```
$ PHONEBOOK=
$ : ${PHONEBOOK:=$HOME/phonebook}
$ echo $PHONEBOOK                          See if it got assigned
/users/steve/phonebook
$ : ${PHONEBOOK:=foobar}                   Shouldn't change it
$ echo $PHONEBOOK
/users/steve/phonebook                     It didn't
$
```

Just as commonly seen, however, are shell programs that use the := notation on the first reference to the variable in a conditional or echo statement. Same effect, but without the null command.

${parameter:?value}

If *parameter* is not null, the shell substitutes its value; otherwise, the shell writes *value* to standard error and then exits (don't worry—if it's done from your login shell, you won't be logged off). If *value* is omitted, the shell writes the default error message

prog: *parameter*: parameter null or not set

Here's an example:

```
$ PHONEBOOK=
$ : ${PHONEBOOK:?"No PHONEBOOK file"}
No PHONEBOOK file
$ : ${PHONEBOOK:?}                    Don't give a value
sh: PHONEBOOK: parameter null or not set
$
```

With this construct, you can easily check to see whether variables needed by a program are all set and not null:

```
: ${TOOLS:?}  ${EXPTOOLS:?}  ${TOOLBIN:?}
```

${parameter:+value}

This one substitutes *value* if *parameter* is not null; otherwise, it substitutes nothing. It's the opposite of :-, of course.

```
$ traceopt=T
$ echo options: ${traceopt:+"trace mode"}
options: trace mode
$ traceopt=
$ echo options: ${traceopt:+"trace mode"}
options:
$
```

The *value* part for any of the constructs in this section can be a command substitution because it's executed only if its value is required. This can get a bit complicated too. Consider this:

```
WORKDIR=${DBDIR:-$(pwd)}
```

Here WORKDIR is assigned the value of DBDIR if it's not null, or the pwd command is executed and the result assigned to WORKDIR. pwd is executed *only if* DBDIR is null.

Pattern Matching Constructs

The POSIX shell offers four parameter substitution constructs that perform pattern matching. Some really old shells do not support this feature, but it's unlikely you'll encounter one of them if you're on a modern Unix, Linux, or Mac system.

The construct takes two arguments: a variable name (or parameter number) and a pattern. The shell searches through the contents of the specified variable to match the supplied pattern. If matched, the shell uses the value of the variable on the command line, *with the matching portion of the pattern deleted*. If the pattern is not matched, the entire contents of the variable are used on the command line. In both cases, the contents of the variable remain unchanged.

The term *pattern* is used here because the shell allows you to use the same pattern matching characters that it accepts in filename substitution and case values: * to match zero or more characters, ? to match any single character, [...] to match any single character from the specified set, and [!...] to match any single character not in the specified set.

When you write the construct

${*variable%pattern*}

the shell looks inside `variable` to see whether it *ends* with the specified `pattern`. If it does, the contents of `variable` are used, with the shortest matching `pattern` removed from the right.

If you use the construct

${*variable%%pattern*}

the shell once again looks inside `variable` to see whether it ends with `pattern`. This time, however, it removes the *longest* matching pattern from the right. This is relevant only if the * is used in `pattern`. Otherwise, the % and %% behave the same way.

The # is used in a similar way to force the pattern matching to start from the left rather than the right. So, the construct.

${*variable#pattern*}

tells the shell to use the value of `variable` on the command line, with `pattern` removed from the left.

Finally, the shell construct

${*variable##pattern*}

works like the # form, except that the longest occurrence of `pattern` is removed from the left.

Remember that in all four cases, no changes are made to the variable itself. You are affecting only what gets used on the command line. Also, remember that the pattern matches are *anchored*. In the case of the % and %% constructs, the values of the variable must *end* with the specified pattern; in the case of the # and ## constructs, the variable must *begin* with it.

Here are some simple examples to show how these constructs work:

```
$ var=testcase
$ echo $var
testcase
$ echo ${var%e}                    Remove e from right
testcas
$ echo $var                        Variable is unchanged
testcase
$ echo ${var%s*e}                  Remove smallest match from right
testca
$ echo ${var%%s*e}                 Remove longest match
te
$ echo ${var#?e}                   Remove smallest match from left
stcase
$ echo ${var#*s}                   Remove smallest match from left
tcase
$ echo ${var##*s}                  Remove longest match from left
```

```
e
$ echo ${var#test}                  Remove test from left
case
$ echo ${var#teas}                  No match
testcase
$
```

There are many practical uses for these constructs. For example, the following tests to see whether the filename stored inside the variable file ends in the two characters .o:

```
if [ ${file%.o} != $file ] ; then
   # file ends in .o
         ...
fi
```

As another example, here's a shell program that works just like the Unix system's basename command:

```
$ cat mybasename
echo ${1##*/}
$
```

The program displays its argument with all the characters up to the last / removed:

```
$ mybasename /usr/spool/uucppublic
uucppublic
$ mybasename $HOME
steve
$ mybasename memos
memos
$
```

But wait, there are more constructs.

${#variable}

Need to figure out how many characters are stored in a variable? That's just what this construct offers:

```
$ text='The shell'
$ echo ${#text}
9
$
```

> **Tip**
>
> Each of the parameter constructs described in this chapter is summarized in Appendix A, Table A.3.

The $0 Variable

Whenever you execute a shell program, the shell automatically stores the name of the program inside the special variable $0. This can be helpful in a number of situations, including when you have a program accessible through different command names through hard links in the file system. It lets you programmatically figure out which one was executed.

It's more commonly used for displaying error messages because it is based on the actual program file name, not whatever's hardcoded in the program itself. If the name of the program is referenced by $0, renaming the program will update the message without requiring the program to be edited:

```
$ cat lu
#
# Look someone up in the phone book
#

if [ "$#" -ne 1 ] ; then
        echo "Incorrect number of arguments"
        echo "Usage: $0 name"
        exit 1
fi

name=$1
grep "$name" $PHONEBOOK

if [ $? -ne 0 ] ; then
        echo "I couldn't find $name in the phone book"
fi
$ PHONEBOOK=$HOME/phonebook
$ export PHONEBOOK
$ lu Teri
Teri Zak        201-393-6000
$ lu Teri Zak
Incorrect number of arguments
Usage: lu name
$ mv lu lookup                      Rename it
$ lookup Teri Zak                   See what happens now
Incorrect number of arguments
Usage: lookup name
$
```

Some Unix systems will automatically make $0 a full pathname including directories, which can lead to some clunky error and usage messages. In that instance, use $(basename $0) or utilize the trick from earlier to chop out the path name:

```
${0##*/}
```

The `set` Command

The shell's `set` command also serves two purposes: it's used both to set various shell options and to reassign the positional parameters $1, $2, and so on... .

The `-x` Option

Earlier, in Chapter 7 we briefly looked at using `sh -x ctype` as a way to help debug problems in a shell program, but the `set` command lets you actually turn on and off trace mode for specific portions of your program.

Within a program, the statement

```
set -x
```

enables trace mode, which means all subsequently executed commands will be printed to standard error by the shell, after filename, variable, and command substitution, as well as I/O redirection have been performed. The traced commands are preceded by plus signs.

```
$ x=*
$ set -x                          Set command trace option
$ echo $x
+ echo add greetings lu rem rolo
add greetings lu rem rolo
$ cmd=wc
+ cmd=wc
$ ls | $cmd -l
+ ls
+ wc -l
      5
$
```

You can turn off trace mode at any time simply by executing `set` with the +x option:

```
$ set +x
+ set +x
$ ls | wc -l
         5                        Back to normal
$
```

Note that the trace option is *not* passed down to subshells. But you can trace a subshell's execution either by invoking the program with the `sh -x` option followed by the name of the program, as in

```
sh -x rolo
```

or you can insert a series of `set -x` and `set +x` commands within the program itself. In fact, you can insert any number of `set -x` and `set +x` commands inside your program to turn trace mode on and off as desired!

set **with No Arguments**

If you don't give any arguments to set, you'll get an alphabetized list of all the variables that exist in the current environment, local or exported:

```
$ set                          Show me all variables
CDPATH=:/users/steve:/usr/spool
EDITOR=/bin/vi
HOME=/users/steve
IFS=

LOGNAME=steve
MAIL=/usr/spool/mail/steve
MAILCHECK=600
PATH=/bin:/usr/bin:/users/steve/bin:.:
PHONEBOOK=/users/steve/phonebook
PS1=$
PS2=>
PWD=/users/steve/misc
SHELL=/usr/bin/sh
TERM=xterm
TMOUT=0
TZ=EST5EDT
cmd=wc
x=*
$
```

Using set **to Reassign Positional Parameters**

You'll recall that there's no way to assign a new value to or reassign the value of a positional parameter. Attempts to reassign $1 to be 100, for example, might be logically written like this:

```
1=100
```

But it won't work. Positional parameters are set upon invocation of the shell program.

However, there's a sneaky trick: you can use set to change the value. If words are given as arguments to set on the command line, the positional parameters $1, $2, ... will be assigned to those words. The previous values stored in the positional parameters will be lost. Within a shell program then, the command

```
set a b c
```

will assign a to $1, b to $2, and c to $3. $# also gets set to 3 as appropriate for the new argument count.

Here's a more involved example:

```
$ set one two three four
$ echo $1:$2:$3:$4
```

```
one:two:three:four
$ echo $#                       This should be 4
4
$ echo $*            What does this reference now?
one two three four
$ for arg; do echo $arg; done
one
two
three
four
$
```

After execution of the set, everything works as expected: $#, $*, and the for loop without a list all reflect the change in positional parameter values.

set is often used in this fashion to "parse" data read from a file or the terminal. Here's a program called words that counts the number of words typed on a line (using the shell's definition of a "word"):

```
$ cat words
#
# Count words on a line
#

read line
set $line
echo $#
$ words                              Run it
Here's a line for you to count.
7
$
```

The program reads the user input, storing the line read in the shell variable line, then executes the command

```
set $line
```

This causes each word stored in line to be assigned to the appropriate positional parameter. The variable $# is also set to the number of words assigned, which is also the number of words on the line.

The -- Option

The above works fine, but what happens if for some reason the user input starts with a - symbol?

```
$ words
-1 + 5 = 4
words: -1: bad option(s)
$
```

Here's what happened: After the line was read and assigned to `line`, the command

```
set $line
```

was executed and after the shell did its substitution, the command looked like this:

```
set -1 + 5 = 4
```

When `set` executed, it saw the - and thought that an invalid option, `-1`, was being selected. That explains the error message.

Another problem with `words` occurs if you give it a line consisting entirely of whitespace characters, or if the line is null:

```
$ words
                 Just Enter is pressed
CDPATH=.:/users/steve:/usr/spool
EDITOR=/bin/vi
HOME=/users/steve
IFS=

LOGNAME=steve
MAIL=/usr/spool/mail/steve
MAILCHECK=600
PATH=/bin:/usr/bin:/users/steve/bin:.:
PHONEBOOK=/users/steve/phonebook
PS1=$
PS2=>
PWD=/users/steve/misc
SHELL=/usr/bin/sh
TERM=xterm
TMOUT=0
TZ=EST5EDT
cmd=wc
x=*
0
$
```

In the latter case the shell saw the `set` command, but no arguments, so it output a list of all variables in the shell.

To protect against both of these problems occurring, use the `--` option to `set`. This tells `set` not to interpret any subsequent dashes or argument-format words it encounters on the command line as options. It also prevents `set` from displaying all your variables if no other arguments follow, as was the case when you typed a null line.

Reflecting this, the `set` command in `words` should be changed to read

```
set -- $line
```

With the addition of a `while` loop and some integer arithmetic, the `words` program can now
be modified to count the total number of words from standard input, essentially offering you
your own version of `wc -w`:

```
$ cat words
#
# Count all of the words on standard input
#

count=0
while read line
do
        set -- $line
        count=$(( count + $# ))
done

echo $count
$
```

After each line is read, the `set` command assigns all the positional parameters to the new line
of information, which resets `$#` to the number of words on the line. The `--` option is included
in case any of the lines begins with a `-` or is blank or lacks any alphanumeric characters.

The value of `$#` is then added to the variable `count`, and the next line is read. When the loop
is exited due to the end of file being encountered, the value of `count` is displayed; that is, the
total number of words read.

```
$ words < /etc/passwd
567
$ wc -w < /etc/passwd          Check against wc
567
$
```

We admit, this is a rather weird way to figure out how many words are in a file, but as you can
see, the `set` command is more versatile than most Unix users realize.

Here's a quick way to count the number of files in your directory:

```
$ set *
$ echo $#
8
$
```

This is much faster than

```
ls | wc -l
```

because the first method uses only shell built-in commands. In general, your shell programs
run much faster if you try to get as much done as you can using the shell's built-in commands.

Other Options to `set`

`set` accepts several other options, each enabled by preceding the option with a -, and disabled by preceding it with a +. The -x option that we have described here is the most commonly used but others are summarized in Appendix A, Table A.9.

The `IFS` Variable

There is a special shell variable called `IFS`, which stands for *internal field separator*. The shell uses the value of this variable when parsing input from the `read` command, output from command substitution (the back-quoting mechanism), and when performing variable substitution. Succinctly, `IFS` contains a set of characters that are used as whitespace separators. If it's typed on the command line, the shell treats it like a normal whitespace character (that is, as a word delimiter).

See what it's set to now:

```
$ echo "$IFS"

$
```

Well, that wasn't very illuminating! To determine the actual characters stored in there, pipe the output from `echo` into the `od` *(octal dump)* command with the -b *(byte display)* option:

```
$ echo "$IFS" | od -b
0000000 040 011 012 012
0000004
$
```

The first column of numbers shown is the relative offset from the start of the input. The following numbers are the octal equivalents of the characters read by `od`. The first such number is 040, which is the ASCII value of the space character. It's followed by 011, the tab character, and then by 012, the newline character. The next character is another newline which was added by `echo`. This set of characters for `IFS` should come as no surprise; they're the whitespace characters we've talked about throughout the book.

Where this gets interesting is the fact that you can change `IFS` to any character or character set desired. This can be particularly useful when you want to parse a line of data whose fields aren't delimited by the normal whitespace characters.

For example, we noted that the shell normally strips leading whitespace characters from the beginning of any line that you read with the `read` command. Change `IFS` to just a newline character before the `read` is executed, however, and it will preserve the leading whitespace (because the shell won't consider it a field delimiter):

```
$ read line                        Try it the "old" way
            Here's a line
$ echo "$line"
Here's a line
```

```
$ IFS="
>  "                                Set it to a just a newline
$ read line                         Try it again
        Here's a line
$ echo "$line"
        Here's a line               Leading spaces preserved
$
```

To change IFS to just a newline, an open quote was typed, followed immediately by pressing the Enter key, followed by the closing quote on the next line. No additional characters can be typed inside those quotes because they'll be stored inside IFS and then used by the shell.

Now let's change IFS to something more visible, the colon:

```
$ IFS=:
$ read x y z
123:345:678
$ echo $x
123
$ echo $z
678
$ list="one:two:three"
$ for x in $list; do echo $x; done
one
two
three
$ var=a:b:c
$ echo "$var"
a:b:c
$
```

Because IFS was changed to a colon, when the line was read, the shell divided it into three words: 123, 345, and 678, which were then stored into the three variables x, y, and z. In the next-to-last example, the shell used IFS when substituting the value of list in the for loop. The last example demonstrates that the shell doesn't use IFS when performing variable assignment.

Changing IFS is often done in conjunction with the set command:

```
$ line="Micro Logic Corp.:Box 174:Hackensack, NJ 07602"
$ IFS=:
$ set $line
$ echo $#                           How many parameters were set?
3
$ for field; do echo $field; done
Micro Logic Corp.
Box 174
Hackensack, NJ 07602
$
```

This technique is a powerful one because it uses all built-in shell commands which makes it very fast. This technique is used in the final version of the rolo program as presented in Chapter 13.

The following program, called number2 is a final version of the line numbering program presented in Chapter 9. This program prints the input lines to standard output, preceded by a line number, modifying IFS to ensure that leading spaces and other whitespace characters on each line of input are faithfully stored and reproduced, unlike the earlier version of the program. Notice also the use of printf to right-align the line numbers.

```
$ cat number2
#
# Number lines from files given as argument or from
# standard input if none supplied (final version)
#

# Modify the IFS to preserve leading whitespace on input

IFS='
'    # Just a newline appears between the quotes

lineno=1

cat $* |
while read -r line
do
        printf "%5d:%s\n" $lineno "$line"
        lineno=$(( lineno + 1 ))
done
```

Here's a sample execution of number:

```
$ number2 words
    1:#
    2:# Count all of the words on standard input
    3:#
    4:
    5:count=0
    6:while read line
    7:do
    8:  set -- $line
    9:  count=$(( count + $# ))
   10:done
   11:
   12:echo $count
$
```

Because IFS has an influence on the way things are interpreted by the shell, if you're going to change it in your program it's usually wise to save the old value first in another variable (such as OIFS) and then restore it after you've finished the operations.

The readonly Command

The readonly command is used to specify variables whose values cannot be subsequently changed. For example,

```
readonly PATH HOME
```

marks both PATH and HOME variables as read-only. Subsequent attempts to assign a value to either variable causes the shell to issue an error message:

```
$ PATH=/bin:/usr/bin:.:
$ readonly PATH
$ PATH=$PATH:/users/steve/bin
sh: PATH: is read-only
$
```

Here you see that after the variable PATH was made read-only, the shell printed an error message when an attempt was made to assign a value to it.

To get a list of your read-only variables, type readonly -p without any arguments:

```
$ readonly -p
readonly PATH=/bin:/usr/bin:.:
$
```

The read-only variable attribute is not passed down to subshells. Also, after a variable has been made read-only in a shell, there is no way to "undo" it.

The unset Command

Sometimes you may want to remove the definition of a variable from your environment. To do so, you type unset followed by the names of the variables:

```
$ x=100
$ echo $x
100
$ unset x              Remove x from the environment
$ echo $x

$
```

You can't unset a read-only variable. Furthermore, the variables IFS, MAILCHECK, PATH, PS1, and PS2 cannot be unset.

12

Loose Ends

We've put commands and features into this chapter that did not fit into earlier chapters. There's no particular rationale for their order of presentation, so this is your chance to simply expand your knowledge of shell programming tricks and techniques.

The `eval` Command

This section describes one of the more unusual shell commands: `eval`. Its format is as follows:

```
eval command-line
```

where `command-line` is a normal command line that you would type at the terminal. When you put `eval` in front of it, however, the effect is that the shell scans the command line *twice* before executing it, which can be very useful if the script is building a command that needs to be invoked, among other purposes.

For the simple case, using `eval` seems to have no effect:

```
$ eval echo hello
hello
$
```

But consider the following example without the use of `eval`:

```
$ pipe="|"
$ ls $pipe wc -l
|: No such file or directory
wc: No such file or directory
-1: No such file or directory
$
```

Those `ls` errors are because the value of `pipe` and the subsequent call to `wc -l` are all interpreted as command arguments. The shell takes care of pipes and I/O redirection *before* variable substitution, so it never properly interprets the pipe symbol inside `pipe`.

Putting `eval` in front of the command sequence gives the desired results, however:

```
$ eval ls $pipe wc -l
     16
$
```

The first time the shell scans the command line, it substitutes | as the value of pipe.
Then eval causes it to rescan the line, at which point the | is recognized by the shell as the
pipe symbol and everything proceeds as desired.

The eval command is frequently used in shell programs that build up command lines inside
one or more variables. If the variables contain any characters that must be interpreted by
the shell, eval is essential. Command terminator (;, |, &), I/O redirection (<, >), and quote
characters are among the characters that must appear directly on the command line to have
special meaning to the shell.

For the next example, consider the program last whose sole purpose is to display the last
argument passed to it. Recall the mycp program from Chapter 9 where we accomplished this
task by shifting all the arguments until only one was left.

It turns out you can accomplish the same result by using eval:

```
$ cat last
eval echo \$$#
$ last one two three four
four
$ last *                         Get the last file
zoo_report
$
```

The first time the shell scans

```
echo \$$#
```

the backslash tells it to ignore the $ that immediately follows. After that, it encounters the
special parameter $#, so it substitutes its value on the command line. The command now looks
like this:

```
echo $4
```

The backslash is removed by the shell after the first scan. When the shell rescans this line, it
substitutes the value of $4 and then executes echo.

This same technique could be used if you had a variable called arg that contained a digit, for
example, and you wanted to display the positional parameter referenced by arg. You could
simply write

```
eval echo \$$arg
```

The only problem with this approach is that only the first nine positional parameters can be
accessed this way because accessing positional parameters 10 and above requires the ${n}
notation. So here's a second attempt:

```
eval echo \${$arg}
```

The eval command can also be used to effectively create "pointers" to variables:

```
$ x=100
$ ptrx=x
$ eval echo \$$ptrx          Dereference ptrx
100
$ eval $ptrx=50              Store 50 in var that ptrx points to
$ echo $x                    See what happened
50
$
```

The wait Command

If you move a command into the background for execution, that command line runs in a subshell independent of your current shell (the job is said to run *asynchronously*). In some situations, however, you may want to wait for the background process (also known as a *child* process because it's spawned from your current shell—the *parent*) to finish execution before proceeding. For example, you may have sent a large sort into the background and need to wait for it to finish before you access the sorted data.

The wait command does the job. Its general format is

```
wait process-id
```

where `process-id` is the process ID of the process you want to complete. If the process ID is omitted, the shell waits for all child processes to complete execution. Execution of your current shell will be suspended until the process or processes finish execution.

You can try the wait command at your terminal:

```
$ sort big-data > sorted_data &          Send it to the background
[1] 3423                                  Job number & process id from the shell
$ date                                    Do some other work
Wed Oct  2 15:05:42 EDT 2002
$ wait 3423                               Now wait for the sort to finish
$                                         When sort finishes, prompt is returned
```

The $! Variable

If you have only one process running in the background, then wait with no argument suffices. However, if you're running more than one background command and you want to wait on the most recently launched, you can access the process ID of the most recent background command as the special variable $!. So the command

```
wait $!
```

waits for the last process sent to the background to complete execution. With some intermediate variables involved, you can also save their process ID values for later access too:

```
prog1 &
pid1=$!
...
prog2 &
pid2=$!
...
wait $pid1        # wait for prog1 to finish
...
wait $pid2        # wait for prog2 to finish
```

Tip: Want to test if a process you've launched is still running? The ps command can check if you use the -p flag and the process ID.

The trap Command

When you press the DELETE or BREAK key at your terminal during execution of a shell program, that program is typically terminated and you're prompted for your next command. This may not always be desirable in shell programs. For instance, you may end up leaving a bunch of temporary files that won't get cleaned up as they would on normal program completion.

Pressing the DELETE key sends what's known as a *signal* to the executing program, and programs can specify what action should be taken on receipt of the signal rather than just relying on default actions like immediately exiting the process.

Signal handling in a shell program is done with the trap command, whose general format is

```
trap commands signals
```

where *commands* is one or more commands that will be executed whenever any of the signals specified by *signals* is received.

Mnemonic names and numbers are assigned to the different types of signals, and the more commonly used ones are summarized in Table 12.1. A more complete list is given under the trap command in Appendix A.

Table 12.1 **Commonly Used Signal Numbers**

Signal	Mnemonic Name	Generated for
0	EXIT	Exit from the shell
1	HUP	Hangup
2	INT	Interrupt (for example, DELETE, *Ctrl+c* key)
15	TERM	Software termination signal (sent by kill by default)

As an example of the `trap` command, the following shows how you can remove some files and then exit if someone tries to interrupt the program from the terminal:

```
trap "rm $WORKDIR/work1$$ $WORKDIR/dataout$$; exit" INT
```

Once this `trap` is executed, the two files `work1$$` and `dataout$$` will be automatically removed if a `SIGINT` (signal number 2) is received by the program. If the user interrupts execution of the program after this `trap` is executed, you can be assured that these two temporary files will be removed, not left around in the file system. The `exit` that follows the `rm` is necessary because without it execution would continue in the program at the point that it left off when the signal was received.

Signal number 1—`SIGHUP` or just `HUP`—is generated for hangup: originally this related to dialup connections, but now more generally refers to an unexpected disconnect like the Internet connection dropping. You can modify the preceding `trap` to also remove the two specified files in this case by adding a `SIGINT` to the list of signals:

```
trap "rm $WORKDIR/work1$$ $WORKDIR/dataout$$; exit'' INT HUP
```

Now these files will be removed if the line gets hung up or if the user interrupts processing with the DELETE key or Ctrl+c.

The sequence specified to `trap` (also known as the *trap handler*) must be enclosed in quotes if it contains more than one command. Also note that the shell scans the command line at the time that the `trap` command gets executed and also again when one of the listed signals is received.

In the preceding example, the value of `WORKDIR` and `$$` will be substituted at the time that the `trap` command is executed. If you wanted this substitution to occur at the time that a signal was received, you can put the commands inside single quotes:

```
trap 'rm $WORKDIR/work1$$ $WORKDIR/dataout$$; exit' INT HUP
```

The `trap` command can be used to make your programs more user friendly too. In a further revision to the `rolo` program in the next chapter, the *Ctrl+c* interrupt signal will be caught by the program and return the user to the main menu, not have the program quit completely.

`trap` with No Arguments

Executing `trap` with no arguments results in the display of any trap handlers that you have defined or modified:

```
$ trap 'echo logged off at $(date) >>$HOME/logoffs' EXIT
$ trap                      List changed traps
trap - 'echo logged off at $(date) >>$HOME/logoffs' EXIT
$ Ctrl+d                    Log off
login: steve                Log back in
Password:
$ cat $HOME/logoffs         See what happened
logged off at Wed Oct  2 15:11:58 EDT 2002
$
```

A trap was set to be executed whenever the shell exited—signal 0, EXIT—was received by the shell. Because this was set in the login shell, the trap handler is used when you log off to write the time you logged off into the file $HOME/logoffs. The command is enclosed in single quotes to prevent the shell from executing date when the trap is defined.

The trap command is then executed with no arguments which lists the new action to be taken for signal 0 (EXIT). When steve then logs off and back on again, the file $HOME/logoffs verifies that the echo command was executed and the trap worked.

Ignoring Signals

If the command listed for trap is null, the specified signal will be ignored when received. For example, the command

```
trap "" SIGINT
```

specifies that the interrupt signal is to be ignored. You might want to ignore certain signals when performing some operation that you don't want interrupted.

Note that trap lets you specify signals by signal number, by shortened name (INT) or by the full signal name (SIGINT). We encourage you to use mnemonic names to help produce readable code, but it is, of course, up to you which you prefer.

In the above example, the first argument must be specified as a null value for a signal to be ignored and is not equivalent to writing the following, which has a separate meaning of its own:

```
trap 2
```

If you ignore a signal, all subshells also ignore that signal. If you specify a signal handler action, however, all subshells will automatically take the *default* action on receipt of that signal, not the new code sequence.

Suppose that you execute the command

```
trap "" 2
```

and then start a subshell, which in turn executes other shell programs as subshells. If an interrupt signal is then generated, it will have no effect on the shells or subshells that are executing because they will all ignore the signal by default.

If instead of executing the previous trap command you execute

```
trap : 2
```

and then execute your subshells, then the current shell will do nothing on receipt of an interrupt (it will execute the null command), while subshells will be terminated (the default action).

Resetting Traps

After you've changed the default action to be taken on receipt of a signal, you can change it back again with `trap` if you simply omit the first argument; so

```
trap HUP INT
```

resets the action to be taken on receipt of the SIGHUP or SIGINT signals back to the default behavior for the shell.

Many shell programs also use a construct like this

```
trap "/bin/rm -f $tempfile; exit" INT QUIT EXIT
```

to ensure that the `rm` command won't produce an error message if the temporary file hasn't yet been created upon exit. The trap handler removes the temporary file if it exists and does nothing if it doesn't.

More on I/O

You know about the standard constructs `<`, `>`, and `>>` for input redirection, output redirection, and output redirection with append, respectively. You also know that you can redirect standard error from any command simply by writing `2>` instead of just `>`:

```
command 2> file
```

Sometimes you may want to explicitly write to standard error in your program. With a slight variation on the above, you can redirect standard output to standard error by writing

```
command >&2
```

The notation `>&` specifies output redirection to a file associated with the *file descriptor* that follows. File descriptor 0 is standard input, descriptor 1 is standard output, and descriptor 2 is standard error. It's important to remember that no space is permitted between the `>` and the `&`.

To write a message to standard error:

```
echo "Invalid number of arguments" >&2
```

You may want to redirect both standard output (often abbreviated "stdout") and standard error output ("stderr") from a program into the same file. If you know the name of the file, this is straightforward:

```
command > foo 2>> foo
```

Here both stdout and stderr will be written to `foo`.

You can also write

```
command > foo 2>&1
```

to achieve the same effect; standard output is redirected to `foo`, and standard error is redirected to standard output (which has already been redirected to `foo`). Because the shell evaluates redirection from left to right on the command line, the last example won't work properly if the stderr redirection sequence appears first on the command line

```
command 2>&1 > foo
```

because this would first redirect standard error to standard output then standard output to `foo`.

You can also dynamically redirect standard input or output in a program using the `exec` command:

```
exec < datafile
```

redirects standard input from the file `datafile`. Subsequent commands executed that read from standard input will read from `datafile` instead. The command

```
exec > /tmp/output
```

does the same thing with standard output: all commands that subsequently write to standard output will write to `/tmp/output` unless explicitly redirected elsewhere.

Naturally, standard error can be reassigned as well:

```
exec 2> /tmp/errors
```

All subsequent output to standard error will go to `/tmp/errors`.

`<&-` and `>&-`

The sequence `>&-` has the effect of closing standard output. If preceded by a file descriptor, the associated file is closed instead. So writing

```
ls >&-
```

causes the output from `ls` to go nowhere because standard output is closed by the shell before `ls` is executed. Not hugely useful, we admit!

In-line Input Redirection

If the `<<` characters follow a command in the format

```
command <<word
```

the shell uses the lines that follow as the input for *command*, until a line that contains just *word* is found. Here's a simple example:

```
$ wc -l <<ENDOFDATA          Use lines up to ENDOFDATA as standard input
> here's a line
> and another
> and yet another
> ENDOFDATA
      3
$
```

The shell fed every line typed into the shell as the standard input stream of wc until it encountered the line containing just ENDOFDATA.

In-line input redirection—also referred to as *here documents* by some programmers—is a powerful feature when used inside shell programs. It lets you specify the standard input to a command directly in the program, thus obviating the need to write it into a separate file, or to use echo to get it into the standard input of the command.

Here's a common example of how this feature is used within a shell program:

```
$ cat mailmsg
mail $* <<END-OF-DATA

Attention:

Our monthly computer users group meeting
will take place on Friday, March 4, 2016 at
8pm in Room 1A-308. Please try to attend.

END-OF-DATA
$
```

To send this message to all members of the group as stored in the file users_list, you could invoke

```
mailmsg $(cat users_list)
```

The shell performs parameter substitution for the redirected input data, executes back-quoted commands, and recognizes the backslash character.

Special characters within a *here document* are generally ignored, but if you include dollar signs, back quotes, or backslashes in these lines, they can be interpreted. To have them ignored, precede them with a backslash character. Alternatively, if you want the shell to leave all input lines completely untouched, precede the end of document word that follows the << with a backslash.

Let's highlight the difference between the two:

```
$ cat <<FOOBAR
> $HOME
> *****
>     \$foobar
> `date`
> FOOBAR                          Terminates the input
/users/steve
*****
    $foobar
Wed Oct  2 15:23:15 EDT 2002
$
```

Since the shell supplies all the lines up to FOOBAR as the input to cat it substitutes the value for HOME but not for foobar because the latter is prefaced with a backslash. The date command is also executed because back quotes are interpreted by the shell.

To side-step all the issues with the shell interpreting the contents of the lines, use backslash *on the end-of-document word* instead:

```
$ cat <<\FOOBAR
> \\\\
> `date`
> $HOME
> FOOBAR
\\\\
`date`
$HOME
$
```

Use care when selecting the word that follows the <<. Generally, just make sure that it's weird enough so that the chances of it accidentally appearing in the subsequent lines of data are miniscule.

You now know about the <<\ sequence, but there's another one that most modern shells understand: If the first character that follows the << is a dash (-), any leading tab characters in the input will be removed by the shell. This is useful for visually indenting the redirected text for readability while still having it output appear in normal left-aligned form:

```
$ cat <<-END
>            Indented lines
>            because tabs are cool
> END
Indented lines
because tabs are cool
$
```

Shell Archives

One of the best uses of the in-line input redirection feature is for creating *shell archive* files. With this technique, one or more related shell programs can be put into a single file and then sent to someone else using the standard Unix mail commands. When the archive is received, it can be "unpacked" by invoking it as a shell program.

For example, here's an archived version of the lu, add, and rem programs used by rolo:

```
$ cat rolosubs
#
# Archived programs used by rolo.
#

echo Extracting lu
```

```
cat >lu <<\THE-END-OF-DATA
#
# Look someone up in the phone book
#

if [ "$#" -ne 1 ]
then
        echo "Incorrect number of arguments"
        echo "Usage: lu name"
        exit 1
fi

name=$1
grep "$name" $PHONEBOOK

if [ $? -ne 0 ]
then
        echo "I couldn't find $name in the phone book"
fi
THE-END-OF-DATA

echo Extracting add
cat >add <<\THE-END-OF-DATA
#
# Program to add someone to the phonebook file
#

if [ "$#" -ne 2 ]
then
        echo "Incorrect number of arguments"
        echo "Usage: add name number"
        exit 1
fi

echo "$1     $2" >> $PHONEBOOK
sort -o $PHONEBOOK $PHONEBOOK
THE-END-OF-DATA

echo Extracting rem
cat >rem <<\THE-END-OF-DATA
#
# Remove someone from the phone book
#

if [ "$#" -ne 1 ]
then
        echo "Incorrect number of arguments"
```

```
            echo "Usage: rem name"
            exit 1
fi

name=$1

#
# Find number of matching entries
#

matches=$(grep "$name" $PHONEBOOK | wc -1)

#
# If more than one match, issue message, else remove it
#

if [ "$matches" -gt 1 ]
then
        echo "More than one match; please qualify further"
elif [ "$matches" -eq 1 ]
then
        grep -v "$name" $PHONEBOOK > /tmp/phonebook
        mv /tmp/phonebook $PHONEBOOK
else
        echo "I couldn't find $name in the phone book"
fi
THE-END-OF-DATA
$
```

To be complete, this archive would include rolo as well, but we didn't include it here to conserve space in the book.

This shell archive offers one portable file, rolosubs, that contains the source for all three programs lu, add, and rem, and can be sent to someone else using mail:

`$ mail tony@aisystems.com < rolosubs`	*Mail the archive*
`$ mail tony@aisystems.com`	*Mail tony a message*

```
Tony,
     I mailed you a shell archive containing the programs
     lu, add, and rem. rolo itself will be sent along shortly.
Pat
Ctrl+d
$
```

When tony receives the file in his mail, she can extract the three programs by saving the message, then running the shell on the file (after having first removed any email header lines that might have ended up in the beginning of the file):

```
$ sh rolosubs
Extracting lu
Extracting add
Extracting rem
$ ls lu add rem
add
lu
rem
$
```

To generalize this process, here's a simple shell program, shar, that can produce a shell archive that contains every specified script in a neat, ready-to-email format:

```
$ cat shar
#
# Program to create a shell archive
# from a set of files
#

echo "#"
echo "# To restore, type sh archive"
echo "#"

for file
do
    echo
    echo "echo Extracting $file"
    echo "cat >$file <<\THE-END-OF-DATA"
    cat $file
    echo "THE-END-OF-DATA"
done
```

Flip back to look at the contents of the rolosubs file when studying the operation of this shar program and remember, shar actually creates a shell program, not just a generic output file.

More sophisticated archiving programs allow entire directories to be included and use various techniques to ensure that no data is lost in the transmission (see Exercises 2 and 3 at the end of this chapter).

The sum and cksum commands can be used to generate a *checksum* for a program too. This checksum can be generated on the sending end for each file in the archive, and then the shell archive can verify the checksum for each unpacked file on the receiving end. If they don't match, an error message can be displayed and the user will be alerted something went wrong with the process.

Functions

All modern shells support functions—long or short sequences of commands that can be referenced or reused as often as desired in a shell program.

To define a function, you use the general format:

name () { *command*; ... *command*; }

where *name* is the name of the function, the parentheses denote that a function is being defined, and the commands enclosed between the curly braces define the body of the function. These commands will be executed whenever the function is executed.

Note that at least one whitespace character must separate the { from the first command, and that a semicolon must separate the last command from the closing brace if they occur on the same line.

The following defines a function called nu that displays the number of logged-in users:

nu () { who | wc -l; }

You execute a function the same way you execute an ordinary command: by typing its name into the shell:

```
$ nu
     22
$
```

Functions are really useful for shell programmers and can alleviate lots of tedium in developing solutions. One key feature: arguments listed after the function on the command line are assigned to the positional parameters $1, $2, ..., within the function, just as with any other command.

Here's a function called nrrun that runs tbl, nroff, and lp on the file specified:

```
$ nrrun () { tbl $1 | nroff -mm -Tlp | lp; }
$ nrrun memo1                    Run it on memo1
request id is laser1-33 (standard input)
$
```

Functions exist only in the shell in which they're defined so they can't be passed to subshells. Because the function is executed in the current shell, changes made to the current directory or to variables remain after the function has completed execution, as if it had been invoked with the . command explored earlier in the book:

```
$ db () {
>        PATH=$PATH:/uxn2/data
>        PS1=DB:
>        cd /uxn2/data
>        }
$ db                             Execute it
DB:
```

A function definition can continue over as many lines as necessary. The shell will continue to prompt for commands within the function with the secondary command prompt until you complete the function definition with the }.

You can put definitions for commonly used functions inside your .profile so that they'll be available whenever you log in. Alternatively, you can group the definitions in a file, say myfuncs, and then execute the file in the current shell by typing

. myfuncs

As you now know, this causes any functions defined inside myfuncs to become available in the current shell.

The following function, called mycd, takes advantage of the fact that functions are run in the current environment. It mimics the operation of the Korn shell's cd command, which has the capability of substituting portions of the current directory's path (see the discussion of cd in Chapter 14 for more explanation).

```
$ cat myfuncs                    See what's inside
#
# new cd function:
#      mycd dir Switches dir
#      mycd old new  Substitute new for old in current directory's path
#
mycd ()
{
        if [ $# -le 1 ] ; then
                # normal case -- 0 or 1 argument
                cd $1
        elif [ $# -eq 2 ] ; then
                # special case -- substitute $2 for $1
                cd $(echo $PWD | sed "s|$1|$2|")
        else
                # cd can't have more than two arguments
                echo mycd: bad argument count
                exit 1
        fi
}

$ . myfuncs                      Read in definition
$ pwd
/users/steve
$ mycd /users/pat                Change directory
$ pwd                            Did it work?
/users/pat
$ mycd pat tony                  Substitute tony for pat
$ pwd
/users/tony
$
```

Functions execute faster than an equivalent shell program because the shell doesn't have to search the disk for the program, open the file, and read its contents into memory; it can just jump right into executing the individual commands directly.

Another advantage of functions is the capability to group related shell programs in a single file. For example, the add, lu, and rem programs from Chapter 10 can now be defined as individual functions within the rolo program file. The template for such an approach is shown:

```
$ cat rolo
#
# rolo program written in function form
#

#
# Function to add someone to the phonebook file
#

add () {
        # put commands from add program here
}

#
# Function to look someone up in the phone book
#

lu () {
        # put commands from lu program here
}

#
# Function to remove someone from the phone book
#

rem () {
        # put commands from rem program here
}

#
# rolo - rolodex program to look up, add, and
#        remove people from the phone book
#

# put commands from rolo here
$
```

None of the commands inside the original add, lu, rem, or rolo programs would have to be changed. The first three are turned into functions by including them inside rolo, sandwiched between the function header and the closing curly brace. Defining them as functions would, however, make them inaccessible as standalone commands.

Removing a Function Definition

To remove the definition of a function from the shell, use the `unset` command with the `-f` option. Look familiar? It is the same command you use to remove the definition of a variable from the shell.

```
$ unset -f nu
$ nu
sh: nu: not found
$
```

The `return` Command

If you use `exit` from inside a function, its effect is not only to terminate execution of the function but also of the shell program that called the function. It exits all the way back to the command line. If you instead want to just exit the function, use the `return` command, whose format is

```
return n
```

The value *n* is used as the return status of the function. If omitted, the status is that of the last command executed. This is also what gets returned if you don't include a `return` statement in your function. The return status is in all other ways equivalent to the exit status: you can access its value through the shell variable `$?`, and you can test it in `if`, `while`, and `until` commands.

The `type` Command

When you type in the name of a command to execute, it's useful to know whether the command is a function, a shell built-in function, a standard Unix command or even a shell alias. This is where the `type` command comes in handy. The `type` command takes one or more command names as its argument and tells you what it knows about it. Here are some examples:

```
$ nu () { who | wc -l; }
$ type pwd
pwd is a shell builtin
$ type ls
ls is aliased to `/bin/ls -F'
$ type cat
cat is /bin/cat
$ type nu
nu is a function
$
```

## 13

Rolo Revisited

This chapter presents the final, much improved version of the `rolo` program enhanced with additional options and also allows for more general types of entries (other than just names and numbers). The sections in this chapter discuss the individual components of `rolo`, starting with the main `rolo` program itself. At the end of this chapter, sample output is shown.

Data Formatting Considerations

While the initial name-and-number `rolo` program shown earlier in the book is handy, there's no question that a more useful program would allow more than just the names and numbers to be stored. You'd probably want to save addresses and email addresses too, for example. The new `rolo` program allows entries in the phone book to consist of multiple lines. A typical entry might be

```
Steve's Ice Cream
444 6th Avenue
New York City 10003
212-555-3021
```

To increase the flexibility of the program, an individual entry can now contain as many lines as desired. Another entry in the phone book might read

```
YMCA
(201) 555-2344
```

To logically separate entries in the phone book file, each entry is "packed" into a single line by replacing the terminating newline characters in an entry with a different character. We arbitrarily chose the caret ^ as it appears very rarely in regular user input, addresses, etc. The only repercussion of this decision is that this character cannot be used as part of the entry itself.

Using this technique, the first entry shown would be stored in the phone book file as

```
Steve's Ice Cream^444 6th Avenue^New York City 10003^212-555-3021^
```

and the second entry as

```
YMCA^(201) 555-2344^
```

It now becomes quite easy to work with entries when they're stored in this format, a testament to how really thinking through a problem and solution can reap great benefits as it's developed further.

rolo

```
#
# rolo - rolodex program to look up, add,
#         remove and change entries from the phone book
#


#
# Set PHONEBOOK to point to the phone book file
# and export it so other progs know about it
# if it's set on entry, then leave it alone
#

: ${PHONEBOOK:=$HOME/phonebook}
export PHONEBOOK
if [ ! -e "$PHONEBOOK" ] ; then
      echo "$PHONEBOOK does not exist!"
      echo "Should I create it for you (y/n)? \c"
      read answer

      if [ "$answer" != y ] ; then
            exit 1
      fi

      > $PHONEBOOK || exit 1        # exit if the creation fails
fi


#
# If arguments are supplied, then do a lookup
#

if [ "$#" -ne 0 ] ; then
      lu "$@"
      exit
fi


#
# Set trap on interrupt (DELETE key) to continue the loop
#
```

```
trap "continue" SIGINT

#
# Loop until user selects 'exit'
#

while true
do
        #
        # Display menu
        #

        echo '
Would you like to:

        1. Look someone up
        2. Add someone to the phone book
        3. Remove someone from the phone book
        4. Change an entry in the phone book
        5. List all names and numbers in the phone book
        6. Exit this program

Please select one of the above (1-6): \c'

        #
        # Read and process selection
        #

        read choice
        echo
        case "$choice"
        in
            1) echo "Enter name to look up: \c"
               read name

               if [ -z "$name" ] ; then
                        echo "Lookup ignored"
               else
                        lu "$name"
               fi;;
            2) add;;
            3) echo "Enter name to remove: \c"
               read name
               if [ -z "$name" ] ; then
                        echo "Removal ignored"
               else
                        rem "$name"
               fi;;
```

```
       4) echo "Enter name to change: \c"
          read name
          if [ -z "$name" ] ; then
                  echo "Change ignored"
          else
                  change "$name"
          fi;;
       5) listall;;
       6) exit 0;;
       *) echo "Bad choice\a";;
    esac
done
```

One improvement appears in the very beginning of the new code: Instead of requiring that the user already have a phone book file in their home directory, the program checks to see whether the variable PHONEBOOK has been set. If it has, it's assumed that it contains the name of the phone book file. If it hasn't, it's set to $HOME/phonebook as the default.

The program then checks to see whether the actual file exists, and if it doesn't, asks the user whether they would like to have it created. This greatly improves that first use experience, as you can imagine.

This version of rolo also has a couple of new choices on the menu too. Because individual entries can be rather long, an edit option now allows the user to update a particular entry. Prior to this, of course, the only way to change an entry was to remove it, then add a completely new entry.

Another option lists the entire phone book. With this option, just the first and last lines (fields) of each entry are displayed. This assumes that the user follows some convention such as putting the name on the first line and the number on the last.

The entire menu selection code block is also now inside a while loop so that rolo will continue to display menus until the user chooses to exit the program.

As per our discussion last chapter, notice that a trap command is executed before the loop is entered. This trap specifies that a continue command is to be executed if an interrupt (SIGINT) is generated by the user. If the user presses Ctrl+c in the middle of an operation (such as listing the entire phone book), the program will stop the current operation and redisplay the main menu.

Because entries can now span as many lines as desired, the action performed when add is selected has been changed too. Instead of asking for the name and number, rolo invokes the add program to get the entry and lets the function take care of prompting the user and figuring out when the data input is done.

For the lookup, change, and remove options, a check is now made to ensure that the user doesn't end a null value by pressing the Enter key when asked to type in the name. This avoids the regular expression error that grep would otherwise issue if given a null first argument.

Now let's look at the individual programs that `rolo` utilizes, with particular attention paid to how the change in data format ripples through the entire design. Each of the original programs has been changed to accommodate the new entry format and also to be more user friendly.

add

```
#
# Program to add someone to the phonebook file
#

echo "Type in your new entry"
echo "When you're done, type just a single Enter on the line."

first=
entry=

while true
do
      echo ">> \c"
      read line

      if [ -n "$line" ] ; then
              entry="$entry$line^"

              if [ -z "$first" ] ; then
                      first=$line
              fi
      else
              break
      fi
done


echo "$entry" >> $PHONEBOOK
sort -o $PHONEBOOK $PHONEBOOK
echo
echo "$first has been added to the phone book"
```

This program adds an entry to the phone book. It continually prompts the user to enter lines until a line with just an Enter is typed (that is, a completely blank line). Each line that is entered is appended to the variable entry, with the special ^ character used to logically separate fields.

When the while loop is exited, the new entry is added to the end of the phone book, and the file is sorted.

lu

```
#
# Look someone up in the phone book
#

name="$1"
grep -i "$name" $PHONEBOOK > /tmp/matches$$

if [ ! -s /tmp/matches$$ ] ; then
      echo "I can't find $name in the phone book"
else
      #
      # Display each of the matching entries
      #

      while read line
      do
              display "$line"
      done < /tmp/matches$$
fi

rm /tmp/matches$$
```

This is the program to look up an entry in the phone book. Now, however, matching entries are written to the file /tmp/matches$$ so we can improve the user experience in the situation where there are no matches.

If the size of this output file is zero (test -s), no match was found. Otherwise, the program enters a loop to read each matching line from the file and display it to the user. A new program called display is used to unwrap ^-separated fields and turn them into multi-line output entries. This new program is also used by the rem and change programs to display entries.

Also note the addition of the -i flag to grep in the script. This allows case-insensitive matches, so a search for "steve" will match "Steve." A good example of how a working knowledge of the flags to key Unix commands can easily make your scripts more powerful and easier to use.

display

```
#
# Display entry from the phonebook
#

echo
echo "--------------------------------------"
```

```
entry=$1
IFS="^"
set $entry

for line in "$1" "$2" "$3" "$4" "$5" "$6"
do
        printf "| %-34.34s |\n" $line
done
echo "|        o                    o       |"
echo "---------------------------------------"
echo
```

This program displays the caret-separated entry passed as its argument. To make the output more aesthetically interesting, the program actually "draws" a rolodex card. Typical output from display looks like this:

```
---------------------------------------
| Steve's Ice Cream                    |
| 444 6th Avenue                       |
| New York City  10003                 |
| 212-555-3021                         |
|                                      |
|                                      |
|        o                    o        |
---------------------------------------
```

Look at the code again and notice how after skipping a line and displaying the top of the card, display changes IFS to ^, then executes the set command to assign each "line" to a different positional parameter. For example, if entry is equal to

Steve's Ice Cream^444 6th Avenue^New York City 10003^212-555-3021^

executing the set command assigns Steve's Ice Cream to $1, 444 6th Avenue to $2, New York City 10003 to $3, and 212-555-3021 to $4.

After breaking down the fields with set, the program enters a for loop that, with this version of the code, will output six lines of data, no matter how many lines are contained in the entry. This ensures uniformity of rolodex cards and the program can be easily modified to "draw" larger-sized cards if desired.

If the set command was executed on Steve's Ice Cream as shown previously, $5 and $6 would be null, thus resulting in two blank lines to "fill out" the bottom of the card.

To ensure that the output is properly aligned on both left and right edges, the printf command is used to display a line exactly 38 characters wide: the leading | followed by a space followed by the first 34 characters of $line followed by a space and a |.

rem

```
#
# Remove someone from the phone book
#

name=$1

#
# Get matching entries and save in temp file
#

grep -i "$name" $PHONEBOOK > /tmp/matches$$
if [ ! -s /tmp/matches$$ ] ; then
        echo "I can't find $name in the phone book"
        exit 1
fi


#
# Display matching entries one at a time and confirm removal
#

while read line
do
        display "$line"
        echo "Remove this entry (y/n)? \c"
        read answer < /dev/tty

        if [ "$answer" = y ] ; then
                break
        fi
done < /tmp/matches$$

rm /tmp/matches$$

if [ "$answer" = y ] ; then
        if grep -i -v "^$line$" $PHONEBOOK > /tmp/phonebook$$
        then
                mv /tmp/phonebook$$ $PHONEBOOK
                echo "Selected entry has been removed"
        elif [ ! -s $PHONEBOOK ] ; then
                echo "Note: You now have an empty phonebook."
        else
                echo "Entry not removed"
        fi
 fi
```

The rem program collects all matching entries into a temporary file, then tests the result: If the size of the file is zero, no match was found and an error message is issued. Otherwise, for each matching entry, the program displays the entry and asks the user whether that entry should be removed.

From a user experience perspective, this type of coding practice provides reassurance to the user that the entry they intend to remove is the same one that the program is going to remove, even in the single match case.

After the user has answered the prompt with y, a break command exits the loop. Outside the loop, the program then tests the value of answer to determine how the loop was exited. If its value is not equal to y, then the user doesn't want to remove an entry after all (for whatever reason). Otherwise, the program proceeds with the requested removal by greping all lines that don't match the specified pattern. Note that grep matches only entire lines by anchoring the regular expression to the start and end of the line.

Note also that in the edge case of the user removing the last entry in their phonebook, the script now recognizes the situation (by testing to see if the file exists and is non-zero in size) and outputs an informative message. It's not an error, but it ensures that the failure message that would otherwise be triggered by the grep -v invocation isn't displayed.

change

```
#
# Change an entry in the phone book
#

name=$1

#
# Get matching entries and save in temp file
#

grep -i "$name" $PHONEBOOK > /tmp/matches$$
if [ ! -s /tmp/matches$$ ] ; then
        echo "I can't find $name in the phone book"
        exit 1
fi

#
# Display matching entries one at a time and confirm change
#

while read line
do
        display "$line"
        echo "Change this entry (y/n)? \c"
```

```
        read answer < /dev/tty

        if [ "$answer" = y ] ; then
                break
        fi
done < /tmp/matches$$

rm /tmp/matches$$

if [ "$answer" != y ] ; then
        exit
fi

#
# Start up editor on the confirmed entry
#

echo "$line\c" | tr '^' '\012' > /tmp/ed$$

echo "Enter changes with ${EDITOR:=/bin/vi}"
trap "" 2           # don't abort if DELETE hit while editing
$EDITOR /tmp/ed$$

#
# Remove old entry now and insert new one
#

grep -i -v "^$line$" $PHONEBOOK > /tmp/phonebook$$
{ tr '\012' '^' < /tmp/ed$$; echo; } >> /tmp/phonebook$$
# last echo was to put back trailing newline translated by tr

sort /tmp/phonebook$$ -o $PHONEBOOK
rm /tmp/ed$$ /tmp/phonebook$$
```

The change program allows the user to edit an entry in the phone book. The first portion of the code ends up virtually identical to rem: it finds the matching entries and then prompts the user to select which one to change.

The selected entry is then written into the temporary file /tmp/ed$$, with the ^ characters translated to newlines. This "unfolds" the entry into separate lines to be consistent with how rolo displays the entry and for easier editing. The program then displays the message

```
echo "Enter changes with ${EDITOR:=/bin/vi}"
```

This serves a dual purpose: it tells the user what editor will be used to make the change and sets the variable EDITOR to /bin/ed vi if it's not already set. This technique allows the user to use their preferred editor by simply assigning its name to the variable EDITOR before executing rolo:

$ **EDITOR=emacs rolo**

The signal generated by the DELETE key (2) is ignored so that if the user presses this key while in the editor, the change program won't abort. The editor is then launched so that the user can make whatever changes are required. Once done, the program continues by removing the old entry from the phone book file with grep, then the modified entry is converted back to having ^ field separators and appended to the end of the file. An extra newline character must be added here to make sure that a newline is stored in the file after the new entry, easily done with an echo with no arguments.

Finally, the phone book file is sorted and the temporary files removed.

listall

```
#
# list all of the entries in the phone book
#

IFS='^'       # to be used in set command below
echo "-------------------------------------------------------"
while read line
do
     #
     # Get the first and last fields, presumably names and numbers
     #

     set $line

     #
     # display 1st and last fields (in reverse order!)
     #

     eval printf "\"%-40.40s %s\\n\"" "\"$1\"" "\"\${$#}\""
done < $PHONEBOOK
echo "-------------------------------------------------------"
```

The listall program lists all entries in the phone book, printing just the first and last lines of each entry. The internal field separator characters (IFS) is set to a ^, to be used inside the loop. Each line from the file is then read and assigned to the variable line. The set command assigns each field to the appropriate positional parameter as shown earlier.

The challenge is to get the value of the first and last positional parameters. The first is easy because it can be directly referenced as $1. To get the last one, the program taps the power of eval as explained in Chapter 12. Specifically, the command

```
eval echo \${$#}
```

displays the value of the last positional parameter. In this particular program, it shows up in the command

```
eval printf "\"%-40.40s %-s\\n\"" "\"$1\"" "\"\${$#}\""
```

This is evaluated, for example, to

```
printf "%-40.40s %-s\n" "Steve's Ice Cream" "${4}"
```

using the entry shown previously, and then rescanned to substitute the value of ${4} before executing printf.

Sample Output

Now it's time to see how the new, much improved rolo works. We'll start with an empty phone book and add a few entries to it. Then we'll list all the entries, look up a friend, then change their entry. To conserve space here in the book, we'll show only the full menu that rolo displays the first time.

```
$ PHONEBOOK=/users/steve/misc/book
$ export PHONEBOOK
$ rolo                          Start it up
/users/steve/misc/book does not exist!
Should I create it for you (y/n)? y

        Would you like to:

            1. Look someone up
            2. Add someone to the phone book
            3. Remove someone from the phone book
            4. Change an entry in the phone book
            5. List all names and numbers in the phone
            6. Exit this program

Please select one of the above (1-6): 2

Type in your new entry
When you're done, type just a single Enter on the line.
>> Steve's Ice Cream
>> 444 6th Avenue
>> New York City 10003
>> 212-555-3021
>>

Steve's Ice Cream has been added to the phone book

        Would you like to:
            ...
        Please select one of the above (1-6): 2

Type in your new entry
```

```
When you're done, type just a single Enter on the line.
>> YMCA
>> 973-555-2344
>>


YMCA has been added to the phone book
      Would you like to:

        . . .
      Please select one of the above (1-6): 2


Type in your new entry
When you're done, type just a single Enter on the line.
>> Maureen Connelly
>> Hayden Book Companu
>> 10 Mulholland Drive
>> Hasbrouck Heights, N.J. 07604
>> 201-555-6000
>>


Maureen Connelly has been added to the phone book

      Would you like to:
      . . .
      Please select one of the above (1-6): 2


Type in your new entry
When you're done, type just a single Enter on the line.
>> Teri Zak
>> Hayden Book Company
>> (see Maureen Connelly for address)
>> 201-555-6060
>>


Teri Zak has been added to the phone book

      Would you like to:
      . . .
      Please select one of the above (1-6): 5



-------------------------------------------------------------
Maureen Connelly                    201-555-6000
Steve's Ice Cream                   212-555-3021
Teri Zak                            201-555-6060
YMCA                                973-555-2344
-------------------------------------------------------------
```

```
        Would you like to:
          ...
        Please select one of the above (1-6): 1
Enter name to look up: Maureen


--------------------------------------
| Maureen Connelly                    |
| Hayden Book Companu                 |
| 10 Mulholland Drive                 |
| Hasbrouck Heights, NJ 07604         |
| 201-555-6000                        |
|       o                  o          |
--------------------------------------


--------------------------------------
| Teri Zak                            |
| Hayden Book Company                 |
| (see Maureen Connelly for address)  |
| 201-555-6060                        |
|                                     |
|       o                  o          |
--------------------------------------


        Would you like to:
          ...
        Please select one of the above (1-6): 4

Enter name to change: Maureen


--------------------------------------
| Maureen Connelly                    |
| Hayden Book Companu                 |
| 10 Mulholland Drive                 |
| Hasbrouck Heights, NJ 07604         |
| 201-555-6000                        |
|       o                  o          |
--------------------------------------


Change this person (y/n)? y
Enter changes with /bin/ed
101
1,$p
Maureen Connelly
Hayden Book Companu
10 Mulholland Drive
Hasbrouck Heights, NJ 07604
201-555-6000
```

```
2s/anu/any                        Change the misspelling
Hayden Book Company
w
101
q

    Would you like to:
      . . .
    Please select one of the above (1-6): 6
$
```

Hopefully this complex shell programming example offers you some insight into how to develop larger shell programs and how the many different programming tools provided by the system can work together.

Other than shell built-ins, `rolo` relies on `tr`, `grep`, an editor, `sort`, and the standard file system commands such as `mv` and `rm` to get the job done.

The simplicity and elegance that enable you to easily tie all these tools together account for the deserved popularity of the Unix system.

See Appendix B for more information on downloading the `rolo` programs.

Chapter 14 introduces you to interactive features of the shell and two shells that have some nice features not found in the POSIX standard shell.

Interactive and Nonstandard Shell Features

In this chapter you'll learn about shell features that are useful to interactive users or not part of the POSIX shell standard. These features are available in Bash and the Korn shell, the two most commonly available POSIX-compliant shells across Unix, Linux, and Mac systems.

The Korn shell was developed by David Korn of AT&T Bell Laboratories and was designed to be "upward compatible" with both the System V Bourne shell and the POSIX standard shell. It is now widely available across all major *nix platforms and if you have access to a command line, you probably have ksh available to you.

Bash (short for Bourne-Again Shell) was developed by Brian Fox for the Free Software Foundation. It was also designed to be compatible with the System V Bourne shell and the POSIX standard shell, and additionally contains many extensions from the Korn and C shells. Bash is the standard shell on Linux systems and on most modern Unix and Mac systems it has replaced the Bourne shell (in fact, if you are using sh you're probably really using bash and just don't know it).

Except for a few minor differences, Bash and the Korn shell provide all the POSIX standard shell's features and add many new ones. To give you an idea of the compatibility of these shells with the POSIX standard, all shell programs presented in this book work under both Bash and the Korn shell.

We'll note any non-standard features that we discuss in this chapter, and Table 14.4 at the end of this chapter lists the features supported by the different shells.

Getting the Right Shell

Up to this point we've dropped commands into a file and run it as a shell program without really discussing what shell will actually read the lines and run the program. By default, shell programs are run by your login shell, so it hasn't been a big issue.

It turns out that all the major interactive shells allow you to specify which shell—actually, which program of the thousands included in a Unix or Linux distribution—should be used to run the file. If the first two characters on the first line of a file are #!, the remainder of the line specifies an interpreter for the file. So

```
#!/bin/ksh
```

specifies the Korn shell and

```
#!/bin/bash
```

specifies Bash. If you use constructs or notational conventions specific to one shell, you can use this feature to force that shell to run your programs, avoiding compatibility problems.

Since you can specify any program you want, a Perl program beginning with

```
#!/usr/bin/perl
```

forces the shell to invoke /usr/bin/perl to interpret the lines within the file.

You have to use this feature with caution, however, because many programs, such as Perl, don't reside in a standard place on every Unix system. Also, this is not specified by the POSIX standard, even though it's found in every modern shell and is even implemented at the operating system level on many Unix versions.

Most commonly you'll see system shell programs use this notation to ensure that Bourne Shell is used regardless of the user's login shell by beginning with

```
#!/bin/sh
```

The ENV File

When you start the shell, one of the first things it does is look in your environment for a variable called ENV. If it finds it and it's non-null, the file specified by ENV will be executed, much like the .profile is executed when logging in. The ENV file contains commands to set up the shell's environment. Throughout this chapter, we'll mention various things that you may want to put into this file.

If you do decide to have an ENV file, you should set and export the ENV variable inside your .profile file:

```
$ cat .profile
...
export ENV=$HOME/.alias
...
$
```

Note the shortcut in use above: Instead of assigning the variable a value, then calling export, it turns out you can do both on the same line for efficiency.

For Bash users, the ENV file is read only when Bash is invoked with the name sh, with the --posix command-line option, or after set -o posix is executed (all of which force POSIX standard compliance). By default, when a non-interactive Bash shell is started (for example, when you run a shell program), it reads commands from the file specified by the BASH_ENV environment variable, and when an interactive Bash shell is started (for example, by typing bash at the command prompt), it doesn't.

If you're running an older system, you should also export a variable called SHELL inside your .profile file.

```
$ grep SHELL .profile
SHELL=/bin/ksh ; export SHELL
$
```

This variable is used by certain applications (such as vi) to determine what shell to start up when you execute a shell escape. In such cases, you want to make sure that each time you start up a new shell, you get the shell you want and not an older Bourne shell.

Probably, though, SHELL will already be set by your login shell. You can test it with

```
$ echo $SHELL
/bin/bash
$
```

Also note that the previous example demonstrates yet another way to set and export a variable, this time by having two separate commands on the same line, separated by a semicolon. Why the inconsistency? Because Unix is so flexible that you'll find it's common for shell programs you read—and users you work with—to accomplish the same task multiple ways. Might as well get used to variations in notation!

Command-Line Editing

Line edit mode is a feature of the shell that allows you to edit a command line in a manner that mimics features found in two popular screen editors. The POSIX standard shell provides the capability to mimic vi and both Bash and the Korn shell also support an emacs line edit mode. We list the complete set of vi commands in Table A.4 in Appendix A.

If you've used either of these screen-based text editors, you'll find that the built-in line editors in the shell are faithful reproductions from a functional perspective. This capability is one of the most useful features in the shell.

To turn on a line edit mode, use the set command with the -o *mode* option, where *mode* is either vi or emacs:

```
$ set -o vi                    Turn on vi mode
```

Put this in your .profile or ENV file to automatically start up the shell with one of the edit modes turned on.

Command History

Regardless of which shell you use, it keeps a history of all your previously entered commands. Each time you press the `Enter` key to execute a command, that command gets added to the end of your history list.

Depending on your settings, your command history could even be saved to a file and restored between login sessions, so you can quickly access commands from previous sessions.

By default, the history list is kept in a file in your home directory under the name `.sh_history` (`.bash_history` for Bash). You can change this filename to anything you want by setting the variable `HISTFILE` to the name of your history file. This variable can be set and exported in your `.profile` file.

There is a limit to the number of commands the shell stores. The minimum value is 128 commands but most modern shells save 500 or more of your commands on the list. Each time you log in, the shell automatically truncates your history file to this length.

You can control the size of your history file through the `HISTSIZE` variable. If the default size isn't adequate for your needs, set the `HISTSIZE` variable to a larger value, such as 500 or 1000. The value you assign to `HISTSIZE` can be set and exported in your `.profile` file:

```
$ grep HISTSIZE .profile
HISTSIZE=500
export HISTSIZE
$
```

Don't go crazy with a massive history size, however: The larger the value, the more disk space you will need to store the history file, and the longer it will take the shell to search through the list when you access previous commands.

The `vi` Line Edit Mode

After turning on the `vi` line editor feature, you will be typing all subsequent commands in what `vi` users would think of as *input* mode. You probably won't even notice anything different because you can type in and execute commands exactly the same way that you do with the default shell input prompt:

```
$ set -o vi
$ echo hello
hello
$ pwd
/users/pat
$
```

To make use of the line editor, you must switch to *command* mode by pressing the `ESCAPE` or `Esc` key, usually in the upper-left corner of the keyboard. When you enter command mode, the cursor moves to the left one space, to the last character typed in.

The *current character* is whatever character the cursor is on; we'll say more about the current character in a moment. You can enter `vi` commands only in command mode and that the commands are interpreted immediately upon typing them in, no `Enter` needed.

A typical problem you may encounter when typing in long commands is that it's only after typing it all in that you notice an error. Inevitably, the error is at the beginning of the line!

In command mode, you can move the cursor around and fix the errors without disturbing the command line. After you've moved the cursor to the place where the error is, you can change the letter or letters to whatever you want. Then press `Enter` (regardless of where the cursor is on the line) and it'll be given to the shell for interpretation.

In the following examples, the underline (_) represents the cursor. A command line will be shown, followed by one or more keystrokes, followed by what the line looks like after applying the keystrokes:

> *before keystrokes after*

First, let's look at moving the cursor around. Many systems will let you use the arrow keys on your keyboard, which makes it easy: left arrow to move left, right arrow to move right.

The more general `vi`-inspired movement commands, however, are `h` to move the cursor to the left and the `l` key moves it to the right. Try this out by entering command mode (press `Esc`) and pressing the `h` and `l` keys a few times. The cursor should move around on the line. If you try to move the cursor past the left or right side of the line, the shell "beeps" at you.

```
$ mary had a little larb_      Esc    $ mary had a little larb
$ mary had a little larb       h      $ mary had a little larb
$ mary had a little larb       h      $ mary had a little larb
$ mary had a little larb       l      $ mary had a little larb
```

After the cursor is on the character you want to change, you can use the `x` command to delete the current character ("X" it out).

```
$ mary had a little larb       x      $ mary had a little lab
```

Note that the `b` moved to the left when the `r` was deleted and is now the current character.

To add characters to the command line, you can use the `i` or `a` commands. The `i` command inserts characters *before* the current character, and the `a` command adds characters *after* the current character. Both of these commands put you back into input mode, so remember to press `Esc` to go back to command mode.

```
$ mary had a little lab        im     $ mary had a little lamb
$ mary had a little lamb       m      $ mary had a little lammb
$ mary had a little lammb      Esc    $ mary had a little lammb
$ mary had a little lammb      x      $ mary had a little lamb
$ mary had a little lamb       a      $ mary had a little lamb_
$ mary had a little lamb_      da     $ mary had a little lambda_
```

If you think that moving the cursor around by repeatedly pressing h and l is slow, you're right. The h and l commands may be preceded by a number that specifies the number of spaces to move the cursor.

```
$ mary had a little lambda_   Esc   $ mary had a little lambda
$ mary had a little lambda    10h   $ mary had a little lambda
$ mary had a little lambda    13h   $ mary had a little lambda
$ mary had a little lambda    5x    $ had a little lambda
```

As you see, the x command can also be preceded by a number to tell it how many characters to delete.

You can then easily move to the end of the line by typing the $ command:

```
$ had a little lambda          $     $ had a little lambda
```

To move to the beginning of the line, you use the 0 (that's a zero) command:

```
$ had a little lambda          0     $ had a little lambda
```

Two other useful cursor movement commands are w and b. The w command moves the cursor forward to the beginning of the next word, where a word is a string of letters, numbers, and underscores delimited by blanks or punctuation. The b command moves the cursor backward to the beginning of the previous word. These commands may also be preceded by a number to specify the number of words to move forward or backward.

```
$ had a little lambda          w     $ had a little lambda
$ had a little lambda          2w    $ had a little lambda
$ had a little lambda          3b    $ had a little lambda
```

At any time you can press Enter and the current line will be executed as a command.

```
$ had a little lambda                Hit Enter
ksh: had: not found
$ _
```

After a command is executed, you are placed back in input mode.

Accessing Commands from Your History

So far, you've learned how to edit the current command line. But there's more to vi mode because you can use the vi commands k and j to retrieve commands from your history. The k command replaces the current line on your terminal with the previously entered command, putting the cursor at the beginning of the line. Let's assume that these commands have just been entered:

```
$ pwd
/users/pat
$ cd /tmp
$ echo this is a test
this is a test
$ _
```

Now go into command mode (Esc) and use k to access previous commands from the command history:

```
$ _                            Esc k      $ echo this is a test
```

Every time k is used, the line is replaced by the previous line from the command history, as far back as you want to go, within the constraints set with HISTSIZE, as discussed earlier.

```
$ echo this is a test          k          $ cd /tmp
$ cd /tmp                      k          $ pwd
```

To execute the command being displayed, just press the Enter key.

```
$ pwd                          Hit Enter
/tmp
$ _
```

The j command is the reverse of the k command and is used to display the next most recent command in the history. In other words, k moves you "back" in time, and j moves you "forward" in time. Try them a few times and you'll immediately see what we mean.

The / command searches through the command history for a command containing the specified string. If the / is entered followed by a string, the shell searches backward through its history to find the most recently executed command that contains that string. The command will then be displayed.

If no line in the history contains the specified string, the shell "beeps" to indicate the error. When the / is entered, the current line is replaced by a /.

```
/tmp
$ _                            Esc /test   /test_
```

The search is begun when the Enter key is pressed.

```
/test_                         Enter      $ echo this is a test
```

To execute the command that results from the search, Enter must be pressed again.

```
$ echo this is a test                    Hit Enter again
this is a test
$ _
```

If the command that's displayed isn't the one you seek, continue the search by typing in / *without* a pattern and pressing Enter. The shell is smart enough to use the string that you entered the last time you executed the search command and continue from the last match shown further back in your command list.

When you've found the command in the history (either by k, j, or /), you can edit the command using the other vi commands we've already discussed. Worth noting is that by making these changes, you don't actually change the command in the history. You're editing a copy of the command, which will then be entered in the history as the most recent command when you press Enter.

Table 14.1 summarizes the basic vi line edit commands.

Table 14.1   **Basic** vi **Line Edit Commands**

Command	Meaning
h	Move left one character.
l	Move right one character.
b	Move left one word.
w	Move right one word.
0	Move to start of line.
$	Move to end of line.
x	Delete character at cursor.
dw	Delete word at cursor.
rc	Change character at cursor to c.
a	Enter input mode and enter text after the current character.
i	Enter input mode and insert text before the current character.
k	Get previous command from history.
j	Get next command from history.
/string	Search history for the most recent command containing string; if string is null, the previous string will be used.

It seems like a lot, but don't get too anxious: j and k to move up and down your history list, h and l to move around on the command line, i to insert and Enter to invoke are all you really need to get going with command line editing in vi mode.

The emacs Line Edit Mode

Not a fan of the vi visual editor but prefer emacs, an editor much beloved by the open source developer community? The shell has a line edit mode for you too. After turning on the emacs line editor, you again won't notice anything different because you'll type in and execute commands exactly as before:

```
$ set -o emacs
$ echo hello
hello
$ pwd
/users/pat
$
```

This time, however, to use the emacs line editor you will enter emacs *commands*. emacs commands are either *control* characters—characters typed in by holding down the Ctrl key and pressing another character—or they are characters preceded by the Esc key. You may enter emacs commands any time you want because there are no separate "modes" like the vi line editor. *Note that* emacs *commands are not followed by an* Enter.

(For a complete list of emacs commands, refer to the documentation for Bash or the Korn shell.)

First, let's look at how to move the cursor around on the command line. *Ctrl+b* moves the cursor back (to the left), and the *Ctrl+f* command moves it forward (to the right). Try this by pressing *Ctrl+b* and *Ctrl+f* a few times while entering a command on the command line. The cursor should move around on the line. If you try to move the cursor past the left or right side of the line, the shell simply ignores your command.

```
$ mary had a little larb_      Ctrl+b      $ mary had a little larb
$ mary had a little larb       Ctrl+b      $ mary had a little larb
$ mary had a little larb       Ctrl+b      $ mary had a little larb
$ mary had a little larb       Ctrl+f      $ mary had a little larb
```

After the cursor is on the character you want to change, you can use the *Ctrl+d* command to delete the current character.

```
$ mary had a little larb       Ctrl+d      $ mary had a little lab
```

Note that the b moved to the left when the r was deleted and is now the current character.

To add characters to the command line, you simply type them in. The characters are inserted *before* the current character.

```
$ mary had a little lab        m        $ mary had a little lamb
$ mary had a little lamb       m        $ mary had a little lammb
$ mary had a little lammb      Ctrl+h   $ mary had a little lamb
```

Note that the current erase character (usually either Backspace or *Ctrl+h*) will *always* delete the character to the left of the cursor.

The *Ctrl+a* and *Ctrl+e* commands may be used to move the cursor to the beginning and end of the command line, respectively.

```
$ mary had a little lamb       Ctrl+a      $ mary had a little lamb
$ mary had a little lamb       Ctrl+e      $ mary had a little lamb_
```

Note that the *Ctrl+e* command places the cursor one space to the right of the last character on the line. (When you're not in emacs mode, the cursor is always at the end of the line, one space to the right of the last character typed in.)

This is handy because when you're at the end of the line, anything you type will be appended to whatever is already on the line.

```
$ mary had a little lamb_      da        $ mary had a little lambda_
```

Two other useful cursor movement commands are the Esc f and Esc b commands. The Esc f command moves the cursor forward to the end of the current word. The Esc b command moves the cursor backward to the beginning of the previous word. Note that for these commands you press *and release* the Esc key, *then* press the key that corresponds to the desired command (f, b, and so on).

```
$ mary had a little lambda_    Esc b        $ mary had a little lambda
$ mary had a little lambda     Esc b        $ mary had a little lambda
$ mary had a little lambda     Esc b        $ mary had a little lambda
$ mary had a little lambda     Esc f        $ mary had a_little lambda
$ mary had a_little lambda     Esc f        $ mary had a little_lambda
```

You can press the Enter key at any time and the current line will be executed as a command.

```
$ mary had a little_lambda              Hit Enter; enter command
ksh: mary: not found
$ _
```

Accessing Commands from Your History

You've learned how to edit the current command line, but the shell keeps a history of recently entered commands. To access these commands from the history list, use the emacs commands *Ctrl+p* and *Ctrl+n*. The *Ctrl+p* command replaces the current line on your terminal with the previously entered command, putting the cursor at the end of the line. *Ctrl+n* does the same action, but with the *next* command in the history list.

Let's assume that these commands have just been entered:

```
$ pwd
/users/pat
$ cd /tmp
$ echo this is a test
this is a test
$ _
```

Now use *Ctrl+p* to access them:

```
$ _                      Ctrl+p        $ echo this is a test_
```

Every time *Ctrl+p* is used, the current line is replaced by the previous line from the command history.

```
$ echo this is a test_    Ctrl+p        $ cd /tmp_
$ cd /tmp_                Ctrl+p        $ pwd_
```

To execute the command being displayed, just press Enter.

```
$ pwd_                   Hit Enter
/tmp
$ _
```

The *Ctrl+r* command is used to search through the command history for a command containing the specified string. The *Ctrl+r* is entered followed by the search pattern, followed by the Enter key. The shell then searches the command history for the most recently executed command that contains that string. If found, the command line is displayed; otherwise, the shell "beeps."

When the *Ctrl+r* is typed, the shell replaces the current line with the prompt ^R:

```
$ _                         Ctrl+r test    $ ^Rtest_
```

The search is initiated when Enter is pressed.

```
$ ^Rtest_                   Enter          $ echo this is a test_
```

To execute the command that is displayed as a result of the search, Enter must be pressed again.

```
$ echo this is a test_      Hit Enter again
this is a test
$ _
```

To continue the search through the command history, keep typing *Ctrl+r* followed by an Enter.

Bash handles *Ctrl+r* a little differently. When you type *Ctrl+r*, Bash replaces the current line with (reverse-i-search)`':

```
$ _                         Ctrl+r         (reverse-i-search)`': _
```

As you type text, the line is updated inside the `' with the text you type, and the rest of the line is updated with the matching command:

```
(reverse-i-search)`': _                        c      (reverse-i-search)`c': echo this is a
test
(reverse-i-search)`c': echo this is a test    d      (reverse-i-search)`cd': cd /tmp
```

Note how Bash highlights the matching part of the command by placing the cursor on it. As with the Korn shell, the command is executed by pressing Enter.

When you've found the command in the history (either by *Ctrl+p, Ctrl+n,* or *Ctrl+r*), you can also edit the command using the other emacs commands already discussed. As with the vi edit mode, you won't actually change the command in the history but are editing a copy of the command, which will then be entered in the history list when you press Enter.

Table 14.2 summarizes the basic emacs line edit commands.

Table 14.2 **Basic emacs Line Edit Commands**

Command	Meaning
Ctrl+b	Move left one character.
Ctrl+f	Move right one character.
Esc f	Move forward one word.
Esc b	Move back one word.
Ctrl+a	Move to start of line.
Ctrl+e	Move to end of line.
Ctrl+d	Delete current character.

Chapter 14 Interactive and Nonstandard Shell Features

Command	Meaning
Esc d	Delete current word.
erase char	(User-defined erase character, usually # or *Ctrl+h*), delete previous character.
Ctrl+p	Get previous command from history.
Ctrl+n	Get next command from history.
Ctrl+r `string`	Search history for the most recent command line containing `string`.

Other Ways to Access Your History

There are several other ways to access your command history that are worth noting if you don't find that either the vi or emacs line edit modes work for you.

The history Command

The easiest way to access your command history is actually to just type in the command history:

```
$ history
507    cd shell
508    cd ch15
509    vi int
510    ps
511    echo $HISTSIZE
512    cat $ENV
513    cp int int.sv
514    history
515    exit
516    cd shell
517    cd ch16
518    vi all
519    run -n5 all
520    ps
521    lpr all.out
522    history
```

The numbers to the left are relative command numbers (command number 1 would be the first, or oldest, command in your history).

Be aware that the history command differs between the Korn and Bash shells: The Korn shell history command writes your last 16 commands to standard output while Bash will list your *entire* command history, even if it's 500 or 1000 lines long.

If you're running Bash and don't want to be inundated with commands, you can specify the number of commands to display as an argument:

```
$ history 10
  513    cp int int.sv
  514    history
  515    exit
  516    cd shell
  517    cd ch16
  518    vi all
  519    run -n5 all
  520    ps
  521    lpr all.out
  522    history 10
$
```

The `fc` Command

The `fc` command allows you to start up an editor on one or more commands from your history or to write a list of history commands to your terminal. In the latter form, which is indicated by giving the `-l` option to `fc`, it is like typing in `history`, only more flexible (you can specify a range of commands to be listed). For example, the command

```
fc -l 510 515
```

writes commands 510 through 515 to standard output, and the command

```
fc -n -l -20
```

writes the last 20 commands to standard output, but omits the command numbers (`-n`). Suppose that you've just executed a long command and decide that it would be nice to turn that command line into a shell program called `runx`. You can use `fc` to get the command from your history and I/O redirection to write that command to a file:

```
fc -n -l -1 > runx
```

That's the letter `l` followed by the number `-1` to get the most recent command (current minus one). `fc` is described in full detail in Appendix A.

The `r` Command

A simple Korn shell command allows you to re-execute previous commands using even fewer keystrokes. Type in the `r` command, and the Korn shell re-executes your last command:

```
$ date
Thu Oct 24 14:24:48 EST 2002
$ r                             Re-execute previous command
date
Thu Oct 24 14:25:13 EST 2002
$
```

When you type in the r command, the Korn shell redisplays the previous command and then immediately executes it.

If you give r the name of a command as an argument, the Korn shell re-executes the most recent command from your history that *begins* with the specified pattern:

```
$ cat docs/planA
...
$ pwd
/users/steve
$ r cat                    Rerun last cat command
cat docs/planA
$
```

Once again, the Korn shell redisplays the command line from its history before automatically re-executing it.

The final form of the r command allows you to substitute the first occurrence of one string with the next. To re-execute the last cat command on the file planB instead of planA you could type:

```
$ r cat planA=planB
cat docs/planB
...
$
```

or even more simply, you could have typed:

```
$ r cat A=B
cat docs/planB
...
$
```

Bash has a similar history shortcut command. !*string* lets you search your history and !! re-executes the previous command:

```
$ !!
cat docs/planB
...
$ !d
date
Thu Oct 24 14:39:40 EST 2002
$
```

No spaces can occur between ! and *string*.

The fc command can be used with the -s option to do the same thing with any POSIX compliant shell (the r command is actually an *alias* to the fc command in the Korn shell—more on that later in this chapter):

```
$ fc -s cat
cat docs/planB
...
```

```
$ fc -s B=C
cat docs/planC
...
$
```

Functions

Bash and the Korn shell both have function features not available in the POSIX standard shell. Let's have a look.

Local Variables

Both Bash and Korn shell functions can have local variables, making recursive functions possible. These variables are defined with the `typeset` command, as in

```
typeset i j
```

If a variable of the same name already exists, it is saved when the `typeset` is executed and restored when the function exits.

After using the shell for a while, you may develop a set of functions that you like to use during your interactive work sessions. A good place to define such functions is inside your ENV file so that they will be defined whenever you start up a new shell.

Automatically Loaded Functions

The Korn shell allows you to set up a special variable called FPATH that is similar to your PATH variable. If you try to execute a function that is not yet defined, the Korn shell searches the colon-delimited list of directories in FPATH for a file that matches the function name. If it finds such a file, it executes it in the current shell with the expectation that somewhere in the file is a definition for the specified function.

Integer Arithmetic

Both Bash and the Korn shell support evaluating arithmetic expressions without arithmetic expansion. The syntax is similar to $((...)) but without the dollar sign. Because expansion is not performed, the construct can therefore be used by itself as a command:

```
$ x=10
$ ((x = x * 12))
$ echo $x
120
$
```

The real value of this construct is that it allows arithmetic expressions to be used in `if`, `while`, and `until` commands. The comparison operators set the exit status to a non-zero value if the result of the comparison is false and to a zero value if the result is true. So writing

```
(( i == 100 ))
```

has the effect of testing `i` to see whether it is equal to 100 and setting the exit status appropriately. This makes integer arithmetic ideal for inclusion in `if` conditionals:

```
if (( i == 100 ))
then
        ...
fi
```

The `(( i == 100 ))` returns an exit status of zero (true) if `i` equals 100 and one (false) otherwise, and has the same effect as writing

```
if [ "$i" -eq 100 ]
then
        ...
fi
```

Another advantage of using `((...))` rather than `test` is the ability to perform arithmetic as part of the test:

```
if (( i / 10 != 0 ))
then
      ...
fi
```

Here the comparison returns TRUE if `i` divided by 10 is not equal to zero.

`while` loops can also benefit from integer arithmetic. For example,

```
x=0
while ((x++ < 100))
do
      commands
done
```

executes *commands* 100 times.

Integer Types

Both the Korn and Bash shells support an integer data type. You can declare variables to be integers by using the `typeset` command with the `-i` option

```
typeset -i variables
```

where *variables* are any valid shell variable names. Initial values can also be assigned to the variables at the time they are declared:

```
typeset -i signal=1
```

The main benefit: arithmetic performed on integer variables with the ((...)) construct is faster than on non-integer values.

However, an integer variable cannot be assigned anything but an integer value or integer expression. If you attempt to assign a non-integer to it, the message bad number is printed by the shell:

```
$ typeset -i i
$ i=hello
ksh: i: bad number
```

Bash simply ignores any strings that don't contain numeric values and generates an error for anything that contains both numbers and other characters:

```
$ typeset -i i
$ i=hello
$ echo $i
0
$ i=1hello
bash: 1hello: value too great for base (error token is "1hello")
$ i=10+15
$ echo $i
25
$
```

The preceding example also shows that integer-valued expressions can be assigned to an integer variable, without even having to use the ((...)) construct. This holds true for both shells.

Numbers in Different Bases

Both Korn and Bash also allow you to perform arithmetic in different numeric bases. To write a number in a different base with these shells, you use the notation

base#number

For example, to express the value 100 in base 8 (octal) you can write

8#100

You can write constants in different bases anywhere an integer value is permitted. To assign octal 100 to the integer variable i, you can write

typeset -i i=8#100

Note that with the Korn shell the base of the first value assigned to an integer variable sets the default base of all subsequent uses of that variable. In other words, if the first value you assign to the integer variable i is an octal number, each time you reference the value of i on the command line, the Korn shell displays it as an octal number using the notation 8#*value*.

```
$ typeset -i i=8#100
$ echo $i
8#100
$ i=50
```

```
$ echo $i
8#62
$ (( i = 16#a5 + 16#120 ))
$ echo $i
8#705
$
```

Because the first value assigned to i is an octal number (8#100), all further references to i will also be in octal. When the base 10 value of 50 is next assigned to i and then i is subsequently displayed, we get the value 8#62, which is the octal equivalent of 50 in base 10.

There's a subtlety in the above example too: while the display value of i is set to octal, the default numeric base for values assigned to the variable remain decimal unless specified otherwise. In other words, i=50 was *not* equivalent to i=8#50 even though the shell knew i was to be referenced as base 8.

In the preceding example, the ((...)) construct is used to add the two hexadecimal values a5 and 120. The result is then displayed, once again in octal. We admit, that's fairly obscure and not likely something you'll encounter in day-to-day shell programming or interactive use!

Bash uses both the *base#number* syntax for arbitrary bases and the C language syntax for octal and hexadecimal numbers—octal numbers are preceded by 0 (zero), and hexadecimal numbers are preceded by 0x:

```
$ typeset -i i=0100
$ echo $i
64
$ i=0x80
$ echo $i
128
$ i=2#1101001
$ echo $i
105
$ (( i = 16#a5 + 16#120 ))
$ echo $i
453
$
```

Unlike the Korn shell, Bash doesn't keep track of the variable's numeric base; integer variables are displayed as decimal values. You can always use printf to print integers in octal or hexadecimal format.

As you can see, with Bash and the Korn shell it's easy to work with different bases which makes it possible to write functions that perform base conversion and non-decimal arithmetic.

The alias **Command**

An *alias* is a shorthand notation provided by the shell to allow command customization. The shell keeps a list of aliases that is searched when a command is entered before any other substitution occurs. If the first word of a command line is an alias, it is replaced by the text of the alias.

An alias is defined by using the alias command. The format is

```
alias name=string
```

where *name* is the name of the alias, and *string* is any string of characters. For example,

```
alias ll='ls -l'
```

assigns ls -l to the alias ll. Now when the command ll is entered by the user, the shell silently replaces it with ls -l. Even better, you can type arguments after the alias name on the command line, as in

```
ll *.c
```

which transforms into this after alias substitution has been performed:

```
ls -l *.c
```

The shell performs its normal command-line processing both when the alias is set and when it is used, so quoting can be tricky. For example, recall that the shell keeps track of your current working directory inside a variable called PWD:

```
$ cd /users/steve/letters
$ echo $PWD
/users/steve/letters
$
```

You can create an alias called dir that gives you the base name of your current working directory by using the PWD variable and one of the parameter substitution constructs:

```
alias dir="echo ${PWD##*/}"
```

This seems reasonable, but let's see how this alias works in practice:

```
$ alias dir="echo ${PWD##*/}"       Define alias
$ pwd                               Where are we?
/users/steve
$ dir                               Execute alias
steve
$ cd letters                        Change directory
$ dir                               Execute the alias again
steve
$ cd /usr/spool                     One more try
$ dir
steve
$
```

No matter the current directory, the `dir` alias prints out `steve`. That's because we weren't careful about quotes when we defined the `dir` alias. Recalling that the shell performs parameter substitution inside double quotes, the problem is that the shell evaluated

```
${PWD##*/}
```

at the time the alias was defined. This means that the `dir` alias was essentially defined as if we'd typed in the following:

```
$ alias dir="echo steve"
```

No wonder it didn't work!

The solution is to use single rather than double quotes when defining the `dir` alias to defer the parameter substitution until the alias is executed:

```
$ alias dir='echo ${PWD##*/}'        Define alias
$ pwd                                Where are we?
/users/steve
$ dir                                Execute alias
steve
$ cd letters                         Change directory
$ dir                                Execute alias again
letters
$ cd /usr/spool                      One more try
$ dir
spool
$
```

If an alias ends with a space, the word following the alias is also checked for alias substitution. For example:

```
alias nohup="/bin/nohup "
nohup ll
```

causes the shell to perform alias checking on the string `ll` after replacing `nohup` with `/bin/nohup`.

Quoting a command or prefacing it with a backslash prevents alias substitution. For example:

```
$ 'll'
ksh: ll: command not found
$
```

The format

```
alias name
```

causes the value of the alias `name` to be listed, and the `alias` command without arguments causes all aliases to be listed.

The following aliases are automatically defined when the Korn shell starts up:

```
autoload='typeset -fu'
functions='typeset -f'
history='fc -l'
integer='typeset -i'
local=typeset
nohup='nohup '
r='fc -e -'
suspend='kill -STOP $$'
```

Note from the preceding example that r is actually an alias for the fc command with the -e option, and history is an alias for fc -l. By comparison, Bash doesn't automatically define any aliases by default.

Removing Aliases

The unalias command is used to remove aliases from the alias list. The format is

```
unalias name
```

which removes the alias *name* and

```
unalias -a
```

which removes all aliases.

If you develop a set of alias definitions that you like to use during your login sessions, you may want to define them inside your ENV file so that they will always be available for you to use, as they don't otherwise migrate to subshells.

Arrays

Both Korn and Bash provide a limited array capability. Bash arrays may contain an unlimited number of elements (subject to memory limitations); Korn shell arrays are limited to 4096 elements. Array indexing in both shells starts at zero.

An array element is accessed with a *subscript*, which is an integer-valued expression enclosed within square brackets. You don't declare the maximum size of a shell array either, you simply assign values to elements as needed. The values that you can assign are the same as for ordinary variables:

```
$ arr[0]=hello
$ arr[1]="some text"
$ arr[2]=/users/steve/memos
$
```

To retrieve an element from an array, you need to write the array name followed by an open bracket, the element number and a close bracket. The entire construct must also be enclosed inside a pair of curly braces, and the whole element is preceded by a dollar sign. Sounds complicated? It's not:

```
$ echo ${array[0]}
hello
$ echo ${array[1]}
some text
$ echo ${array[2]}
/users/steve/memos
$ echo $array
hello
$
```

As you can see from the preceding example, if no subscript is specified, element zero is used.

If you forget the curly braces when performing the substitution, nothing breaks, it just produces a result that's not quite what you expect:

```
$ echo $array[1]
hello[1]
$
```

The value of `array` is substituted (`hello`—the value of `array[0]`) and then echoed along with `[1]`. (Note that because the shell does filename substitution after variable substitution, the shell would attempt to match the pattern `hello[1]` against the files in your current directory.)

The construct `[*]` can be used as a subscript to produce all the elements of an array on the command line, with each element separated by a space.

```
$ echo ${array[*]}
hello some text /users/steve/memos
$
```

The construct `${#array[*]}` can be used to find out the number of elements in *array*.

```
$ echo ${#array[*]}
3
$
```

The number reported is the actual number of values stored within array elements, not the largest subscript used to store an element inside the array.

```
$ array[10]=foo
$ echo ${array[*]}              Display all elements
hello some text /users/steve/memos foo
$ echo ${#array[*]}             Number of elements
4
$
```

An array that has noncontiguous values defined is known as a *sparse array*, in case you've ever heard that phrase before.

You can declare an array of integers by specifying the array name to `typeset -i`:

```
typeset -i data
```

Integer calculations can be performed on array elements using the ((...)) construct:

```
$ typeset -i array
$ array[0]=100
$ array[1]=50
$ (( array[2] = array[0] + array[1] ))
$ echo ${array[2]}
150
$ i=1
$ echo ${array[i]}
50
$ array[3]=array[0]+array[2]
$ echo ${array[3]}
250
$
```

Note that not only can you omit the dollar signs and the curly braces when referencing array elements within double parentheses, you also can omit them outside when the array is declared to be of integer type. Also note that dollar signs are not needed before variables used in subscript expressions.

The following program, called reverse, reads lines from standard input and then writes them back to standard output in reverse order:

```
$ cat reverse
# read lines to array buf

typeset -i line=0

while (({ line < 4096 )) && read buf[line]
do
    (({ line = line + 1 ))
done

# now print the lines in reverse order

while (( line > 0 )) do
    (( line = line - 1 ))
    echo "${buf[line]}"
done

$ reverse
line one
line two
line three
Ctrl+d
line three
line two
line one
$
```

The first while loop executes until end of file or 4096 lines have been read (4096 is a Korn shell buffer limit for arrays).

Another example: The cdh function defined below changes the current directory but also uses an array to keep a history of previous directories. It allows the user to list the directory history and move back to any directory in the list:

```
$ cat cdh
CDHIST[0]=$PWD                        # initialize CDHIST[0]

cdh ()
{
        typeset -i cdlen i
        if [ $# -eq 0 ] ; then        # default to HOME with no arguments
          set -- $HOME
        fi

        cdlen=${#CDHIST[*]}           # number of elements in CDHIST

        case "$@" in
        -1)                           # print directory list
                i=0
                while ((i < cdlen))
                do
                        printf "%3d %s\n" $i ${CDHIST[i]}
                        ((i = i + 1))
                done
                return ;;
        -[0-9]|-[0-9][0-9])           # cd to dir in list
                i=${1#-}              # remove leading '-'
                cd ${CDHIST[i]} ;;
        *)                            # cd to new dir
                cd $@ ;;
        esac

        CDHIST[cdlen]=$PWD
}
$
```

The CDHIST array stores each directory visited by cdh, and the first element, CDHIST[0], is initialized with the current directory when the cdh file is run:

```
$ pwd
/users/pat
$ . cdh                     Define cdh function
$ cdh /tmp
$ cdh -1
  0 /users/pat
  1 /tmp
$
```

When the `cdh` file was first run, `CDHIST[0]` was assigned /users/pat, and the `cdh` function was defined. When `cdh /tmp` was executed, `cdlen` was assigned the number of elements in CDHIST (one), and `CDHIST[1]` was assigned /tmp. The `cdh -1` caused `printf` to display each element of CDHIST (on this invocation, `cdlen` was set to 2, because elements 0 and 1 of CDHIST contained data).

Note that the `if` statement at the beginning of the function sets `$1` to `$HOME` if no arguments are passed. Let's try that out:

```
$ cdh
$ pwd
/users/pat
$ cdh -l
  0 /users/pat
  1 /tmp
  2 /users/pat
$
```

It worked, but now /users/pat shows up twice in the list. One of the exercises at the end of this chapter asks you to come up with a solution for this bug.

The most useful feature of `cdh` is the `-n` option, which changes your current directory to the one specified in the list:

```
$ cdh /usr/spool/uucppublic
$ cdh -l
  0 /users/pat
  1 /tmp
  2 /users/pat
  3 /usr/spool/uucppublic
$ cdh -1
$ pwd
/tmp
$ cdh -3
$ pwd
/usr/spool/uucppublic
$
```

`cdh` can replace the standard `cd` command because alias lookup is performed before built-in commands are executed. If we create a `cd` alias to `cdh`, we now have an enhanced `cd`.

For that to work, however, we will have to quote every use of `cd` in the `cdh` function to prevent unwanted recursion:

```
$ cat cdh
CDHIST[0]=$PWD                          # initialize CDHIST[0]
alias cd=cdh

cdh ()
{
        typeset -i cdlen i
        if [ $# -eq 0 ] ; then          # default to HOME with no arguments
```

```
            set -- $HOME
        fi

        cdlen=${#CDHIST[*]}              # number of elements in CDHIST

        case "$@" in
        -1)                              # print directory list
                i=0
                while ((i < cdlen))
                do
                        printf "%3d %s\n" $i ${CDHIST[i]}
                        ((i = i + 1))
                done
                return ;;
        -[0-9]|-[0-9][0-9])              # cd to dir in list
                i=${1#-}                 # remove leading '-'
                'cd' ${CDHIST[i]} ;;
        *)                               # cd to new dir
                'cd' $@ ;;
        esac

        CDHIST[cdlen]=$PWD
}
$ . cdh                    Define cdh function and cd alias
$ cd /tmp
$ cd -l
  0 /users/pat
  1 /tmp
$ cd /usr/spool
$ cd -l
  0 /users/pat
  1 /tmp
  2 /usr/spool
$
```

Table 14.3 summarizes the various array constructs in the Korn shell and Bash.

Table 14.3 **Array Constructs**

Construct	Meaning
${array[i]}	Substitute value of element i
$array	Substitute value of first element (array[0])
${array[*]}	Substitute value of all elements
${#array[*]}	Substitute number of elements
array[i]=val	Store val into array[i]

Job Control

The shell provides facilities for controlling *jobs* directly from the command line. A job is any command or command sequence in the shell. For example:

```
who | wc
```

When a command is started in the background (that is, with &), the shell prints out the job number inside brackets ([]) as well as the process ID:

```
$ who | wc &
[1]      832
$
```

When a job finishes, the shell prints the message

```
[n] + Done     sequence
```

where *n* is the job number of the finished job, and `sequence` is the text of the command sequence used to create the job.

In its easiest usage, the `jobs` command is used to print the status of jobs that haven't completed.

```
$ jobs
[3] + Running      make ksh &
[2] - Running      monitor &
[1]   Running      pic chapt2 | troff > aps.out &
```

The + and - after the job number mark the current and previous jobs, respectively. The current job is the job most recently sent to the background, and the previous job is the next-to-the-last job sent to the background. A number of built-in commands may be given a job number or the current or previous job as arguments as a convenient shortcut.

For example, the shell's built-in `kill` command can be used to terminate a job running in the background. The argument to it can be a process ID or a percent sign (%) followed by a job number, a + (current job), a - (previous job), or another % (also current job).

```
$ pic chapt1 | troff > aps.out &
[1]      886
$ jobs
[1] + Running         pic chapt1 | troff > aps.out &
$ kill %1
[1]   Done            pic chapt1 | troff > aps.out &
$
```

The preceding `kill` could have used %+ or %% to refer to the same job.

The first few characters of the command sequence can also be used to refer to a job; for example, `kill %pic` would have worked in the preceding example.

Stopped Jobs and the `fg` and `bg` Commands

If you are running a job in the foreground (without an &) and you want to suspend it, you can press *Ctrl+z*. The job stops executing, and the shell prints the message

```
[n] + Stopped (SIGTSTP)     sequence
```

The stopped job becomes the current job. To have it continue executing, use the `fg` or `bg` command: The `fg` command causes the current job to resume execution in the foreground, and `bg` causes the current job to resume execution in the background.

You can also specify a job number, the first few characters of the pipeline, a +, a -, or a % preceded by a % to specify any job to the `fg` and `bg` commands. These commands also print out the command sequence to remind you what is being brought to the foreground or sent to the background.

```
$ troff memo | photo
Ctrl+z
[1] + Stopped (SIGTSTP)       troff memo | photo
$ bg
[1]        troff memo | photo &
$
```

The preceding sequence is one of the most often used with job control: stopping a running foreground job and sending it to the background.

If a job running in the background tries to read from the terminal, it is stopped, and the message

```
[n] - Stopped (SIGTTIN)    sequence
```

is printed. It can then be brought to the foreground with the `fg` command to enter the data required. After entering input, the job can be stopped again (with *Ctrl+z)* and moved to the background to continue running.

Output from a background job normally goes directly to the terminal, which can be confusing if you're doing something else at the time. There's a fix, though: The command

```
stty tostop
```

causes any background job that attempts to write to the terminal to be stopped and the message

```
[n] - Stopped (SIGTTOU)   sequence
```

to be printed. (Bash generates slightly different messages than the ones shown here, but the functionality is identical)

The following shows how job control might be used:

```
$ stty tostop
$ rundb                      Start up data base program
??? find green red           Find green and red objects
Ctrl+z                       This may take a while
```

```
[1] + Stopped        rundb
$ bg                                So put it in the background
[1]      rundb &
...                                 Do some other stuff
$ jobs
[1] + Stopped(tty output)           rundb &
$ fg                                Bring back to foreground
rundb
1973 Ford        Mustang       red
1975 Chevy       Monte Carlo   green
1976 Ford        Granada       green
1980 Buick       Century       green
1983 Chevy       Cavalier      red
??? find blue                       Find blue objects
Ctrl+z                              Stop it again
[1] + Stopped        rundb
$ bg                                Back to the background
[1]      rundb &
...                                 Keep working until it's ready
```

Miscellaneous Features

Just a few more tidbits before we wrap up this chapter...

Other Features of the cd Command

The cd command seems straightforward, but it has a few tricks up its proverbial sleeve. For example, the - argument means "the previous directory" as a convenient shortcut:

```
$ pwd
/usr/src/cmd
$ cd /usr/spool/uucp
$ pwd
/usr/spool/uucp
$ cd -                      cd to previous directory
/usr/src/cmd                cd prints out name of new directory
$ cd -
/usr/spool/uucp
$
```

As you can see, cd - can be used to toggle between two directories with no effort at all.

The Korn shell's cd command has the capability to substitute portions of the current directory's path. (Neither Bash nor the POSIX standard shell support this feature)

The format is

```
cd old new
```

cd attempts to replace the first occurrence of the string *old* in the current directory's path with the string *new*.

```
$ pwd
/usr/spool/uucppublic/pat
$ cd pat steve                          Change pat to steve and cd
/usr/spool/uucppublic/steve             cd prints out name of new directory
$ pwd                                   Confirm location
/usr/spool/uucppublic/steve
$
```

Tilde Substitution

If a word on the command line begins with the tilde ~ character, the shell performs the following substitutions: If the tilde is the only character in the word or if the character following the tilde is a slash /,the value of the HOME variable is substituted:

```
$ echo ~
/users/pat
$ qrep Korn ~/shell/chapter9/ksh
The Korn shell is a new shell developed
by David Korn at AT&T
for the Bourne shell would also run under the Korn
the one on System V, the Korn shell provides you with
idea of the compatibility of the Korn shell with Bourne's,
the Bourne and Korn shells.
The main features added to the Korn shell are:
$
```

If the rest of the word up to a slash is a user's login name in /etc/passwd, the tilde and the user's login name are substituted by the HOME directory of that user.

```
$ echo ~steve
/users/steve
$ echo ~pat
/users/pat
$ qrep Korn -pat/shell/chapter9/ksh
The Korn shell is a new shell developed
by David Korn at AT&T
for the Bourne shell would also run under the Korn
the one on System V, the Korn shell provides you with
idea of the compatibility of the Korn shell with Bourne's,
the Bourne and Korn shells.
The main features added to the Korn shell are:
$
```

In both the Korn and Bash shells, if the ~ is followed by a + or a -, the value of the variable PWD or OLDPWD is substituted, respectively. PWD and OLDPWD are set by cd and are the full pathnames of the current and previous directories, respectively. ~+ and ~- are not supported by the POSIX standard shell.

```
$ pwd
/usr/spool/uucppublic/steve
$ cd
$ pwd
/users/pat
$ echo ~+
/users/pat
$ echo ~-
/usr/spool/uucppublic/steve
$
```

In addition to the preceding substitutions, the shell also checks for a tilde after a colon : and performs tilde substitution on that as well (that's how you can have something like ~/bin in your PATH and have it work correctly).

Order of Search

It's worthwhile understanding the search order that the shell uses when you type in a command name:

1. The shell first checks to see whether the command is a reserved word (such as for or do).

2. If it's not a reserved word and is not quoted, the shell next checks its alias list, and if it finds a match, performs the substitution. If the alias definition ends in a space, it also attempts alias substitution on the next word. The final result is then checked against the reserved word list, and if it's not a reserved word, the shell proceeds to step 3.

3. The shell checks the command against its function list and executes the eponymous function if found.

4. The shell checks to see whether the command is a built-in command (such as cd and pwd).

5. Finally, the shell searches the PATH to locate the command.

6. If the command still isn't found, a "command not found" error message is issued.

Compatibility Summary

Table 14.4 summarizes the compatibility of the POSIX standard shell, the Korn shell, and Bash with the features described in this chapter. In this table, an "X" denotes a supported feature, "UP," an optional feature in the POSIX shell (these are also known as "User Portability" features in the POSIX shell specification), and "POS" a feature supported only by Bash when it is invoked with the name sh or with the --posix command-line option, or after set -o posix is executed.

Table 14.4 **POSIX Shell, Korn Shell, and Bash Compatibility**

	POSIX Shell	Korn Shell	Bash
`ENV` file	X	X	POS
`vi` line edit mode	X	X	X
`emacs` line edit mode		X	X
`fc` command	X	X	X
`r` command			X
`!!`			
`!string`			X
Functions	X	X	X
Local variables		X	X
Autoload via `FPATH`		X	
Integer expressions with `((...))`		X	X
Integer data type		X	X
Integers in different bases		X	X
`0xhexnumber`, `0octalnumber`			X
Aliases	UP	X	X
Arrays		X	X
Job control	UP	X	X
`cd -`	X	X	X
`cd old new`		X	
`~username`, `~/`	X	X	X
`~+`, `~-`		X	X

A

Shell Summary

This appendix summarizes the main features of the standard POSIX shell as per IEEE Std 1003.1-2001.

Startup

The shell can be given the same options on the command line as can be specified with the `set` command. In addition, the following options can be specified:

`-c` *commands*	*commands* are executed.
`-i`	The shell is interactive. Signals 2, 3, and 15 are ignored.
`-s`	Commands are read from standard input.

Commands

The general format of a command typed to the shell is

`command arguments`

where *command* is the name of the program to be executed, and *arguments* are its arguments. The command name and the arguments are delimited by *whitespace* characters, normally the space, tab, and newline characters (changing the variable `IFS` affects this).

Multiple commands can be typed on the same line if they're separated by semicolons `;`.

Every command that gets executed returns a number known as the *exit status*; zero is used to indicate success, and non-zero indicates a failure.

The pipe symbol | can be used to connect the standard output from one command to the standard input of another, as in

`who | wc -l`

The exit status is that of the last command in the pipeline. Placing a ! at the beginning of the pipeline causes the exit status of the pipeline to be the logical negation of the last command in the pipeline.

If the command sequence is terminated by an ampersand &, it is run asynchronously in the background. The shell displays the process ID and job number of the command at the terminal and prompts for the next interactive command to be entered.

Typing of a command can continue to the next line if the last character on the line is a backslash character \.

The characters && cause the command that follows to be executed only if the preceding command returns a zero exit status. The characters || cause the command that follows to be executed only if the preceding command returns a non-zero exit status. As an example, in

```
who | grep "fred" > /dev/null && echo "fred's logged on"
```

the echo is executed only if the grep returns a zero exit status.

Comments

If the character # appears on a line, the shell treats the remainder of the line as a comment and ignores it for interpretation, substitution and execution.

Parameters and Variables

There are three different types of *parameters*: shell variables, special parameters, and positional parameters.

Shell Variables

A shell variable name must start with an alphabetic or underscore _ character, and can be followed by any number of alphanumeric or underscore characters. Shell variables can be assigned values on the command line by writing:

```
variable=value variable=value ...
```

Filename substitution is not performed on *value*.

Positional Parameters

Whenever a shell program is executed, the name of the program is assigned to the variable $0 and the arguments typed on the command line to the variables $1, $2, ..., respectively. Positional parameters can also be assigned values with the set command. Parameters 1 through 9 can be explicitly referenced. Parameters greater than 9 must be enclosed inside braces, as in ${10}.

Special Parameters

Table A.1 summarizes the special shell parameters.

Table A.1   **Special Parameter Variables**

Parameter	Meaning
$#	The number of arguments passed to the program; or the number of parameters set by executing the `set` statement.
$*	Collectively references all the positional parameters as $1, $2, ...
$@	Same as $*, except when double-quoted ("$@") collectively references all the positional parameters as "$1", "$2" , ...
$0	The name of the program being executed.
$$	The process ID of the program being executed.
$!	The process ID of the last program sent to the background for execution.
$?	The exit status of the last command not executed in the background.
$-	The current option flags in effect (see the `set` statement).

In addition to these parameters, the shell has some other variables that it uses. Table A.2 summarizes the more important of these variables.

Table A.2   **Other Variables Used by the Shell**

Variable	Meaning
CDPATH	The directories to be searched whenever `cd` is executed without a full path as argument.
ENV	The name of a file that the shell executes in the current environment when started interactively.
FCEDIT	The editor used by `fc`. If not set, `ed` is used.
HISTFILE	If set, specifies a file to be used to store the command history. If not set or if the file isn't writable, `$HOME/.sh_history` is used.
HISTSIZE	If set, specifies the number of previously entered commands accessible for editing. The default value is at least 128.
HOME	The user's home directory; the directory that `cd` changes to when no argument is supplied.
IFS	The internal field separator characters; used by the shell to delimit words when parsing the command line, for the `read` and `set` commands, when substituting the output from a back-quoted command, and when performing parameter substitution. Normally, it contains the three characters: space, horizontal tab, and newline.

Variable	Meaning
LINENO	Set by the shell to the line number in the script it is executing. This value is set before the line gets executed and starts at 1.
MAIL	The name of a file that the shell periodically checks for the arrival of mail. If new mail arrives, the shell displays a "You have mail" message. See also MAILCHECK and MAILPATH.
MAILCHECK	The number of seconds specifying how often the shell is to check for the arrival of mail in the file in MAIL or in the files listed in MAILPATH. The default is 600. A value of 0 causes the shell to check before displaying each command prompt.
MAILPATH	A list of files to be checked for the arrival of mail. Each file is delimited by a colon and can be followed by a percent sign % and a message to be displayed when mail arrives in the indicated file. (You have mail is often the default.)
PATH	A colon-delimited list of directories to be searched when the shell needs to find a command to be executed. The current directory is specified as :: or :.: (if it heads or ends the list, : suffices).
PPID	The process ID of the program that invoked this shell (that is, the parent process).
PS1	The primary command prompt, normally "$ ".
PS2	The secondary command prompt, normally "> ".
PS4	Prompt used during execution trace (-x option to shell or set -x). Default is "+ ".
PWD	Pathname of the current working directory.

Parameter Substitution

In the simplest case, the value of a parameter can be accessed by preceding the parameter with a dollar sign $. Table A.3 summarizes the different types of parameter substitution that can be performed. Parameter substitution is performed by the shell before filename substitution and before the command line is divided into arguments.

The presence of the colon after *parameter* in Table A.3 indicates that *parameter* is to be tested to see whether it's set and non-null. Without the colon, a test is made to check whether *parameter* is set only.

Table A.3 **Parameter Substitution**

Parameter	Meaning
$parameter or ${parameter}	Substitute the value of parameter.
${parameter:-value}	Substitute the value of parameter if it's set and non-null; otherwise, substitute value.
${parameter-value}	Substitute the value of parameter if it's set; otherwise, substitute value.
${parameter:=value}	Substitute the value of parameter if it's set and non-null; otherwise, substitute value and also assign it to parameter.
${parameter=value}	Substitute the value of parameter if it's set; otherwise, substitute value and also assign it to parameter.
${parameter:?value}	Substitute the value of parameter if it's set and non-null; otherwise, write value to standard error and exit. If value is omitted, write parameter: parameter null or not set instead.
${parameter?value}	Substitute the value of parameter if it's set; otherwise, write value to standard error and exit. If value is omitted, write parameter: parameter null or not set instead.
${parameter:+value}	Substitute value if parameter is set and non-null; otherwise, substitute null.
${parameter+value}	Substitute value if parameter is set; otherwise, substitute null.
${#parameter}	Substitute the length of parameter. If parameter is * or @, the result is not specified.
${parameter#pattern}	Substitute the value of parameter with pattern removed from the left side. The smallest portion of the contents of parameter matching pattern is removed. Shell filename substitution characters (*, ?, [. . .], !, and @) may be used in pattern.
${parameter##pattern}	Same as #pattern except the largest matching pattern is removed.
${parameter%pattern}	Same as #pattern except pattern is removed from the right side.
${parameter%%pattern}	Same as ##pattern except the largest matching pattern is removed from the right side.

Command Re-entry

The shell keeps a history list of recently entered commands. The number of commands available is determined by the HISTSIZE variable (default is typically 128), and the file in which the history is kept is determined by the HISTFILE variable (default is $HOME/ .sh_history). Because the command history is stored in a file, these commands are available after you log off and back on.

There are three ways you can access the command history.

The fc Command

The built-in command fc allows you to run an editor on one or more commands in the command history. When the edited command is written and you leave the editor, the edited version of the command is then executed. The editor is determined by the FCEDIT variable (default ed). The -e option may be used with fc to specify the editor rather than FCEDIT.

The -s option causes commands to be executed without first invoking an editor. A simple editing capability is built in to the fc -s command; an argument of the form

old=new

may be used to change the first occurrence of the string *old* to the string *new* in the command(s) to be re-executed.

vi Line Edit Mode

The shell has a vi editor compatible edit mode. When vi mode is turned on, you are placed in a state that duplicates vi's *input* mode. You can press the ESC key to be placed in *edit* mode, at which point most vi commands will be properly interpreted by the shell. The current command line can be edited, as can any of the lines in the command history. Pressing Enter at any point in either command or input mode causes the command being edited to be executed.

Table A.4 lists all the editing commands in vi mode. Note: [*count*] is an integer and can be omitted.

Table A.4   vi **Editing Commands**

Input Mode Commands	
Command	**Meaning**
erase	(Erase character, usually *Ctrl+h* or #); delete previous character.
Ctrl+w	Delete the previous blank-separated word.
kill	(Line kill character, normally *Ctrl+u* or @); delete the entire current line.
eof	(End-of-file character, normally *Ctrl+d*); terminate the shell if the current line is empty.

Ctrl+v	Quote next character; editing characters and the erase and kill characters may be entered in a command line or in a search string if preceded by a *Ctrl+v*.
`Enter`	Execute the current line.
`ESC`	Enter edit mode.

Edit Mode Commands

Command	Meaning
`[count]k`	Get previous command from history.
`[count]-`	Get previous command from history.
`[count]j`	Get next command from history.
`[count]+`	Get next command from history.
`[count]G`	Get the command number `count` from history; the default is the oldest stored command.
`/string`	Search history for the most recent command containing `string`; if `string` is null, the previous string will be used (`string` is terminated by an `Enter` or a *Ctrl+j*); if `string` begins with ^, search for line beginning with `string`.
`?string`	Same as / except that the search will be for the least recent command.
`n`	Repeat the last / or ? command.
`N`	Repeat the last / or ? command but reverse the direction of the search.
`[count]l` or	
`[count]`*space*	Move cursor right one character.
`[count]w`	Move cursor right one alphanumeric word.
`[count]W`	Move cursor right to next blank-separated word.
`[count]e`	Move cursor to end of word.
`[count]E`	Move cursor to end of current blank-separated word.
`[count]h`	Move cursor left one character.
`[count]b`	Move cursor left one word.
`[count]B`	Move cursor left to previous blank-separated word.
`0`	Move cursor to start of line.
`^`	Move cursor to first nonblank character.
`$`	Move cursor to end of line.
`[count]|`	Move cursor to column `count`; 1 is default.
`[count]fc`	Move cursor right to character `c`.
`[count]Fc`	Move cursor left to character `c`.

Command	Meaning
[count]tc	Same as fc followed by h.
[count]Tc	Same as Fc followed by l.
;	Repeats the last f, F, t, or T command.
,	Reverse of ;.
a	Enter input mode and enter text after the current character.
A	Append text to the end of the line; same as $a.
[count]c motion	Delete current character through character specified by motion and enter input mode; if motion is c, the entire line is deleted.
C	Delete current character through end of line and enter input mode.
S	Same as cc.
[count]d motion	Delete current character through the character specified by motion; if motion is d, the entire line is deleted.
D	Delete current character through the end of line; same as d$.
i	Enter input mode and insert text before the current character.
I	Enter input mode and insert text before the first word on the line.
[count]P	Place the previous text modification before the cursor.
[count]p	Place the previous text modification after the cursor.
[count]y motion	Copy current character through character specified by motion into buffer used by p and P; if motion is y, the entire line is copied.
Y	Copy current character through the end of line; same as y$.
R	Enter input mode and overwrite characters on the line.
[count]rc	Replace the current character with c.
[count]x	Delete current character.
[count]X	Delete preceding character.
[count].	Repeat the previous text modification command.
~	Invert the case of the current character and advance the cursor.
[count]_	Append the count word from the previous command and enter input mode; the last word is the default.
	Attempt filename generation on the current word; if a match is found, replace the current word with the match and enter input mode.
=	List files that begin with current word.

\	Complete pathname of current word; if current word is a directory, append a /; if current word is a file, append a space.
u	Undo the last text modification command.
U	Restore the current line to its original state.
@letter	Soft function key—if an alias of the name _letter is defined, its value will be executed.
[count]v	Executes vi editor on line count; if count is omitted, the current line is used.
Ctrl+l	Linefeed and print current line.
L	Reprint the current line.
Ctrl+j	Execute the current line.
Ctrl+m	Execute the current line.
Enter	Execute the current line.
#	Insert a # at the beginning of the line and enter the line into the command history (same as I#Enter).

Quoting

Four different types of quoting mechanisms are recognized, as summarized in Table A.5.

Table A.5   **Summary of Quotes**

Quote	Description
'...'	Removes special meaning of all enclosed characters.
"..."	Removes special meaning of all enclosed characters except $, ', and \.
\c	Removes special meaning of character c that follows; inside double quotes removes special meaning of $, ', ", newline, and \ that follows, but is otherwise not interpreted; used for line continuation if it appears as last character on line (newline is removed).
'command' or $(command)	Executes command and inserts standard output at that point.

Tilde Substitution

Each word and shell variable on a command line is checked to see whether it begins with an unquoted ~. If it does, the rest of the word or variable up to a / is considered a login name and is looked up in a system file, typically /etc/passwd. If that user exists, their home directory replaces the ~ and the login name. If that user doesn't exist, the text is unchanged. A ~ by itself or followed by a / is replaced by the HOME variable.

Arithmetic Expressions

General Format: $((\text{expression}))$

The shell evaluates the integer arithmetic *expression*. *expression* can contain constants, shell variables (which don't have to be preceded by dollar signs), and operators. The operators, in order of decreasing precedence, are

-	unary minus
~	bitwise NOT
!	logical negation
* / %	multiplication, division, remainder
+ -	addition, subtraction
<< >>	left shift, right shift
<= >= < >	comparison
== !=	equal, not equal
&	bitwise AND
^	bitwise exclusive OR
|	bitwise OR
&&	logical AND
||	logical OR
$expr_1$? $expr_2$: $expr_3$	conditional operator
=, *=, /=, %=	assignment
+=, <<=, >>=,	
&=, ^=, |=	

Parentheses may be used to override operator precedence.

The exit status is zero (true) if the last expression is nonzero and one (false) if the last expression is zero.

The C operators sizeof, ++, and -- may be available in your shell implementation but are not required by the standard. Check by typing sizeof and see what happens.

Examples

```
y=$((22 * 33))
z=$((y * y / (y - 1)))
```

Filename Substitution

After parameter substitution and command substitution are performed on the command line, the shell looks for the special characters *, ?, and [. If they're not quoted, the shell searches the current directory, or another directory if preceded by a /, and substitutes the names of all files that match. If no match is found, the characters remain untouched.

Note that filenames beginning with a . must be explicitly matched (in other words, echo * won't display your hidden files but echo .* will).

The filename substitution characters are summarized in Table A.6.

Table A.6   **Filename Substitution Characters**

Character(s)	Meaning
?	Matches any single character.
*	Matches zero or more characters.
[chars]	Matches any single character in chars; the format c_1-c_2 can be used to match any character in the range c_1 through c_2, inclusive (for example, [A-Z] matches any uppercase letter).
[!chars]	Matches any single character not in chars; a range of characters may be specified as above.

I/O Redirection

When scanning the command line, the shell looks for the special redirection characters < and >. If found, they are processed and removed (with any associated arguments) from the command line. Table A.7 summarizes the different types of I/O redirection that the shell supports.

Table A.7   **I/O Redirection**

Construct	Meaning
< file	Redirect standard input from file.
> file	Redirect standard output to file; file is created if it doesn't exist and zeroed if it does.
>| file	Redirect standard output to file; file is created if it doesn't exist and zeroed if it does; the noclobber (-C) option to set is ignored.
>> file	Like >, except that output is appended to file if it already exists.
<< word	Redirect standard input from lines that follow up until a line containing just word; parameter substitution occurs on the lines, and back-quoted commands are executed and the backslash character interpreted; if any character in word is quoted, none of this processing occurs and the lines are passed through unaltered; if word is preceded by a -, leading tabs on the lines are removed.
<& digit	Standard input is redirected from the file associated with file descriptor digit.

Construct	Meaning
`>& digit`	Standard output is redirected to the file associated with file descriptor `digit`.
`<&-`	Standard input is closed.
`>&-`	Standard output is closed.
`<> file`	Open `file` for both reading and writing.

Note that filename substitution is not performed on `file`. Any of the constructs listed in the first column of the table may be preceded by a file descriptor number to have the same effect on the file associated with that file descriptor.

The file descriptor 0 is associated with standard input, 1 with standard output, and 2 with standard error.

Exported Variables and Subshell Execution

Commands other than the shell's built-in commands are normally executed in a new instantiation of the shell called a *subshell*. Subshells cannot change the values of variables in the parent shell, and they can only access variables from the parent shell that were *exported*—either implicitly or explicitly—by the parent. If the subshell changes the value of one of these variables and wants to have its own subshells know about it, it must explicitly export the variable before executing the subshell.

When the subshell finishes execution, any variables that it may have set are inaccessible by the parent.

The (...) Construct

If one or more commands are placed inside parentheses, those commands will be executed in a subshell.

The { ...; } Construct

If one or more commands are placed inside curly braces, those commands will be executed by the *current* shell.

With this construct and the (...) construct, I/O can be redirected and piped into and out of the set of enclosed commands, and the set can be sent to the background for execution by placing an & at the end. For example,

```
(prog1; prog2; prog3) 2>errors &
```

submits the three listed programs to the background for execution, with standard error from all three programs redirected to the file `errors`.

More on Shell Variables

A shell variable can be placed into the environment of a command by preceding the command name with the assignment to the parameter on the command line, as in

```
PHONEBOOK=$HOME/misc/phone rolo
```

Here the variable PHONEBOOK will be assigned the indicated value and then placed in rolo's environment. The environment of the current shell remains unchanged, as if

```
(PHONEBOOK=$HOME/misc/phone; export PHONE BOOK; rolo)
```

had been executed instead.

Functions

Functions take the following form:

```
name () compound-command
```

where `compound-command` is a set of commands enclosed in (...), {...} or can be a for, case, until, or while command. Most often, the function definition takes this form:

```
name () { command; command; ...command; }
```

where `name` is the name of the function defined to the *current* shell (functions can't be exported). The function definition can span as many lines as needed. A return command can be used to cause execution of the function to be terminated without also terminating the shell (see the return command description).

For example,

```
nf () { ls | wc -l; }
```

defines a function called nf to count the number of files in your current directory.

Job Control

Shell Jobs

Every command sequence run in the background is assigned a job number, starting at one. A job can be referenced by a *job_id*, which is a % followed by the job number, %+, %-, %%, % followed by the first few letters of the pipeline, or %?*string*.

The following built-in commands can be given a *job_id* as an argument: kill, fg, bg, and wait. The special conventions %+ and %- refer to the current and previous jobs, respectively; %% also refers to the current job. The current job is the most recent job placed in the background or the job running in the foreground. The convention %*string* refers to the job whose name begins with *string*; %?*string* refers to the job whose name contains *string*. The jobs command may be used to list the status of all currently running jobs.

If the monitor option of the set command is turned on, the shell prints a message when each job finishes. If you still have jobs when you try to exit the shell, a message is printed to alert you of this. If you immediately try to exit again, the shell exits. The monitor option is enabled by default for interactive shells.

Stopping Jobs

If the shell is running on a system with job control, and the monitor option of the set command is enabled, jobs that are running in the foreground may be placed in the background and vice versa. Normally, *Ctrl+z* stops the current job and the bg command puts a stopped job in the background. The fg command brings a background or stopped job to the foreground.

Whenever a job in the background attempts to read from the terminal, it is stopped until it is brought to the foreground. Output from background jobs normally comes to the terminal. If stty tostop is executed, output from background jobs is disabled, and a job writing to the terminal is stopped until it is brought to the foreground. When the shell exits, all stopped jobs are killed.

Command Summary

This section summarizes the shell's built-in commands. Actually, some of these commands (such as echo and test) may not be built in to the shell or might have a streamlined version built-in and a more sophisticated version as a separate program. In all cases, these functions must be provided as a utility by a POSIX-compliant system. They are built in to Bash and the Korn shell and are used in almost all shell scripts.

The : Command

General Format: :

This is essentially a *null* command. It is frequently used to satisfy the requirement that a command appear.

Example

```
if who | grep jack > /dev/null ; then
        :
else
        echo "jack's not logged in"
fi
```

The : command returns an exit status of zero.

The . Command

General Format: . *file*

The "dot" command causes the indicated file to be read and executed by the shell, just as if the lines from the file were typed at that point. Note that `file` does not have to be executable, only readable. Also, the shell uses the PATH variable to find `file`.

Example

```
. progdefs                Execute commands in progdefs
```

The preceding command causes the shell to search the current PATH for the file `progdefs`. When it finds it, it reads and executes the commands from the file.

Note that because `file` is not executed by a subshell, variables set and/or changed within `file` remain in effect after execution of the commands in `file` is complete.

The `alias` Command

General Format: `alias name=string [name=string ...]`

The `alias` command assigns `string` to the alias `name`. Whenever `name` is used as a command, the shell substitutes `string`, performing command-line substitution after `string` is in place.

Examples

```
alias ll='ls -l'
alias dir='basename $(pwd)'
```

If an alias ends with a blank, the word following the alias is also checked to see whether it's an alias.

The format

```
alias name
```

causes the alias for `name` to be printed out.

`alias` with no arguments lists all aliases.

`alias` returns an exit status of zero unless a `name` is given (as in `alias name`) for which no alias has been defined.

The `bg` Command

General Format: `bg job_id`

If job control is enabled, the job identified by `job_id` is put into the background. If no argument is given, the most recently suspended job is put into the background.

Example

```
bg %2
```

The `break` Command

General Format: `break`

Execution of this command causes execution of the innermost `for`, `while`, or `until` loop to be immediately terminated. Execution continues with the commands that immediately follow the loop.

If the format

`break n`

is used, execution of the *n* innermost loops is automatically terminated.

The `case` Command

General Format:

```
case value in
     pat₁)  command
            command
            . . .
            command;;
     pat₂)  command
            command
            . . .
            command;;
            . . .
     patₙ)  command
            command
            . . .
            command;;
esac
```

The word `value` is successively compared against *pat₁*, *pat₂*, ..., *patₙ* until a match is found. The commands that appear immediately after the matching pattern are then executed until a double semicolon (`;;`) is encountered. At that point, execution of the `case` is terminated.

If no pattern matches `value`, none of the commands inside the case are executed. The pattern `*` matches *anything* and is often used as the last pattern in a `case` as the default or "catch-all" case.

The shell metacharacters

`*` (match zero or more characters),

`?` (match any single character), and

`[...]` (match any single character enclosed between the brackets)

can be used in patterns. The character `|` can be used to specify a logical ORing of two patterns, as in *pat₁| pat₂*

which means to match either pat_1 or pat_2.

Examples

```
case $1 in
    -1) lopt=TRUE;;
    -w) wopt=TRUE;;
    -c) copt=TRUE;;
     *) echo "Unknown option";;
esac
case $choice in
    [1-9]) valid=TRUE;;
        *) echo "Please choose a number from 1-9";;
esac
```

The cd Command

General Format: cd *directory*

Execution of this command causes the shell to make *directory* the current directory. If directory is omitted, the shell makes the directory specified in the HOME variable the current directory.

If the shell variable CDPATH is null, *directory* must be a full directory path (for example, /users/steve/documents) or specified relative to the current directory (for example, documents or ../pat).

If CDPATH is non-null and *directory* is not a full path, the shell searches the colon-delimited directory list in CDPATH for a directory containing *directory*.

Examples

$ **cd documents/memos**	*Change to* documents/memos *directory*
$ **cd**	*Change to* HOME *directory*

An argument of - causes the shell to move the user back to the previous directory. The pathname of the new current directory is printed out.

Examples

```
$ pwd
/usr/lib/uucp
$ cd /
$ cd -
/usr/lib/uucp
$
```

The cd command sets the shell variable PWD to the new current directory, and OLDPWD to the previous directory.

The `continue` Command

General Format: `continue`

Execution of this command from within a `for`, `while`, or `until` loop causes any commands that follow the `continue` to be skipped. Execution of the loop then continues as normal.

If the format

`continue n`

is used, the commands within the *n* innermost loops are skipped. Execution of the loops then continues as normal.

The `echo` Command

General Format: `echo args`

This command causes *args* to be written to standard output. Each word from *args* is delimited by a blank space. A newline character is written at the end. If *args* is omitted, the effect is to simply skip a line.

Certain backslashed characters have a special meaning to `echo` as shown in Table A.8.

Table A.8   `echo` **Escape Characters**

Character	Prints
`\a`	Alert
`\b`	Backspace
`\c`	The line without a terminating newline
`\f`	Formfeed
`\n`	Newline
`\r`	Carriage return
	Tab character
`\v`	Vertical tab character
`\\`	Backslash character
`\0nnn`	The character whose ASCII value is *nnn*, where *nnn* is a one- to three-digit octal number that starts with a zero

Remember to quote these characters so that the `echo` command, rather than the shell, interprets them.

Examples

```
$ echo *                        List all files in the current directory
bin docs mail mise src
$ echo                          Skip a line

$ echo 'X\tY'                   Print X and Y, separated by a tab
X       Y
$ echo "\n\nSales Report"       Skip two lines before displaying Sales Report

Sales Report
$ echo "Wake up!!\a"            Print message and beep terminal
Wake up!!
$
```

Examples

$ echo * — *List all files in the current directory*
$ echo — *Skip a line*
$ echo 'X\tY' — *Print* X *and* Y, *separated by a tab*
$ echo "\n\nSales Report" — *Skip two lines before displaying* Sales Report
$ echo "Wake up!!\a" — *Print message and beep terminal*

The `eval` Command

General Format: `eval args`

Execution of this command causes the shell to evaluate `args` and then execute the results. This is useful for causing the shell to effectively "double-scan" a command line.

Example

```
$ x='abc def'
$ y='$x'                Assign $x to y
$ echo $y
$x
$ eval echo $y
abc def
$
```

The `exec` Command

General Format: `exec command args`

When the shell executes the `exec` command, it initiates execution of the specified `command` with the indicated arguments. Unlike other commands, `command` replaces the current process (that is, no new process is created). After `command` starts execution, there is no return to the program that initiated the `exec`.

If just I/O redirection is specified, the input and/or output for the shell is accordingly redirected.

Examples

```
exec /bin/sh            Replace current process with sh
exec < datafile         Reassign standard input to datafile
```

The `exit` Command

General Format: `exit  n`

Execution of `exit` causes the current shell program to be immediately terminated. The exit status of the program is the value of the integer *n*, if supplied. If *n* is not supplied, the exit status is that of the last command executed prior to the `exit`.

An exit status of zero is used to indicate success, and non-zero to indicate failure (such as an error condition). This convention is used by the shell in evaluation of conditions for `if`, `while`, and `until` commands, and with the `&&` and `||` constructs.

Examples

```
who | grep $user > /dev/null
exit
exit 1
if finduser
then
     ...
fi
```
Exit with status of last `grep`
Exit with status of 1
If `finduser` *returns an exit status of zero then...*

Note that executing `exit` directly from a login shell has the effect of logging you off.

The `export` Command

General Format: `export  variables`

The `export` command tells the shell that the indicated variables are to be marked as exported; that is, their values are to be passed down to subshells.

Examples

```
export PATH PS1
export dbhome x1 y1 date
```

Variables may be set when exported using the form

```
export variable=value...
```

So lines such as

```
PATH=$PATH:$HOME/bin; export PATH
CDPATH=.:$HOME:/usr/spool/uucppublic; export CDPATH
```

can be rewritten as

```
export PATH=$PATH:$HOME/bin CDPATH=.:$HOME:/usr/spool/uucppublic
```

The output of `export` with a `-p` argument is a list of the exported variables and their values in the form

```
export variable=value
```

or

```
export variable
```

if *variable* has been exported but does not yet have its value set.

The `false` Command

General Format: `false`

The `false` command returns a nonzero exit status.

The `fc` Command

General Format: `fc -e editor -lnr first last`

```
         fc -s old=new first
```

The `fc` command is used to edit commands in the command history. A range of commands is specified from *first* to *last*, where *first* and *last* can be either command numbers or strings; a negative number is taken as an offset from the current command number, while a string specifies the most recently entered command beginning with that string. The commands are read into the editor and executed upon exit from the editor. If no editor is specified, the value of the shell variable `FCEDIT` is used; if `FCEDIT` is not set, `ed` is used.

The `-l` option lists the commands from *first* to *last* (that is, an editor is not invoked). If the `-n` option is also selected, these commands are not preceded by command numbers.

The `-r` option to `fc` reverses the order of the commands.

If *last* is not specified, it defaults to *first*. If *first* is also not specified, it defaults to the previous command for editing and to `-16` for listing.

The `-s` option causes the selected command to be executed without editing it first. The format

```
fc -s old=new first
```

causes the command *first* to be re-executed after the string *old* in the command is replaced with *new*. If *first* isn't specified, the previous command is used, and if *old=new* isn't specified, the command is not changed.

Examples

`fc -l`	*List the last 16 commands*
`fc -e vi sed`	*Read the last* `sed` *command into* `vi`
`fc 100 110`	*Read commands 100 to 110 into* `$FCEDIT`
`fc -s`	*Re-execute the previous command*
`fc -s abc=def 104`	*Re-execute command 104, replacing* `abc` *with* `def`

The `fg` Command

General Format: `fg job_id`

If job control is enabled, the job specified by `job_id` is brought to the foreground. If no argument is given, the most recently suspended job or the job last sent to the background is brought to the foreground.

Example

```
fg %2
```

The `for` Command

General Format:

```
for var in word₁ word₂ ... wordₙ
do
    command
    command
    . . .
done
```

Execution of this command causes the commands enclosed between the `do` and `done` to be executed as many times as there are words listed after the `in`.

The first time through the loop, the first word—$word_1$—is assigned to the variable `var` and the commands between the `do` and `done` executed. The second time through the loop, the second word listed—$word_2$—is assigned to `var` and the commands in the loop executed again.

This process continues until the last variable in the list—$word_n$—is assigned to `var` and the commands between the `do` and `done` executed. At that point, execution of the `for` loop is terminated. Execution then continues with the command that immediately follows the `done`.

The special format

```
for var
do
    . . .
done
```

indicates that the positional parameters "$1", "$2", ... are to be used in the list and is equivalent to

```
for var in "$@"
do
    . . .
done
```

Example

```
# nroff all of the files in the current directory
for file in *
```

```
do
    nroff -Tlp $file | lp
done
```

The `getopts` Command

General Format: `getopts` *options var*

This command processes command-line arguments. *options* is a list of valid single letter options. If any letter in *options* is followed by a `:`, that option requires an additional argument on the command line which must be separated from the option by at least one space.

Each time `getopts` is called, it processes the next command-line argument. If a valid option is found, `getopts` stores the matching option letter inside the specified variable *var* and returns a zero exit status.

If an invalid option is specified (one not listed in options), `getopts` stores a `?` inside *var* and returns with a zero exit status. It also writes an error message to standard error.

If an option takes an argument, `getopts` stores the matching option letter inside *var* and stores the command-line argument inside the special variable OPTARG. If no arguments are left on the command line, `getopts` sets *var* to `?` and writes an error message to standard error.

If no more options remain on the command line (if the next command-line argument does not begin with a `-`), `getopts` returns a nonzero exit status.

The special variable OPTIND is also used by `getopts`. It is initially set to 1 and is adjusted each time `getopts` returns to indicate the number of the next command-line argument to be processed.

The argument `--` can be placed on the command line to specify the end of the command-line arguments.

`getopts` supports stacked arguments, as in

`repx -iau`

which is equivalent to

`repx -i -a -u`

Options that have required arguments may not be stacked.

If the format

`getopts` *options var args*

is used, `getopts` parses the arguments specified by *args rather than* the command-line arguments.

Example

```
usage="Usage: foo [-r] [-O outfile] infile"

while getopts ro: opt
```

```
do
        case "$opt"
        in
                r) rflag=1;;
                O) oflag=1
                   ofile=$OPTARG;;
                \?) echo "$usage"
                    exit 1;;
        esac
done

if [ $OPTIND -gt $# ]
then
        echo "Needs input file!"
        echo "$usage"
        exit 2
fi

shift $((OPTIND - 1))
ifile=$1
...
```

The `hash` Command

General Format: `hash` `commands`

This command tells the shell to look for the specified commands and to remember what directories they are located in. If `commands` is not specified, a list of the hashed commands is displayed.

If the format

`hash -r`

is used, the shell removes all commands from its hash list. Next time any command is executed, the shell uses its normal search methods to find the command.

Examples

`hash rolo whoq`	*Add* rolo *and* whoq *to hash list*
`hash`	*Print hash list*
`hash -r`	*Remove hash list*

The `if` Command

General Format:

```
if   command_t
then
```

```
        command
        command
 . . .
fi
```

command$_t$ is executed and its exit status tested. If it is zero, the commands that follow up to the fi are executed. Otherwise, the commands that follow up to the fi are skipped.

Example

```
if grep $sys sysnames > /dev/null
then
        echo "$sys is a valid system name"
fi
```

If the grep returns an exit status of zero (which it will if it finds $sys in the file sysnames), the echo command is executed; otherwise it is skipped.

The built-in command test is often used as the command following the if, either by explicitly calling test or using its mnemonic shortcut [, the latter of which requires a matching].

Example

```
if [ $# -eq 0 ] ; then
        echo "Usage: $0 [-1] file ..."
        exit 1
fi
```

An else clause can be added to the if to be executed if the command returns a nonzero exit status. In this case, the general format of the if becomes

```
if command_t
then
        command
        command
        . . .
else
        command
        command
        . . .
fi
```

If *command$_t$* returns an exit status of zero, the commands that follow up to the else are executed, and the commands between the else and the fi are skipped. Otherwise, *command$_t$* returns a nonzero exit status and the commands between the then and the else are skipped, and the commands between the else and the fi are executed.

Example

```
if [ -z "$line" ]
then
        echo "I couldn't find $name"
```

```
else
        echo "$line"
fi
```

In the preceding example, if `line` has zero length, the `echo` command that displays the message `I couldn't find $name` is executed; otherwise, the `echo` command that displays the value of `line` is executed.

A final format of the `if` command is useful when more than a two-way decision has to be made. Its general format is

```
if command₁
then
        command
        command
        . . .
elif command₂
then
        command
        command
        . . .
elif commandₙ
then
        command
        command
        . . .
else
    command
        command
        . . .
fi
```

command₁, *command₂*, ..., *commandₙ* are evaluated in order until one of the commands returns an exit status of zero, at which point the commands that immediately follow the `then` (up to another `elif`, `else`, or `fi`) are executed. If none of the commands returns an exit status of zero, the commands listed after the `else` (if present) are executed.

Example

```
if [ "$choice" = a ] ; then
        add $*
elif [ "$choice" = d ] ; then
        delete $*
elif [ "$choice" = l ] ; then
        list
else
        echo "Bad choice!"
        error=TRUE
fi
```

The `jobs` Command

General Format: `jobs`

The list of active jobs is printed. If the `-l` option is specified, detailed information about each job, including its process ID, is listed as well. If the `-p` option is specified, only process IDs are listed.

If an optional *job_id* is supplied to the `jobs` command, just information about that job is listed.

Example

```
$ sleep 100 &
[1] 1104
$ jobs
[1] + Running         sleep 100 &
$
```

The `kill` Command

General Format: `kill -signal job`

The `kill` command sends the signal *signal* to the specified process, where *job* is a process ID or *job_id*, and *signal* is a number or one of the signal names specified in `<signal.h>` (see the description of `trap` later in the chapter). `kill -l` lists these names. A signal number supplied with the `-l` option lists the corresponding signal name. A process ID used with the `-l` option lists the name of the signal that terminated the specified process (if it was terminated by a signal).

The `-s` option can also be used when a signal name is supplied, in which case the dash before the name is not used (see the following example).

If *signal* isn't specified, SIGTERM (TERM) is used.

Examples

```
kill -9 1234
kill -HUP %2 3456
kill -s TERM %2
kill %1
```

Note that more than one process ID can be supplied to the `kill` command on the command line.

The `newgrp` Command

General Format: `newgrp group`

This command changes your real group id (GID) to *group*. If no argument is specified, it changes you back to your default group.

Examples

`newgrp shbook`	*Change to group* `shbook`
`newgrp`	*Change back to default group*

If a password is associated with the new group, and you are not listed as a member of the group, you will be prompted to enter it.

`newgrp -l` changes you back to your login group.

The `pwd` Command

General Format: `pwd`

This command tells the shell to print your working directory, which is written to standard output.

Examples

```
$ pwd
/users/steve/documents/memos
$ cd
$ pwd
/users/steve
$
```

The `read` Command

General Format: `read vars`

This command causes the shell to read a line from standard input and assign successive whitespace-delimited words from the line to the variables *vars*. If fewer variables are listed than there are words on the line, the additional words are stored in the last variable.

Specifying just one variable has the effect of reading and assigning an entire line to the variable.

The exit status of `read` is zero unless an end-of-file condition is encountered.

Examples

```
$ read hours mins
10 19
$ echo "$hours:$mins"
10:19
$ read num rest
39 East 12th Street, New York City 10003
$ echo "$num\n$rest"
39
East 12th Street, New York City 10003
```

```
$ read line
      Here      is an entire          line \r
$ echo "$line"
Here      is an entire          line r
$
```

Note in the final example that any leading whitespace characters get "eaten" by the shell when read. You can change IFS if this poses a problem.

Also note that backslash characters get interpreted by the shell when you read the line, and any that make it through (double backslashes will get through as a single backslash) get interpreted by echo if you display the value of the variable.

A -r option to read says to not treat a \ character at the end of a line as line continuation.

The readonly Command

General Format: readonly *vars*

This command tells the shell that the listed variables cannot be assigned values. These variables may be optionally assigned values on the readonly command line. If you subsequently try to assign a value to a readonly variable, the shell issues an error message.

readonly variables are useful for ensuring that you don't accidentally overwrite the value of a variable. They're also good for ensuring that other people using a shell program can't change the values of particular variables (for example, their HOME directory or their PATH). The readonly attribute is not passed down to subshells.

readonly with a -p option prints a list of your readonly variables.

Example

```
$ readonly DB=/users/steve/database      Assign value to DB and make it readonly
$ DB=foo                                 Try to assign it a value
sh: DB: is read-only                     Error message from the shell
$ echo $DB                               But can still access its value
/users/steve/database
$
```

The return Command

General Format: return *n*

This command causes the shell to stop execution of the current function and immediately return to the caller with an exit status of *n*. If *n* is omitted, the exit status returned is that of the command executed immediately prior to the return.

The `set` Command

General Format: `set options args`

This command is used to turn on or off options as specified by *options*. It is also used to set positional parameters, as specified by *args*.

Each single letter option in *options* is enabled if the option is preceded by a minus sign -, or disabled if preceded by a plus sign +. Options can be grouped, as in

`set -fx`

which enables the `f` and `x` options.

Table A.9 summarizes the options that can be selected.

Table A.9   `set` **Options**

Meaning	Option
`--`	Don't treat subsequent *args* preceded by a - as options. If there are no arguments, the positional parameters are unset.
`-a`	Automatically export all variables that are subsequently defined or modified.
`-b`	If supported by the implementation, causes the shell to notify you when background jobs finish.
`-C`	Don't allow output redirection to overwrite existing files. `>|` can still be used to force individual files to be overwritten even if this option is selected.
`-e`	Exit if any command that gets executed fails or has a nonzero exit status.
`-f`	Disable filename generation.
`-h`	Add commands inside functions to the hash list as they are defined, and not as they are executed.
`-m`	Turn on the job monitor.
`-n`	Read commands without executing them (useful for checking for balanced do...dones, and if ... fis).
`+o`	Write current option mode settings in command format.
`-o m`	Turn on option mode *m* (see Table A.10).
`-u`	Issue an error if a variable is referenced without having been assigned a value or if a positional parameter is referenced without having been set.
`-v`	Print each shell command line as it is read.
`-x`	Print each command and its arguments as it is executed, preceded by a +.

Shell modes are turned on or off by using the `-o` and `+o` options, respectively, followed by an option name. These options are summarized in Table A.10.

Table A.10   **Shell Modes**

Mode	Meaning
allexport	Same as -a.
errexit	Same as -e.
ignoreeof	The exit command must be used to leave the shell.
monitor	Same as -m.
noclobber	Same as -C.
noexec	Same as -n.
noglob	Same as -f.
nolog	Don't put function definitions in the history.
nounset	Same as -u.
verbose	Same as -v.
vi	The in-line editor is set to vi.
xtrace	Same as -x.

The command `set -o` without any options has the effect of listing all shell modes and their current settings.

The shell variable `$-` contains the current options setting.

Each word listed in *args* is set to the positional parameters $1, $2, ..., respectively. If the first word might start with a minus sign, it's safer to specify the `--` option to `set` to avoid interpretation of that value.

If *args* is supplied, the variable $# will be set to the number of parameters assigned after execution of the command.

Examples

`set -vx`	*Print all command lines as they are read, and each command and its arguments as it is executed*
`set "$name" "$address" "$phone"`	*Set* $1 *to* $name, $2 *to* $address, *and* $3 *to* $phone
`set --  -1`	*Set* $1 *to* -1
`set -o vi`	*Turn on* vi *mode*
`set +o verbose -o noglob`	*Turn* verbose *mode off,* noglob *on*

The `shift` Command

General Format: `shift`

This command causes the positional parameters $1, $2, ..., $n to be "shifted left" one place. That is, $2 is assigned to $1, $3 to $2, ..., and $n to $n-1. $# is adjusted accordingly.

If the format

`shift n`

is used instead, the shift is to the left *n* places.

Examples

```
$ set a b c d
$ echo "$#\n$*"
4
a b c d
$ shift
$ echo "$#\n$*"
3
b c d
$ shift 2
$ echo "$#\n$*"
1
d
$
```

The `test` Command

General Format:

`test condition`

or

`[ condition ]`

The shell evaluates `condition` and if the result of the evaluation is *TRUE*, returns a zero exit status. If the result of the evaluation is *FALSE*, a nonzero exit status is returned. If the format `[ condition ]` is used, a space must appear immediately after the `[` and before the `]`.

`condition` is composed of one or more operators as shown in Table A.11. The `-a` operator has higher precedence than the `-o` operator. In any case, parentheses can be used to group subexpressions. Just remember that the parentheses are significant to the shell and so must be quoted. Operators and operands (including parentheses) must be delimited by one or more spaces so that `test` sees them as separate arguments.

`test` is most often used to test conditions in an `if`, `while`, or `until` command.

Examples

```
# see if perms is executable

if test -x /etc/perms
then
        . . .
fi
# see if it's a directory or a normal file that's readable

if [ -d $file -o \( -f $file -a -r $file \) ]
then
        . . .
fi
```

Table A.11 test **Operators**

Operator	Returns TRUE (zero exit status) if
File Operators	
-b *file*	*file* is a block special file
-c *file*	*file* is a character special file
-d *file*	*file* is a directory
-e *file*	*file* exists
-f *file*	*file* is an ordinary file
-g *file*	*file* has its set group id (SGID) bit set
-h *file*	*file* is a symbolic link
-k *file*	*file* has its sticky bit set
-L *file*	*file* is a symbolic link
-p *file*	*file* is a named pipe
-r *file*	*file* is readable by the process
-S *file*	*file* is a socket
-s *file*	*file* has nonzero length
-t *fd*	*fd* is an open file descriptor associated with a terminal (1 is default)
-u *file*	*file* has its set user id (SUID) bit set
-w *file*	*file* is writable by the process
-x *file*	*file* is executable

Operator	Returns TRUE (zero exit status) if
String Operators	
string	*string* is not null
-n *string*	*string* is not null (and *string* must be seen by test)
-z *string*	*string* is null (and *string* must be seen by test)
string₁ = *string₂*	*string₁* is identical to *string₂*
string₁ != *string₂*	*string₁* is *not* identical to *string₂*
Integer Comparison Operators	
int₁ -eq *int₂*	*int₁* is equal to *int₂*
int₁ -ge *int₂*	*int₁* is greater than or equal to *int₂*
int₁ -gt *int₂*	*int₁* is greater than *int₂*
int₁ -le *int₂*	*int₁* is less than or equal to *int₂*
int₁ -lt *int₂*	*int₁* is less than *int₂*
int₁ -ne *int₂*	*int₁* is not equal to *int₂*
Boolean Operators	
! *expr*	*expr* is FALSE; otherwise, returns TRUE
expr₁ -a *expr₂*	*expr₁* is TRUE, and *expr₂* is TRUE
expr₁ -o *expr₂*	*expr₁* is TRUE, or *expr₂* is TRUE

The times Command

General Format: times

Execution of this command causes the shell to write to standard output the total amount of time that has been used by the shell and by all its child processes. For each, two numbers are listed: first the accumulated user time and then the accumulated system time.

Note that times does not report the time used by built-in commands.

Example

```
$ times            Print time used by processes
1m5s 2m9s          1 min., 5 secs. user time, 2 mins., 9 secs. system time
8m22.23s 6m22.01s  Time used by child processes
$
```

The `trap` Command

General Format: `trap commands signals`

This command tells the shell to execute *commands* whenever it receives one of the signals listed in *signals*. The listed signals can be specified by name or number.

`trap` with no arguments prints a list of the current trap assignments.

If the first argument is the null string, as in

`trap "" signals`

the signals in *signals are* ignored when received by the shell.

If the format

`trap signals`

is used, processing of each signal listed in *signals* is reset to the default action.

Examples

```
trap "echo hangup >> $ERRFILE; exit" HUP     Log message and exit on hangup
trap "rm $TMPFILE; exit" 1 2 15              remove $TMPFILE on signals 1, 2, or 15
trap "" 2                                    Ignore interrupts
trap 2                                       Reset default processing of interrupts
```

Table A.12 lists values that can be specified in the signal list.

Table A.12 **Signal Numbers and Names for** `trap`

Signal #	Signal Name	Generated for
0	EXIT	Exit from the shell
1	HUP	Hangup
2	INT	Interrupt (for example, `Delete` key, *Ctrl+c*)
3	QUIT	Quit
6	ABRT	Abort
9	KILL	Kill
14	ALRM	Alarm timeout
15	TERM	Software termination signal (sent by `kill` by default)

The shell scans *commands* when the `trap` command is encountered and again when one of the listed signals is received. This means, for example, that when the shell encounters the command

```
trap "echo $count lines processed >> $LOGFILE; exit" HUP INT TERM
```

it substitutes the value of count at that point, and *not when one of the signals is received*. You can get the value of count substituted when one of the signals is received if you instead enclose the commands in single quotes:

```
trap 'echo $count lines processed >> $LOGFILE; exit' HUP INT TERM
```

The true Command

General Format: true

This command returns a zero exit status.

The type Command

General Format: type commands

This command prints information about the indicated commands.

Examples

```
$ type troff echo
troff is /usr/bin/troff
echo is a shell builtin
$
```

The umask Command

General Format: umask mask

umask sets the default file creation mask to mask. Files that are subsequently created are ANDed with this mask to determine the mode of the file.

umask with no arguments prints the current mask. The -s option says to produce symbolic output.

Examples

```
$ umask          Print current mask
0002             No write to others
$ umask 022      No write to group either
$
```

The unalias Command

General Format: unalias names

The aliases names are removed from the alias list. The -a option says to remove all aliases.

The `unset` Command

General Format: `unset names`

This causes the shell to erase definitions of the variables or functions listed in `names`. Read-only variables cannot be unset. The `-v` option to `unset` specifies that a variable name follows, whereas the `-f` option specifies a function name. If neither option is used, it is assumed that variable name(s) follow.

Example

`unset dblist files`   *Remove definitions of variables* `dblist` *and* `files`

The `until` Command

General Format:

```
until command_t
do
        command
        command
        . . . .
done
```

`command_t` is executed and its exit status tested. If it is nonzero, the commands enclosed between the `do` and `done` are executed. Then `command_t` is executed again and its status tested. If it is nonzero, the commands between the `do` and `done` are once again executed. Execution of `command_t` and subsequent execution of the commands between the `do` and `done` continues until `command_t` returns a zero exit status, at which point the loop is terminated. Execution then continues with the command that follows the `done`.

Because `command_t` gets evaluated immediately on entry into the loop, the commands between the `do` and `done` may never be executed if the test returns a zero exit status the first time.

Example

```
# sleep for 60 seconds until jack logs on
until who | grep jack > /dev/null
do
        sleep 60
done

echo jack has logged on
```

The preceding loop continues until the `grep` returns a zero exit status (that is, finds `jack` in `who`'s output). At that point, the loop is terminated, and the `echo` command that follows is executed.

The `wait` Command

General Format: `wait job`

This command causes the shell to suspend its execution until the process identified as `job` finishes executing. Job can be a process ID or a *job_id*. If `job` is not supplied, the shell waits for all child processes to finish executing. If more than one process id is listed, `wait` will wait for them all to complete.

`wait` is useful for waiting for processes to finish that have been sent to the background for execution.

Example

```
sort large_file > sorted_file &          sort in the background
        . . .                            Continue processing
wait                                     Now wait for sort to finish
plotdata sorted_file
```

The variable `$!` can be used to obtain the process ID of the last process sent to the background.

The `while` Command

General Format:

```
while command_t
do
        command
        command
        . . .
done
```

`command_t` is executed and its exit status tested. If it is zero, the commands enclosed between the `do` and `done` are executed. Then `command_t` is executed again and its status tested. If it is zero, the commands between the `do` and `done` are once again executed. Execution of `command_t` and subsequent execution of the commands between the `do` and `done` continues until `command_t` returns a non-zero exit status, at which point the loop is terminated. Execution then continues with the command that follows the `done`.

Note that because `command_t` gets evaluated immediately on entry into the loop, the commands between the `do` and `done` may never be executed if the test returns a non-zero exit status the first time.

Example

```
# fill up the rest of the buffer with blank lines

while [ $lines -le $maxlines ]
do
        echo >> $BUFFER
        lines=$((lines + 1))
done
```

B

For More Information

Many sources of information on Unix, Linux and the Mac OS X command line are available, but we have selected titles and Web sites of particular value to shell programmers. All Web sites and URLs are valid as of the publication of this book, but as is often the case on the Internet, some may not be available by the time you read this.

There is one reference that you cannot do without. This is the built-in documentation for your particular system, which offers detailed descriptions of the syntax and various options for each command.

Online Documentation

If a printed version of your system's documentation isn't available, you can use the man command to get information (referred to as the "man pages") about any specific Unix command. The format is

```
man command
```

Not sure of the command name? man -k can help you identify the specific Linux or Unix command you seek, as in this example from Ubuntu Linux:

```
$ man -k dvd
brasero (1)             - Simple and easy to use CD/DVD burning application for ...
btcflash (8)            - firmware flash utility for BTC DRW1008 DVD+/-RW recorder.
dvd+rw-booktype (1)     - format DVD+-RW/-RAM disk with a logical format
dvd+rw-format (1)       - format DVD+-RW/-RAM disk
dvd+rw-mediainfo (1)    - display information about dvd drive and disk
dvd-ram-control (1)     - checks features of DVD-RAM discs
growisofs (1)           - combined genisoimage frontend/DVD recording program.
rpl8 (8)                - Firmware loader for DVD drives
$
```

Some systems have an interactive documentation command called info. To invoke it, simply type info and after it starts up, type h for a tutorial.

Documentation on the Web

The best place on the Web for information on the POSIX standard is at `www.unix.org`. This site is maintained by The Open Group, an international consortium that worked with the IEEE to create the current POSIX specification. The complete specification is available on its Web site. You must register first to read it, but registration is free. The URL for accessing the documentation is `www.unix.org/online.html`.

The Free Software Foundation maintains online documentation for a variety of Linux and Unix utilities, notably including Bash and the C compiler, at `www.fsf.org/manual`.

David Korn, the developer of the Korn shell, maintains `www.kornshell.com`. It contains documentation, downloads, information on books on the Korn shell, and links to information on other shells.

If you only have access to Microsoft Windows systems but still want to try your hand at shell programming, or you just want to get a taste of Linux, we encourage you to install the Cygwin package from `www.cygwin.com`. The base system includes Bash and lots of other command line utilities, offering a system remarkably Linux and Unix like. Best of all, the entire Cygwin package is free to download and use.

Books

O'Reilly & Associates

A good source of books on Linux and Unix-related topics is O'Reilly and Associates (`www.ora.com`). Their books cover a wide variety of subjects and are available from their Web site, from booksellers online, and in book stores. Their Web site also has many useful articles on Unix and Linux.

Two good references on Unix and Linux, respectively:

Unix in a Nutshell, 4th Edition, A. Robbins, O'Reilly & Associates, 2005.

Linux in a Nutshell, 6th Edition, E. Siever, S. Figgins, R. Love and A. Robbins, O'Reilly & Associates, 2009.

Two good books on Perl programming, from beginner to advanced:

Learning Perl, 6th Edition, R. L. Schwartz, B. Foy and T. Phoenix, O'Reilly & Associates, 2011.

Perl in a Nutshell, 2nd Edition, S. Spainhour, E. Siever, and N. Patwardhan, O'Reilly & Associates, 2002

A good book covering both the POSIX standard versions of `awk` and `sed` as well as the GNU versions:

Sed & Awk, 2nd Edition, D. Dougherty and A. Robbins, O'Reilly & Associates, 1997 (ISBN 978-1-56592-225-9).

Want to learn more about the Unix command line from a Mac user's perspective? We recommend:

Learning Unix for OS X, D. Taylor, O'Reilly & Associates

Pearson

Learn the essentials of Unix shell programming from the ground up:

Sams Teach Yourself Shell Programming in 24 Hours, 2nd Edition, S. Veeraraghaven, Sams Publishing, 2002.

A good book for learning Unix and programming in C and Perl on a Unix system:

Sams Teach Yourself Unix in 24 Hours, 5th Edition, D. Taylor, Sams Publishing, 2016.

This title offers a broad range of topics related to FreeBSD, a robust and free UNIX that many demanding enterprises use in place of Linux. It is detailed in its approach and offers information not found anywhere else:

FreeBSD Unleashed, 2nd Edition, M. Urban and B. Tiemann, Sams Publishing, 2003.

Learn FreeBSD from the ground up. This book is the only beginning level tutorial that offers all the ins and outs of the FreeBSD operating system:

Sams Teach Yourself FreeBSD in 24 Hours, Michael Urban and Brian Tiemann, 2002.

The Unix C Shell Field Guide, G. Anderson and P. Anderson, Prentice Hall, 1986.

An in-depth reference to the C shell.

The AWK Programming Language, A. V. Aho, B. W. Kernighan, and P. J. Weinberger, Addison-Wesley, 1988.

A complete description of the awk language authored by its creators.

The Unix Programming Environment, B. W. Kernighan and R. Pike, Prentice Hall, 1984.

An advanced Unix programming book.

Advanced Linux Programming, M. Mitchell, J. Oldham, and A. Samuel, New Riders Publishing, 2001.

An advanced Linux programming book.

Index

Symbols

overview, 48–49, 331–332

in programs, 94

standard error, writing to, 261–262

standard I/O (input/output), 28–30

ison program, 122

J

jobs

asynchronous jobs, 257

bringing to foreground, 342

job control, 315–317

job numbers, 37

killing, 347

printing list of, 347

referencing, 333–334

sending to background, 316–317

stopped jobs, 316–317

stopping, 334

waiting for, 358

waiting for completion

$! variable, 257–258

wait command, 257

jobs command, 315, 347

K

kernel, 1, 39

keyword parameters. *See* **variables (shell)**

kill command, 315, 347

killing jobs, 347

Korn, David, 289, 360

Korn shell. *See also* **nonstandard shell features**

compatibility summary, 319–320

history of, 289

Web documentation, 360

kornshell.com website, 360

L

-L file operator, 142–143

-le operator, 140–142

left-shifting positional parameters, 128–129

line edit modes

emacs

command history, accessing, 296–298

overview, 296–298

overview, 291

vi

command history, accessing, 294–296

overview, 292–294

in-line input redirection

shell archive creation, 264–267

syntax, 262–264

LINENO variable, 324

lines

cutting, 64–66

deleting, 73

duplicate lines, eliminating

sort command, 84

uniq command, 88–89

line continuation, 112

pasting

from different files, 68–69

output delimiters, 69–70

from same file, 70

pattern matching

beginning of line, 53

end of line, 53–54

sorting

arithmetically, 86

delimiter characters, 87–88

duplicate lines, eliminating, 84

M

REGISTER YOUR PRODUCT at informit.com/register

Access Additional Benefits and SAVE 35% on Your Next Purchase

- Download available product updates.

- Access bonus material when applicable.

- Receive exclusive offers on new editions and related products.
  (Just check the box to hear from us when setting up your account.)

- Get a coupon for 35% for your next purchase, valid for 30 days. Your code will
  be available in your InformIT cart. (You will also find it in the Manage Codes
  section of your account page.)

Registration benefits vary by product. Benefits will be listed on your account page
under Registered Products.

InformIT.com—The Trusted Technology Learning Source

InformIT is the online home of information technology brands at Pearson, the world's foremost
education company. At InformIT.com you can

- Shop our books, eBooks, software, and video training.
- Take advantage of our special offers and promotions (informit.com/promotions).
- Sign up for special offers and content newsletters (informit.com/newsletters).
- Read free articles and blogs by information technology experts.
- Access thousands of free chapters and video lessons.

Connect with InformIT—Visit informit.com/community

Learn about InformIT community events and programs.

the trusted technology learning source

Addison-Wesley · Cisco Press · IBM Press · Microsoft Press · Pearson IT Certification · Prentice Hall · Que · Sams · VMware Press

ALWAYS LEARNING   PEARSO